WATERGATE: A CRISIS FOR THE WORLD

Other Pergamon Titles of Interest

DAMMANN, E.
The Future In Our Hands

FITZGERALD, R.
Human Needs and Politics

GARVEY, W.
Communication: The Essence of Science

MENON, B.
Global Dialogue: The New International Economic Order

POWER, J.
Migrant Workers in Western Europe and the United States

SALAS, R.
International Population Assistance: The First Decade

SCHAFF, A.
History and Truth

TALMOR, E.
Mind and Political Concepts

WENK, E.
Margins for Survival: Overcoming Political Limits in Steering
Technology

WIENER, A.
Magnificent Myth: Patterns of Control in Post-Industrial Society

WATERGATE:
A CRISIS FOR THE WORLD

A Survey of British and French Press Reaction
Toward an American Political Crisis

by

JAMES TREZISE
JAMES GLEN STOVALL

and

HAMID MOWLANA

PERGAMON PRESS
Oxford · New York · Toronto · Sydney · Paris · Frankfurt

U.K.	Pergamon Press Ltd., Headington Hill Hall, Oxford OX3 0BW, England
U.S.A.	Pergamon Press Inc., Maxwell House, Fairview Park, Elmsford, New York 10523, U.S.A.
CANADA	Pergamon of Canada, Suite 104, 150 Consumers Road, Willowdale, Ontario M2J 1P9, Canada
AUSTRALIA	Pergamon Press (Aust.) Pty. Ltd., P.O. Box 544, Potts Point, N.S.W. 2011, Australia
FRANCE	Pergamon Press SARL, 24 rue des Ecoles, 75240 Paris, Cedex 05, France
FEDERAL REPUBLIC OF GERMANY	Pergamon Press GmbH, 6242 Kronberg-Taunus, Pferdstrasse 1, Federal Republic of Germany

First edition 1980

British Library Cataloguing in Publication Data

Trezise, James
Watergate, a crisis for the world.
1. Foreign news 2. Watergate Affair, 1972-
3. Press and politics — Great Britain
4. Press and politics — France
I. Title II. Stovall, James Glen
III. Mowlana, Hamid
301.16'1   PN5124.F67   79-40708

ISBN 0-08-020582-8

Printed in Great Britain by
Biddles Ltd, Guildford, Surrey

This book is dedicated to:

Harry and Mona Trezise
Bresee and Martha Stovall
Javad and Maryam Mowlana

The crisis of the Presidency is a
crisis for the world. . . . It is in the
end the actions and attributes of Mr.
Nixon himself which have destroyed
the moral authority of the President.

The *Sunday Times*
October 28, 1973

Contents

Preface

The French press is *lamentable*, but the American press is even worse. It's *scandaleux* that your country's press is powerful enough — and irresponsible enough — to politically assassinate one of your greatest presidents.

A French businessman

Watergate didn't really surprise me. After all, corruption is standard practice in American politics. But I still don't understand why it took you two years to get rid of Nixon.

A British lawyer

This book is not about Watergate. It is about images, national stereotypes, attitudes, perception, press bias, and "freedom of the press". It describes what people from two other nations — similar to each other and to the United States in many ways — heard or read about Watergate and the American political system's functioning during that period. Watergate provides an unique conceptual filter for analyzing British and French attitudes toward the U.S., and a mirror for reflecting many unstated beliefs regarding their own countries.

Comments like those quoted above — from people of diverse socioeconomic backgrounds and political points of view — planted the seed of an idea which grew into this study. The authors mused about conducting a cross-national public opinion study regarding Watergate, but this proved beyond both time and financial limitations. Since newspapers and magazines obviously served as important interpreters between American news event and foreign audience, an equally viable and revealing alternative was to study British and French press coverage of Watergate.

In terms of media selection, we had two alternatives: (a) control for comparative coverage by surveying the same types of media — e.g. a national daily, a regional newspaper, and a newsmagazine — from each country; (b) select a sample representative of each nation's media structure. Since the media structures of Britain and France differ greatly, we felt that the second alternative would better reflect the news consumption of their respective populations.

One conventional method of content analysis involves counting column inches devoted to a story to determine its relative importance as a news item. We have used a more qualitative approach. Though story length and placement are sometimes noted, our analysis emphasized *what* was said rather than how much. In this regard, the reader is reminded that the sections chronicling actual press coverage contain some of the more evaluative reporting which appeared; to include everything would require three or four volumes this size.

The first section provides a broad theoretical framework and review of pertinent international communications literature designed to lend perspective to this study. The sections devoted to French and British press coverage include a general description of these countries' press histories and contemporary characteristics, as well as a review of what they said about Watergate. The "Legitimization" section draws some specific implications related to this coverage and the press's role in shaping and reinforcing attitudes. The final section re-examines the oft-abused and misunderstood concept of "freedom of the press" in relation to this study's findings, and suggests a more comprehensive and empirical alternative for analyzing press systems throughout the world.

This book concerns perception: culturally based and biased ways of looking at the world around us. We have tried to pinpoint some such cultural biases among British and French journalists covering Watergate. But, as hard as we may have tried, we do not pretend to have totally shed our own in so doing.

Since this manuscript was originally prepared, a number of

developments have occurred which have affected some of the topics discussed in the book. At least two of them should be noted. As this book is going to press, *The Times* and the *Sunday Times* have not been published for nearly a year because of industrial disputes, although an early resumption of publication is now planned. The comments made about each paper are still very relevant to our discussion, however. Secondly, the increasing debate concerning the New World Information Order makes many of the issues presented here even more timely. We hope that readers will keep this debate in mind when reading the book.

Finally, some acknowledgements. Jim Trezise wishes to thank his wife Lois for putting up with it all; Dr. George Cole of the University of Connecticut for an initial push; Françoise Courageot and others at the fabulous Centre Culturel Pierre Bayle/Centre de Recherches et d'Information of Besançon; and the staff of the Bibliothèque Municipale de Besançon. Jim Stovall thanks the reference staff of Chiswick Library, and Jane Pope and Terri Callaway for help with the manuscript. Hamid Mowlana is indebted to Mark Rasmuson, and to members of the foreign press corps in Washington and New York, especially the individual journalists from Britain and France who shared their experiences with us. The authors thank Art Buchwald for kind permission to reprint one of his articles. Last but by no means least, we are especially grateful to Glynn and Suzie Wood for lasting inspiration, sympathetic ears, and kind cooperation.

October, 1979

JAMES TREZISE
Philadelphia, Pa.

JAMES GLEN STOVALL
University of Alabama,
Tuscaloosa, Ala.

HAMID MOWLANA
American University,
Washington, D.C.

1. Pictures in Our Heads

I'd like very much to visit the United States, but I simply couldn't stand eating pills for my meals.

A French dentist

I'd never live in New York City. It's much too violent.

A girl in Belfast, Northern Ireland

We live by images. The driver of a car stops for a red light, goes on green, and slams on the brakes if another car runs its red light. But images don't emanate exclusively from our eyes; a prolonged screech of tires followed by a deadening thud, while out of visual range, hollows the stomach just as quickly. For many Americans, the wafting scent of a cooking turkey spells Thanksgiving dinner. The taste of cranberry sauce, corn, mashed potatoes and pumpkin pie may resurrect fond memories of such days past. The shaking of hands means welcome.

Such immediate sensory stimuli by no means supply all images. To the contrary, many are just mental vestiges of past sensations somehow filed and stored in the incredibly complex blend of cells, matter, lobes, electrical impulses, nerves, synapses, chemical substances and other elements comprising the human brain. Through five external senses the brain connects with the outside world to gather, categorize, store and recall perceptions. All persons perceive, but not necessarily the same things or events, nor, more importantly, through the same filter:

> Dynamically conceived, perception is one of the basic integral functions of an on-going adjustment process on the part of any organism viewed as a whole. . . . In our species, therefore, what is learned and the context of acquired experience in one society

1

as compared to another constitute important variables with reference to full understanding, explanation or prediction of the behavior of individuals who have received a *common* preparation for action.[1]

Today's perceptions color tomorrow's just as yesterday's colored today's. In this sense, a person is the sum total of his or her perceptions.

The psychological basis of the established social norms, such as stereotypes, fashions, conventions, customs, and values, is the formation of common frames of reference as a product of the contact of individuals. Once such frames of reference are established and incorporated in the individual they enter as important factors to determine or modify his reactions to the situations he will face later — social, and even non-social, at times, especially if the stimulus field is not well structured.[2]

In other words, past experience often intervenes as a perceptual filter for interpreting present situations, particularly when they are new or ambiguous.

Much of what we "know" comes not from our own experience, but vicariously through a set of vocalized symbols unique to *Homo sapiens*: words. Other "lower" forms of life communicate — that is, send and receive messages — often with very complex and sophisticated methods. In *The Dancing Bees*, Karl von Frisch detailed inter-bee communication of a honey find — specifying direction, distance, and quantity — by an intricate dance step in the hive. Jane Goodall has spent years studying some very distinct communication patterns among chimpanzees. Other researchers gnash their teeth, waiting for dolphins' and whales' communication codes to be cracked by a breakthrough in humans' scientific method. Even one-cell organisms are thought to communicate with one another.[3]

But humans are the only animals who "speak", who have developed systems of symbols representing not only things — water, fire, earth, food — but also ideas:

In short, then, as a communicator man differs from all other animals by his highly developed capacity for conceptual thought, in his capacity for abstraction, for symbol making and symbol usage. Man is what he is because of his capacity to create in his mind, by the use of symbols, an idea about something which has no existence outside his mind, and with that idea proceed to create something according to the instructions given or the pattern constituted by that idea. In this manner ideas, symbols, create realities, give them an existence outside the mind. Symbols objectify subjective processes. Essentially a symbol is a meaning. And it is essentially because man is a symbol-using creature that he means so much. The human world, the world man has created, is the world of meanings, of symbols, and their realization. That realized and realizing world of meanings, the ideas, institutions, pots, pans, and everything else that man has created, the anthropologist calls *culture*, the man-made part of the environment.[4]

Anthropologist Ashley Montagu maintains that language evolved as a necessary invention when climatic changes drove human ancestors from the forest onto the plain, or savanna. Herbivorous instincts from forest life proved useless and even counterproductive for stalking plains animals as food. Rather, hunting required a cooperative effort, and the shedding of dysfunctional instincts simultaneously wrought a prolonged dependency period for offspring.[5] Both factors forced language into existence, so "it was the savanna environment that produced the pressures which transformed an ape into a man".[6]

Since that time, language has evolved into a complex array of symbols, symbols of symbols, abstractions (a word which itself is an abstraction), and countless other offshoots spawning the science of linguistics to make some sense out of it all. As society has grown more specialized, each discipline has developed its own vocabulary, an esoteric set of symbols which often defy translation into lay vocabulary. Ironically, this evolution of symbols, conceived from the necessity of human cooperation, may finally prove the undoing of us all. Strontium 90.

In any case, words serve as more than symbols representing abstract ideas. They also, more importantly, evoke "pictures in our heads".[7] They often elicit emotions, spur involuntary and irrational reactions. Snake. And they continue to facilitate social cooperation: a light bulb behind a red plastic dome obviously cannot physically stop a car, but society has adopted the red light as a visual symbol whose meaning is conveyed to all drivers through other (verbal) symbols. Still, though the fundamental purpose of language is to provide a relatively stable system of images, it cannot guarantee identity of perception: a half-full glass for one person is half-empty for another.

Even more problems of perception arise with the different languages on this earth. According to the biblical version of events, God showed His displeasure to people in the process of constructing a monument in honor of a competitor by suddenly transforming one tongue into several, and thereby wreaking chaos and dissension among the evildoers. Whether one subscribes to the Tower of Babel theory or another based on anthropological findings, there remains no doubt that differences in language have thrown a persistent kink into international understanding and cooperation by guaranteeing different perceptions.

As a starter, people in different geographical locations have different things to perceive — animals, vegetation, weather conditions, food, customs — and assign a culture-specific symbol to them. Many Americans knew little or nothing about monsoon rains — or Vietnam — until the country became embroiled in the war. Then there exist certain words in one language which describe a situation or atmosphere — again, often culturally unique — better than any translation ever could. *Weltschmerz, angst, gemütlich* in German; groovy, smooth, mellow in American. An American once noted, as proof of the Russians' questionable sincerity, that they had no word equal to détente. But neither, it must be noted, did Americans before anglicizing the French *détente*: essentially, to take one's finger off the trigger while still holding the gun.

Worse yet, often the "same" word connotes entirely different things: *Webster's Universal Dictionary* defines "compromise" as follows: (1) To adjust and settle (a difference) by mutual agreement, with concession of claims by the parties, to compound. (2) To agree; to accord. (3) To commit; to pledge in some manner or form; to put to hazard, or endanger (one's character, reputation, etc.) by an action that cannot be revoked. France's counterpart, *Le Petit Larousse*, essentially shifts Webster's third meaning (compromising oneself) into first place in defining "compromettre". So when an American proudly suggests compromise as a solution, a French person naturally balks.

Still, we must communicate. As often noted, the world has shrunk at an incredible rate during the past few decades. The supersonic British—French *Concorde* is capable of jetting travelers from Paris to New York in 3 hours, a trip which not so very long ago meant a full week aboard a transatlantic liner. Advances in communication technology account even more for the planet's shrinkage. For more than four centuries after its 1438 unveiling, Gutenberg's printing press remained the major revolutionary breakthrough in mass communication. Then in rapidfire succession appeared the wireless, transatlantic cable, telephone, radio, photography, moving pictures, television, telex, communications satellites.... People from all corners of the globe can now tune in on the same news event at the same time. The earth has become a global village; we are citizens of the world.

Yet we also remain citizens of nation-states. Social change has lagged far behind technological change. We stay locked into culturally based and biased ways of perceiving; our communication with other peoples suffers from ethnocentric static; "they" are different from "us". Rarely do we really know them, but we know *about* them. They are pictures in our heads, stereotypes which: "... are usually widely held; they tend to remain relatively stable and unresponsive to objective facts; and they involve some degree of evaluation of the groups concerned".[8]

A striking example of stereotyping occurred in a famous "serial reproduction" experiment: the tester described the contents of a projected slide to the first subject, who passed on a verbal description to the second, and so on through a chain of six or seven people. One slide depicted two men — one white, the other black — facing each other in a subway. The white man held an open razor in his left hand. In half of the communication chains, the razor had been transferred to the black man — who was even described as "brandishing" or "threatening" with it — by the time the image reached the last subject. Significantly, no such distortion in this particular situation occurred among Negro subjects, or among children who had not yet learned the stereotype.[9]

Once a stereotype plants itself in our minds, it is usually there to stay because, knowingly or not, we reinforce its existence — and verify its "accuracy". We select certain portions of "reality" to pay attention to, we distort others which are unavoidable but clash with our image, we reinterpret the same behavior to fit different people or actions, and we dismiss as exceptions events which glaringly contradict our preconceptions. Stereotypes represent a cognitive aspect of our relationships with others, but are closely linked with affective attitudes, so become intertwined with our egos.[10]

The black—white—razor experiment also dramatized the source of most stereotypes: "The special quality of the stereotype is that it is based not on carefully collected data but on hearsay, on anecdotes, on partial and incomplete experience, on what 'people' have said."[11] Similarly, national images grow out of a questionably reliable network of information: "One gets virtually all of his information about other nations from books and from other persons. Few people visit foreign nations to see for themselves. Thus, the real stimulus is ambiguous, and it is easy to accept the majority opinion as factual. If 'everybody says so,' it must be true."[12] Given their pervasiveness and influence, we may reasonably add the mass media as an important source of stereotypes in today's world.

Clearly, stereotyping is an inevitable and necessary part of human psychological functioning. To try to assimilate all experiences, sensations and bits of incoming information as unrelated, random occurrences with no reference to anything past would most likely short-circuit the gray matter. Indeed, this may be one cause of what we label mental illness: the inability to connect meaningfully and consistently with the "real world". Rather, we "normals" generalize, categorize, label, and associate incoming data in terms of our past perceptions in order to make some sense out of life. "It scarcely can be denied that stereotypes have the function, which they share with many other kinds of generalizations, of rendering our world more tractable, more manageable. . . . It would be unrealistic to disapprove of stereotyped thinking, for that means disapproval of thinking itself."[13]

Instead of futilely lamenting their existence, the social scientist can contribute more by studying stereotypes. At best they can be very amusing — such as a French dentist sincerely believing that Americans serve up a plateful of pills (with gravy . . .?) for dinner, or a terror-racked Belfast girl's fear of New York violence. And stereotypes work both ways: an American might logically picture a Britisher in spats and bowler toddling along past the foggy silhouette of Big Ben, umbrella warding off the drizzle and — naturally — reserved; the Frenchman leans against a café door, bread under arm, glass of red wine in hand, cigarette glued to lower lip, beret perched on head, gesticulating madly about the latest *scandale.*

These stereotypes are not *totally* without foundation or useless. They are based on perceptions and communicated perceptions, and "perceptions are part of reality"[14] in that, accurate or not, they shape our view of the world. Nor is it impossible that one would see any of the stereotypes above in real life, but it's much more probable that one would see only parts of the stereotypes at any one time. A major characteristic of national images is that they tend to be conglomerates of a very few notable traits, which are then generalized as a package to the entire population. And, they normally take on a derogatory tone.[15]

This "dislike of the unlike"[16] poses the main danger of stereotyping. National images are created in part by different ways of perceiving, which in turn fuel the tendency to hold inaccurate images. "Distortions and conflicts are thus ensured by the selectiveness and parochialism of perceptions."[17] In *Nobody Wanted War*, Ralph White devoted an entire book to the idea that misperceptions on all sides were at least partially responsible for the Vietnam conflict and two world wars:

> . . . a central hypothesis which the evidence seems to justify, in all three of the wars studied here, is that each side is highly unrealistic

in perceiving — empathizing with — what is in the minds of those on the other side. In the psychologist Hadley Cantril's phrase, they live in different "reality worlds." On each side, men assume that what seems real to them seems real to the enemy also.[18]

We simply don't know each other. In one UNESCO-sponsored study, 1000 persons from each of nine countries were asked to rate their own and other countries by choosing, in order of descriptive accuracy, from among 12 adjectives — such as industrious, intelligent, courageous, peace-loving, practical, etc. All nine groups agreed on only one national characteristic: their own country was the most peace-loving of all.[19]

Some social scientists explain mutual misperceptions in terms of a "mirror-image phenomenon":

> The analogy lies in the fact that a mirror creates much the same kind of similarity-in-reverse; what is black-and-white in one group's image-system becomes white-and-black in the other group's imagery, just as, when any object is held up to a mirror, what originally appeared as left-and-right appears in the mirror as right-and-left . . . . Always there seems to be a tendency to exaggerate the virtues on one's own side and the diabolical character of the opposite side, and especially of the leaders of the opposite side. Distortion in these directions may be great on one side and small on the other, but it appears to be always present.[20]

Regarding the origins of this tendency, Robert LeVine asserts that "most human populations are ethnocentric (i.e. hostile to some outside groups and carrying negative images of them)"; that "intersocietal behavior of a population is functionally related to its social system and varies concomitantly with it"; and that:

> Customary patterns of intersocietal behavior are transmitted from one generation to the next, and each individual acquires the customary attitudes and images in the course of his socialization and personality development. Thus, certain aspects of childhood experience covary with certain patterns of intersocietal behavior.[21]

In a word: communication. Images are passed on by social communication, which Davis Bobrow defines as "the transfer of meaning between persons and groups".[22] Not just words, but *meaning*, an important distinction because, as Karl Deutsch said: "We can measure the 'integration' of individuals in a people by their ability to receive and transmit information on wide ranges of definite topics with relatively little delay or loss of relevant detail."[23]

By definition, a society is an integration of individuals, and its cohesiveness depends largely upon the success of social communication. To a great extent, this involves interpersonal communication, particularly during a child's dependency period and during peer-pressure adolescent years. But in modern society, mass media must be added as an important socializing force — if not always a desirable or unifying one. In the United States, children spend hours watching cartoon shows interlaced with toy and cereal advertisements; adolescents tune in to programs offering guidance about sex roles in society; troubled or physically fatigued adults often seek "escape" in the blue light.[24] Virtually all countries have some form of print and/or electronic press system supplying political, economic, and social information and models, not to mention entertainment. Rarely do mass media definitively create attitudes and images among a population, but they normally reflect and reinforce those already in existence.

Harold Lasswell devised a simple if somewhat dated model for analyzing mass communications:[25]

> Who
> Says What
> In Which Channel
> To Whom
> With What Effect?

The overriding purpose of this book is to examine some of the images which other peoples hold about the United States, as reflected and reinforced by their mass media. Put in terms of Lasswell's formula:

> British and French Journalists
> Said What About Watergate
> In Newspapers and Magazines
> To British and French Audiences
> With What Effect?

WHY WATERGATE?

Watergate provided a story which only a fledgling political novelist would dare submit to a publisher. The plot and characters shattered the plausibility which makes political fiction saleable. There were too many convenient coincidences, the political intrigues were much too convoluted, the happy ending waxed too romantic, there was too little explanation of motive — like why a superpower president would keep tapes that would incriminate him. The idea of two greenhorn suburban-beat reporters catalyzing a chain of events leading to the fall of the most powerful person on earth stretches the imagination too far for an American — not to mention its implausibility for a European. A Watergate novel would snap credibility. It simply wouldn't happen.

But, stranger than fiction, it did happen. Watergate unfolded like a captivating political thriller, with the exposés of political maneuvering at top levels of government in the world's most powerful country. All branches of government played major roles in the story, and the "Fourth Branch" not only reported it, but got it off the ground in the first place. Several anticlimaxes appeared before the grand finale. There were good guys, bad guys, and enough ambiguity to keep the reader guessing who was which. Two other factors multiplied the suspense: whereas a novel inevitably includes an ending before its back cover, nothing guaranteed that Watergate would continue beyond today's scandal. Several times the investigation seemed to run out of steam when, suddenly, a new chapter hit the front page. Secondly, Watergate was not fiction, it was "true", happening in real life, and it would undoubtedly affect the entire world.

More than its appeal to reader interest, Watergate's unusual characteristics as a news event account for its selection in this study. Though it technically involved an American domestic political crisis, it included international consequences, and: ". . . international communications comprises those transactions taking place either across national boundaries or else within a national actor but affecting the ecology within which international transactions take place."[26] Watergate was one of relatively few examples falling into the latter category, and its worldwide political and economic impact guaranteed a broad, international audience.

Watergate was a long story, encompassing more than two years from start to finish. Accordingly, it lends itself well to analysis in reference to one variation of what Ulf Himmelstrand calls "time perspective": "In principle, it consists in asking what happens to the international flow of news about a given event or, rather, a given sequence of events (e.g. a crisis of some sort), as time passes by and new events are added to the 'first' one."[27] Himmelstrand suggests four phases: hard and hot news with little interpretation; then, as the pattern of events develops, the basis for interpretation grows more firm; reduced news value leads to the event's oblivion or latency; in a possible fourth phase, the issue resurfaces and, with background already provided, the media provide a more complete picture right from the start.[28]

Relatedly, Rosengren hypothesizes that interpretation of news events is a function of their importance and predictability:

> . . . the more unpredictable the event, the more factual and the less interpretative its report. And the more important the event, the greater the need for interpretation. From this follows:
> 1) Important and predictable events will be reported at once factually and interpretatively.
> 2) Events that are important and unpredictable tend to be reported at first predominantly factually, then more and more interpretatively.
> 3) Less important events will be reported mainly factually, regardless of whether they are predictable or not.[29]

Watergate's long duration and cumulative tide of events clearly favored — and necessitated — interpretative reporting by foreign journalists covering an American political crisis.

Furthermore, Watergate's pervasive political consequences on various levels made this crisis a near-perfect candidate for exemplifying various forms of international communication. Richard Merritt has proposed the model shown in Table 1 to categorize "types of international political communication flows".[30]

Table 1
Recipients

Source	Governmental actors	Nongovernmental actors	Cultures
Governmental actors	GG	GN	GC
Nongovernmental actors	NG	NN	NC
Cultures	CG	CN	CG

Considering the Nixon Administration as "Source" of actions and France as "Recipient," it becomes obvious that Watergate stimulated all nine types, given the following off-hand examples:

GG: Watergate's effect on foreign policy.
NG: American press's Watergate reportage followed by French officialdom.
CG: American public opinion and behavior monitored by French officialdom.
GN: Nixon's behavior reported by French press.
NN: American press's role seen by French press.
CN: American public opinion reported by French press.
GC: Nixon's actions as seen (through media) by French people.
NC: American press's actions seen by French people.
CC: American public opinion and behavior seen by French people.

As a gauge of its profound influence in international communication, it deserves note that the press served as either the instigator or intermediary in all of these flows.

Somewhat paradoxically, Watergate also permits examination of what Paul Lazarsfeld considers the two main classes of comparative research opportunities: ". . . first the possibility of studying the same social phenomena in different cultural contexts; secondly, the possibility of studying topics so unique to particular countries that they are not generally available to the social scientist."[31] On the one hand, a major underlying cause of Watergate pinpoints a contemporary problem in many modern democracies:

> Each executive tends to surround himself with like-minded associates and assistants. The individual who differs often with his superior soon finds himself excluded from the decision-making process, if not from government employment. The executive consequently is not protected from the hazard of one-sided reports; he receives an illusory impression of objectivity because his informants confirm one another.[32]

On the other hand, as often noted in British and French media, the Watergate prosecution reflected unique dynamics of American political institutions, power relationships, public attitudes and other slippery variables which differ from their counterparts in other societies. For example, a certain attitude toward authority: "Power accrues to the occupant of a social role in so far as the persons affected by this role accept it as having power."[33] True enough, but there's also a question of the occupant's behavior within that role. Though it is highly doubtful that most Americans seriously questioned the validity or power of the Presidency because of Watergate, Nixon's political and moral actions (and inactions) during his tenure precipitated his fall from power.

Finally, Watergate proved unique as an international news story in that it revolved around one country's domestic political functioning. Other than during electoral campaigns, most international news focuses on foreign policy, relationships between countries, the world balance of power. But Watergate affected all these elements, and so required recounting — and interpretation — to foreign audiences. Whereas a country's foreign policy typically elicits evaluation and/or criticism — since it more directly affects other peoples — its domestic system normally remains private property.

Watergate altered all this, allowing foreign journalists to judge the American system first-hand and simultaneously reveal some beliefs about their own countries' systems. As a rough analogy, Watergate represents the difference between every-day dealings with a married couple presenting a common, unified front, versus having the opportunity — and obligation — to observe severe interpersonal difficulties and prescribing ego-centric solutions. What, in other words, did the British and French have to say about the American divorce?

WHY BRITAIN AND FRANCE?

Britain and France share important historical and geopolitical ties with the "New World". People from both nations actively explored, exploited, settled in and contributed to growth of the American continent. According to American history books, religious oppression drove the first English settlers across the Atlantic to an eventual thirteen new colonies, extending the vast British empire — until the rebellious refugees decided to shed an unrepresentative Crown. Right across Pennsylvania Avenue from the White House, Lafayette Square commemorates a maverick Frenchman for his support during the Revolution. A large region of America owes its annexation to a major French property sale called the Louisiana Purchase, and New Orleans still exhibits a deep-rooted French influence. These three countries also fought shoulder to shoulder in two world wars, and the United States reimbursed its Lafayette debt with substantial help in liberating France from Nazi occupation. Britain and France both basked in golden eras of worldwide empire, much as the U.S. — in a thinly veiled update of semantics — boasts "superpower" status.

But contemporary socio-political similarities and differences account for the major criteria used in selecting these two countries for study. Like the U.S., they operate under a tripartite system of government containing executive, legislative and judicial branches. An elected president (or prime minister) normally governs for a set term before new elections take place, a bicameral legislature with upper and lower houses enacts laws, and a judicial network interprets them. Each nation regards its "free press" as an indispensable "Fourth Power" representing the public by keeping a journalistic eye on the government, warning citizens about imminent oppression, and rallying a public outcry to counter it.

. In short, all three countries are advanced industrial Western democracies sharing numerous historical, philosophical and cultural roots which have shaped their contemporary societies. These institutional similarities should have provided a conceptual foundation through which the British and French could understand Watergate more easily than, say, people living under a one-party dictatorship. But, as the most neophyte political science major knows, a country's "organizational chart" yields only a broad framework within which the real dynamics of political behavior occur. This textbook similarity in institutions thus serves as an important control for this study: British and French attitudes about Watergate as a political process reflect assumptions about the proper functioning of parallel institutions — the press, Parliament, executive branch, etc. — within their own societies.

Some of these attitudes, to be discussed later, reflect differences among the three countries. The British Parliament's House of Lords, with a built-in Tory majority due to the right of hereditary peers to sit in the upper chamber, serves as little more than a rubber-stamp council for legislation initiated by the popularly elected House of Commons; the U.S. Senate truly is the "upper house" in terms of political muscle, and often serves as a stepping-stone to the Presidency. Relative to the American Congress, the French Parliament wields negligible influence vis à vis the Presidency. Whereas England and the United States continue along relatively entrenched two-party systems, in France political parties of every imaginable stripe compete for loyalty among small constituencies, then regroup under "Left" and "Right" banners come election time. England and the U.S. have experienced gradual, steady historical evolutions with variations on a political theme, while France has been racked by turnovers from one form of government to another for centuries. Finally, and perhaps most importantly, Britain and the U.S. are predominantly Anglo-Saxon cultures, while France is predominantly Latin.

The latter merits special mention since "the values by which men live are relative to the particular kind of cultural learning they have experienced",[34] and: ". . . the extent of intercultural understanding, misunderstanding or non-understanding is determined by the extent of likenesses and differences in frames-of-reference, value systems, or World Views of the cultures involved, from their cognitive and affective distance from each other."[35] These ideas carry important implications regarding the mass media, since: ". . . the way the society in question is organized, its social constraints, popular beliefs and customs, and so on, exercises an important influence on the way communications are received and the effect they have."[36] One may fairly presume, then, that Britain has a sounder basis for intercultural understanding with the United States than does France, and political history lends support to this idea.

Historically, Britain has maintained a "special relationship" with the United States, often eliciting derision and/or jealousy from other nations. Colonial ties, philosophical and systemic roots, and a certain paternal curiosity regarding a rebellious and prodigious offspring may account for a large part of this.

But France, particularly since World War II and America's emergence as a superpower, remains an uneasy ally of the U.S. — bound by certain goals, aspirations, and dependence to the U.S. while simultaneously demanding and parading its "independence". U.S.—French relations since 1946, and especially since 1958, have provided a classic case of mutual misperceptions. In a brilliant essay, Stanley Hoffman detailed several of these and their roots thus:

The U.S. approaches international affairs in terms of a duel between two groups, with other countries being either "for or against", and operates with crisis or step-by-step diplomacy. The French see, rather, a multiple contest with a gradation of other nations scattered along a broad friendly—hostile spectrum, and consider action in the international arena — whether their own actions or others' — as part of an overriding, long-range policy. So France views the fruits of America's crisis diplomacy as the gradual — and often sinister —

unfolding of an all-encompassing plan.[37]

> France's perceptions . . . are largely dictated by her position in the postwar world. . . . France is also a power that has suffered enormous losses from the "political collapse" of Europe and of empire; she is inevitably worried about any policy that would tend to perpetuate the partition and divided dependence of Europe, and to dismiss as anachronistic France's residual pretensions as a world power. If America's position is that of the global defensive, France's is that of a global revisionist. For the very existence of Britain as a kind of favored American ally makes it impossible for France to play the smooth (and not very successful) role Britain has tried to play in an effort to return to high rank through cooperating with rather than defying the U.S.[38]

For these and other reasons, France and the United States have steadily and predictably accused each other of impeding European unity. France, looking through a multipolar filter, resents and distrusts superpower politics and the Atlantic "monolithism" of the U.S. America regards French actions as unrealistic given the present world situation and, even worse, as setting a bad precedent for other European nations to follow.[39]

> Moreover, France's position is resented both because it encourages the enemy and because France's advice comes cheap, her present responsibilities being as small as her past responsibility looms large. . . . The very fact that (in the U.S., by contrast with Europe) French views are deprived of immediate potency deepens the rift: for while they increase American resentment, they give good conscience to the French, who are moved to heights of self-righteous and indignant lucidity now that their own record has been swept clean by decolonization, and convinced that their very disinterestedness ought to make American officialdom pay special attention to their analysis.[40]

So Britain and France, despite many similarities, offer vastly different perspectives in regard to American foreign policy. The logical question: Does this hold true for Watergate as well?

The most accessible gauge of prevalent attitudes were their respective mass media. And a related criterion for selecting these countries was the specific characteristics of their mass media systems. The printed press, and particularly the daily newspaper, remains a major source of news and information in

Europe: "A regional breakdown shows that Europeans buy 38% of the world's daily papers and North Americans 23%, while Africans, Asians and South Americans, representing nearly 70% of the world population, together command only 26%."[41]
Not only do France and Britain account for a large chunk of this European consumption, but each country boasts an international press agency on the level of Associated Press and United Press International. *Agence France Presse* (AFP) and Britain's Reuters keep French and English readers up to date on international events and exchange national news with other wire services. In addition, both countries have specialized and advanced journalist training programs.[42]

Though similar in some broad ways, the British and French presses diverge at several points: while the former can reasonably be considered the father of the libertarian press system, the latter has been tossed back and forth among various forms of government; the British press is a national press, the French predominantly regional; daily and Sunday newspapers dominate British news media, whereas weekly newsmagazines and general information weeklies play a much larger role in France. . . .

These and other structural characteristics, to be discussed later, determined which publications were to be surveyed in this study and highlighted the differences between British and French societies. What all of the publications had in common was that they were acting as interpreters, perceptual filters through which readers in these countries form and reinforce their impressions of the United States:

> . . . the volume and rate of transactions within a nation-state are vastly greater than those across national boundaries. The consequence is that much of our information about events outside our country is filtered through mediating agents such as the press or governmental spokesmen, compounding the effects of psychological processes on the formation and change of image about the outside world.[43]

Finally, these perceptual filters were not confined to the national boundaries of Britain and France. Though formally "decolonized", both countries maintain special relationships with most of their former colonies, including press distribution.

Compared with the United States, Britain and France remain "world communicators", spreading their perceptions throughout Africa and Asia and, in relation to this study, magnifying the perspective in which they viewed Watergate.

LEGITIMIZATION

British and French press reactions to Watergate provide a unique research opportunity for uncovering some latent and not-so-latent attitudes about the American political system and its crisis functioning. Contrary to U.S. foreign policy, Watergate had virtually no precedent as a story. Foreign journalists were obliged to create a new framework for analysis which, without a well-established pattern of American behavior to fall back on, required more personal interpretations and speculation.

Once interpretation of an enduring news story begins, Himmelstrand suggests that it most often gets locked into a vicious circle which serves to:

> ... bias the total reporting of the event by a given newspaper or group of newspapers. What interpretation is made in the first phase (hard and hot news), is rather like a projective test of the prejudices of the commentator. In the second phase (background and interpretation) these biased interpretations direct the choice among and the play up of the various news items available by then. The biased news, in return, helps create new biased interpretation, and so on, till the third phase, that of oblivion or latency, is entered. Thus, very often the second phase is characterized not so much by "better", i.e., more unbiased interpretation, as by just more interpretation than during the first phase.[44]

As noted earlier, a news item's importance often determines whether or not it must be interpreted. But *how* it is interpreted is another story altogether.

To a certain degree, British and French journalists' interpretations of Watergate lend themselves to prediction simply by reference to the major "pictures in our heads" which people from each country hold about the United States. In an extensive cross-national survey called *How Nations See Each Other: A Study in Public Opinion*, William Buchanan and Hadley Cantril concluded, among other things, that the stereotypes

different nationalities maintain about each other are sympto-
matic — rather than causative — of political relations between
the countries.[45] The same relationship could be postulated
between stereotypes and press coverage, although there might
also exist a two-way casual link: journalists' culturally based
preconceptions slant their reportage, which then reinforces
existing stereotypes within the reading public. As Otto Klineberg
put it:

> The question of cause and effect also arises in connection with
> the suggestion that the mass media — newspapers, magazines, books,
> the cinema and, more recently, television — represent a significant
> source of ethnic stereotypes. Most probably the relation is a circular
> one, with the mass media reflecting stereotypes already in the public
> domain, and at the same time giving them a wider dissemination
> and additional credence.[46]

Years of often frustrating "effects" research in communication encourage caution before jumping to any conclusions
about mass media representing a hypodermic needle injecting
attitudes into its audience. Of the factors in Harold Lasswell's
communication model — Who Says What to Whom in Which
Channel with What Effect? — the last has proven most difficult to pin down. Too many intervening variables — cultural
conditioning, personal experience and attitudes, other sources
of information — muddle the results.

The most important of these — or at least the most studied —
is interpersonal communication of news. The "two-step flow"
idea maintains that local opinion leaders screen the mass media
and then influence others not so attentive to news, by word-of-
mouth.[47] James Rosenau posits a more complex pattern:

> News and interpretations of an event are first carried by, say, a
> newspaper; this is then read and adapted by opinion-makers, who
> assert (step 2) their opinions in speeches on the subject that are
> reported (step 3) by the press and thereupon picked up by "opinion
> leaders" in the general public who in turn pass on (step 4) the
> opinions through word-of-mouth.[48]

Whether directly or indirectly, the mass media wield a profound influence on our perception of the world. Journalists,
editors, news broadcasters, television producers, advertisers,

commentators and other media professionals serve as "gate-keepers" of information, selecting from an enormous number of possibilities what the public will have the opportunity to read, hear or see as "the news" or entertainment. They cannot force people to think in a certain way, but they can — and do — determine what their audiences will think about.

And, knowingly or not, admittedly or not, most readers place a certain amount of trust in journalists reporting for the publications they read. After all, a journalist is a professional — like a pharmacist or lawyer — trained through years of education and hard-knocks experience to carry out a certain specialized function within the society. Limitations of space and time prevent people from witnessing all the events which, directly or indirectly, influence their lives. The journalist's job essentially involves acting as their representative: being in the right place at the right time, then describing what happened. Though an incognito journalist's recounting of an event at a cocktail party might easily draw criticism as rumor-mongering, the same story in black and white normally passes for "the facts".

In short, the mass media lend a journalist's reportage or opinions "legitimization". Recognized as a necessary institution for gathering and disseminating information within the socio-political confines of a given society, the press legitimizes certain attitudes of its members, multiplying their influence by spreading these ideas more widely through the general public.

British and French press coverage of Watergate reveal several such attitudes passed on to the reading public in those countries. Most of these involved journalistic assumptions and preconceptions about life and political behavior in the United States, and about Watergate as a cataclysmic scenario. Even more interestingly, Watergate provided a mirror — if one not looked into by many — for these reporters. In the sense that "What Peter says about Paul tells you more about Peter than Paul", British and French Watergate reportage — particularly regarding the American press's role in the affair — reveals some subtle attitudes about these journalists' perceived roles in their own societies.

. . . there is potentially much to be learned about the culture, values and living ideology of a society from the totality of mass communication content. The basic consensual elements, the unspoken and unacknowledged assumptions, the models of conduct to be followed, the knowledge selected as important for a culture or sub-culture are open to view and even to systematic observation in what is disseminated, or attended to, in mass communications. It would be possible and desirable to conduct those kinds of analysis of mass media content which could help to answer fundamental questions about the society and culture in which mass communications are located.[49]

Newsmen from both countries claimed that Watergate "couldn't happen here", but with entirely different meanings. Their attitudes contain some important implications in relation to the universally claimed "freedom of the press." Chapter 4 details these issues.

FREEDOM OF THE PRESS . . .?

"Capitalism is a system of society in which man exploits man. Under Communism, the reverse is true."[50] This wry Iron Curtain quip could just as easily be applied to press systems in various countries. For years, one of the most acrimonious international debates has focused on alleged exploitation of mass media as political weapons. The latest forum on this heated issue took place at the 1975 Helsinki Conference, during which the Soviet Union supposedly bartered a freer flow of people and ideas for formal Western recognition of post-World War II European boundaries dividing East from West.

"Freedom of the press" is probably one of the most misused, abused, and ultimately meaningless phrases in the field of communication. Politicians, journalists, and laypeople alike often tout the "freedom" of their country's press for reasons ranging from demagoguery to professional pride to cultural ethnocentricism. Both the American and Soviet Constitutions guarantee "freedom of the press," in almost identical language. Meanwhile, these countries acidly accuse each other of denying its practice for "the people", whoever they may be.

Freedom of the press is a slippery concept to define. As reflected by the First Amendment to the Constitution, the

American connotation mainly involves separation and independence from the government, thereby assuring the "public" a voice to guard against and actively counter government oppression. So for Americans, the state-controlled Soviet press system represents the extreme opposite of press freedom. The Soviets, with their own logic, argue that a capitalist press system provides access to only a wealthy and influential elite, intentionally short-circuiting true representation of the masses and thereby maintaining the status quo. A free press, according to the Soviet definition, is a representative of the people. The people are represented by the Communist Party. The Communist Party just happens to run the government. Therefore, a free press is a state-controlled press. "Lenin's Marxist outlook was that freedom of the press was guaranteed not only, and not primarily, by government protection of the right to say what one would, but by public ownership of the economic structure of the press — its capital, newsprint, printing equipment, buildings and distribution network.[51]

Of course, glaring holes in logic — and practice — fuel the continual hurling of mutual accusations regarding "freedom of the press". And variations on these themes make a viable definition even more elusive. The democratic and socially liberal Scandinavian countries often combine a statistically representative political party press with state-controlled electronic media systems. Since 1974, when the Labour government proposed to make union membership compulsory for journalists, Great Britain has been suffering still another "freedom of the press" argument. Compulsory membership would restrict the press freedom of those journalists who did not want to join unions, it is argued. It would also hinder the freedom of editors in hiring persons without union cards. These hindrances could even extend to unions dictating the content of publications. The proposal will do nothing of the kind, says the other side. It will simply enable union members to deal more effectively with management. The debate goes on.[52] The limits of pornography, postal rates for printed matter, and confidentiality of sources remain major issues which continually define "press freedom" in the United States.

In sum, "freedom of the press" involves much more than constitutional guarantees, freedom from government interference or capitalist control. Labor unions, libel laws, advertising forces, political representation, editorial slants, media costs, distribution systems, journalistic preconceptions, deadline pressures, media financing, access to sources and readership preferences are but a handful of the almost innumerable influences defining a press system.

Still, the concept dies hard. Even bias-wary social scientists doggedly pursue a meaningful definition, invariably injecting their own cultural prejudices into the formula:

> There is nothing new, of course, in being able to say that a "free press system" like that of the United States usually is found only in countries with a high rate of literacy and per capita income.[53]

> ... the chief criterion (in distinguishing between a "free press system" and an "authoritarian regime") is the degree of control exercised by any official agency which has the power to interfere with the dissemination and discussion of news.[54]

> The violent upheavals so frequent in the Middle East can be attributed, indeed, to the fact that the demands and expectations of the people, stimulated in part by the mass media, greatly exceed their socioeconomic and cultural capacity for achievement. But if they continue to improve their economic status and their capacity for genuine media and political participation, they too may eventually succeed in establishing the conditions that make true press freedom possible.[55]

> Although the press in the newly-developing nations is burdened with the additional task of mobilizing the people toward national development goals, its political role should be much the same as the press in the West.[56]

Such cultural biases only guarantee an ethnocentric skewing of research results. In an international press survey using essentially the American model to define a "free press" and the Soviet model a "controlled press", the author of the last statement found, not surprisingly, that "the Western Hemisphere [has] the highest degree of press freedom of all five regions".[57]

Other social scientists have abandoned the "prescriptive" in favor of a "descriptive" approach by filing press systems under different categories. According to Communist dogma, "the newspaper [is] more than simply a channel of communication, but a political force in itself,"[58] as best exemplified by Lenin's idea that "A newspaper is not only a collective propagandist and a collective agitator, but also a collective organizer".[59] The government and/or ruling party completely controls the press under an "authoritarian" system. A "libertarian" press system provides a marketplace of ideas theoretically accessible to all sectors of a given population and self-regulating through philosophical, economic and political forces. Since World War II, a "social responsibility" theory has joined — and often overshadowed — the others.[60]

At first glance, the latter seems to present a viable solution to the judgmental problems posed by its predecessors. Under this theory, any press system reflecting its country's sociopolitical system rates the "socially responsible" label. It follows that: ". . . *all* conscientious and serious newspapers — regardless of what nation or political ideology they may represent — are 'socially responsible' ".[61] In this sense: "A capitalistic press, operating in a pluralistic and competitive context, would be socially *irresponsible* if suddenly transplanted into the Communist society."[62] And, the social responsibility theory might even serve to justify Lenin's change of mind "before and after" fathering the Russian revolution: "True freedom (of the press) will be found only in that future system . . . in which any worker (or group of workers) will be able to possess and exercise the right, enjoyed equally by all, of using the public printing works and the public paper. . . ."[63] Once ensconced in power, he wrote:

> Freedom of the press is freedom for the political organization of the bourgeoisie and their agents the Social Democrats and the Social Revolutionaries. To give these people such a weapon as freedom of the press would mean facilitating the task of the adversary. We do not wish to find ourselves committing suicide, and for this reason we shall not introduce freedom of the press.[64]

Most importantly and most damagingly, as John Merrill

noted, the social responsibility theory simply degenerates into a tautological dead-end: "Assuming that a nation's socio-political philosophy determines its press system, and undoubt-edly it does, then it follows that every nation's press system is socially responsible."[65] But then Merrill lapses into a defensive argument that Western presses often suffer charges of irresponsi-bility while their state-controlled Eastern counterparts never undergo similar attacks. This leads him to hypothesize: "The amount of social responsibility present in a press system is closely correlated to the amount of 'control' some outside group exercises over that press system."[66] So, when all is said and done, the social responsibility theory favors authoritarian and Communist systems, but:

> Responsibility to our society implies a continuance of this very pluralistic communication — with all of its virtues and evils — and a constant guard against any encroachments by government on any level to "define" what is "responsible" to society and further to align the press to its definition.
>
> This "press pluralism" concept seems much sounder, and certainly more meaningful, than "social responsibility." All press systems can claim to be responsible to their societies, but the idea of a pluralistic media system injecting a variety of opinions and ideas into the social fabric is one which only the libertarian system can reasonably claim.[67]

All of which implies, at best, that a pluralistic press is socially responsible for a pluralistic society and, at worst, that all responsible societies should adopt a pluralistic press system. In other words, we've come full circle, back to the futile sniping that "our press is better than yours".

Even discounting the press's role for a moment, the defini-tion of "freedom" most often betrays cultural conditioning. Says an American historian: ". . . man can seem to be free in any society, no matter how authoritarian, as long as he accepts the postulates of the society." But with a Western touch he adds: ". . . man can only be free in a society that is willing to allow its basic postulates to be questioned."[68] Perhaps the final word belongs to cultural relativist Melville Herskovits, who wrote: "There is, indeed, some reason to feel that the concept of freedom should be realistically redefined as the right to be exploited in terms of the patterns of one's own culture."[69]

In a sense, then, what we are suggesting is that "freedom" and particularly "freedom of the press" are no more than Cold-War anachronisms, and that it's time to move on to a more genuinely descriptive and sophisticated approach toward analyzing international press systems. Communications pioneer Paul Lazarsfeld said that:

> . . . the social scientist could have a great therapeutic effect if he were to call attention to the possibilities for other solutions to social problems than the ones to which we have become accustomed. International communications research should be looked to for a large share of such contributions.[70]

It is precisely to this spirit that this book owes its inspiration. Traditional frameworks and methods of press analysis prove to be, at best, outdated and, at worst, culturally biased. The final chapter re-examines the concept of "freedom of the press" and cites some of its analytical shortcomings as exemplified through French and British press coverage of Watergate. As an alternative solution, a comprehensive paradigm is presented which provides a method for nonevaluative analysis of press systems throughout the world.

REFERENCES

1. A. I. Hallowell, "Cultural Factors and the Structuralization of Perception," in J. H. Rohrer and M. Sherif (eds.), *Social Psychology at the Crossroads*, New York, Harper, 1951, pp. 166—67.
2. M. Sherif, *The Psychology of Social Norms*, New York, Harper, 1936, p. 32.
3. H. S. Jennings, *Behavior of the Lower Organisms*, New York, Columbia University Press, 1906, Reprinted, Bloomington, Indiana University Press, 1962.
4. Ashley Montagu, in Floyd Matson and Ashley Montagu (eds.), *The Human Dialogue: Perspectives on Communication*, New York, The Free Press, 1967, pp. 446—47.
5. Montagu in Matson and Montagu, pp. 447—50.
6. Montagu in Matson and Montagu, p. 448.
7. Otto Klineberg, *The Human Dimension in International Relations*, New York, Holt, Rinehart & Winston, 1964, p. 33.
8. Klineberg, p. 35.
9. G. W. Allport and L. Postman, *The Psychology of Rumor*, New York, Holt, Rinehart & Winston, 1947.

10. Klineberg, pp. 46—48.
11. Klineberg, p. 34.
12. Ross Stagner, *Psychological Aspects of International Conflict*, Belmont, California, Brooks/Cole, 1967, p. 42.
13. H. C. J. Duijker and N. H. Frijda, *National Character and National Stereotypes*, Amsterdam, North-Holland Publishing Co., 1960, p. 125.
14. Stanley Hoffman, in John C. Farrell and Asa P. Smith (eds.), *Image and Reality in World Politics* . . ., New York, Columbia University Press, 1967, p. 57.
15. William A. Scott, "Psychological and Social Correlates of International Images," in Herbert C. Kelman (ed.), *International Behavior: A Social-Psychological Approach*, New York, Holt, Rinehart & Winston, 1965, pp. 71—100.
16. Klineberg, p. 22.
17. Hoffman in Farrell and Smith, p. 57.
18. Ralph K. White, *Nobody Wanted War*, Garden City. N.Y., Anchor Books, 1970, p. 6.
19. W. Buchanan and H. Cantril, *How Nations See Each Other*, Urbana, University of Illinois Press, 1953.
20. Ralph K. White, "Images in the Context of International Conflict: Soviet Perceptions of the U.S. and U.S.S.R.," in Kelman, p. 255.
21. Robert A. LeVine, "Socialization, Social Structure, and Intersocietal Images," in Kelman, pp. 45—46.
22. Davis Bobrow, "Transfer of Meaning Across National Boundaries," in Richard L. Merritt (ed.), *Communication in International Politics*, Urbana, University of Illinois Press, 1972, p. 57.
23. Karl Deutsch, *The Nerves of Government; Models of Political Communication and Control*, New York, Free Press, 1963, p. 150.
24. Jack Lyle, "Contemporary Functions of the Mass Media," in *Mass Media and Violence*, Volume IX, A Report to the National Commission on the Causes and Prevention of Violence, prepared by Robert K. Baker and Sandra J. Ball, Washington, U.S. Government Printing Office, 1969, pp. 207—10.
25. Harold Lasswell, "The Structure and Function of Communication in Society," in Lyman Bryson (ed.), *The Communication of Ideas*, New York, Harper, 1948, p. 37.
26. Richard L. Merritt, "Transmission of Values across National Boundaries," in Richard Merritt (ed.), p. 12.
27. Karl Erik Rosengren, "International News: Time and Type of Report," in Heinz-Dietrich Fischer and John C. Merrill (eds.), *International Communication: Media, Channels, Functions*, New York, Hastings House Publishers, 1970, pp. 75—76.
28. Rosengren in Fischer and Merrill, p. 76.
29. Rosengren in Fischer and Merrill, p. 78.
30. Merritt in Merritt, p. 17.
31. Paul F. Lazarsfeld, "The Prognosis for International Communications Research," in Fischer and Merrill, p. 456.
32. Stagner, pp. 129—30.
33. Stagner, p. 136.

34. Melville J. Herskovits, *Cultural Relativism: Perspectives in Cultural Pluralism*, New York, Random House, 1972, p. 93.
35. Herskovits, p. 48.
36. W. Phillips Davidson and Alexander L. George, "An Outline for the Study of International Political Communication," in Fischer and Merrill, p. 468.
37. Hoffman in Farrell and Smith, pp. 60—66.
38. Hoffman in Farrell and Smith, p. 65.
39. Hoffman in Farrell and Smith, p. 68.
40. Hoffman in Farrell and Smith, pp. 70—71.
41. UNESCO, "The Structure of the World's Press," in Fischer and Merrill, p. 271.
42. John C. Merrill, "Global Patterns of Elite Daily Journalism," in Fischer and Merrill, p. 286.
43. Merritt in Merritt, p. 18.
44. Rosengren in Fischer and Merrill, p. 76.
45. Buchanan and Cantril, p. 57.
46. Klineberg, p. 38.
47. Elihu Katz, "The Two-step Flow of Communication: An up-to-date Report on a Hypothesis," *Public Opinion Quarterly*, number 21 (Spring 1957), pp. 61—78.
48. James Rosenau, *Public Opinion and Foreign Policy: An Operational Formulation*, New York, Random House, 1961, pp. 7—8.
49. Denis McQuail (ed.), *Sociology of Mass Communications*, Harmondsworth (U.K.), Penguin, 1972, p. 14.
50. Stagner, p. 90.
51. Mark W. Hopkins, "Three Soviet Concepts of the Press," in Fischer and Merrill, p. 30.
52. *Newsweek International*, Nov. 17, 1975, p. 19.
53. Raymond B. Nixon, "Factors Related to Freedom in National Press Systems," in Fischer and Merrill, p. 116.
54. Nixon in Fischer and Merrill, p. 119.
55. Nixon in Fischer and Merrill, p. 128.
56. Ralph L. Lowenstein, "Press Freedom as a Political Indicator," in Fischer and Merrill, p. 129.
57. Lowenstein in Fischer and Merrill, p. 135.
58. Hopkins in Fischer and Merrill, p. 33.
59. Hopkins in Fischer and Merrill, p. 35.
60. Fred S. Siebert, Theodore Peterson and Wilbur Schramm, *Four Theories of the Press*, Urbana, University of Illinois Press, 1956, pp. 73—103.
61. Merrill in Fischer and Merrill, p. 280.
62. Merrill in Fischer and Merrill, p. 280.
63. Fernand Terrou and Lucien Solal, *Legislation for Press, Film and Radio*, UNESCO, Paris, 1951, p. 51.
64. *The Press in Authoritarian Countries, IPI Survey*, Zurich, International Press Institute, 1959, p. 14.
65. John C. Merrill, "The Press and Social Responsibility," in Fischer and Merrill, p. 15.

66. Merrill, 1970b, p. 19.
67. Merrill, 1970b, p. 20.
68. John B. Wolf, "Man's Struggle for Freedom Against Authority," in *Social Sciences and Freedom*, Minneapolis, University of Minnesota Press, 1955, p. 1.
69. Herskovits, p. 9.
70. Lazarsfeld in Fischer and Merrill, p. 457.

2. The British Press and Watergate: The View from Fleet Street

One Congressman suggests Nixon should have a Japanese guard (instead of a German one). 'They make better electronic equipment, and they commit suicide when things get rough.'

The *Sunday Times*

The afternoon of August 8, 1974 was a short one for Louis Heren. The squat, mustachioed deputy editor of *The Times* of London was awaiting word from Washington that Richard Nixon, under siege from the continuous revelations of Watergate, was going to resign.

Nixon had admitted his guilt in the cover-up scheme on Monday of that week. Sometime during each succeeding day he had felt compelled to issue a message no one any longer believed: he wasn't going to resign; he was going to stay and fight. By Thursday, however, Nixon had gotten another message. He could not remain in office. If he did not resign now, he would soon be impeached by the House of Representatives and convicted by the Senate. His days in the Oval Office were numbered.

Heren knew that, too. He, perhaps more than any other newsman in Europe, understood what was happening in Washington. He had spent many years there as a working reporter, had revisited there regularly, and had maintained many contacts there. Just a year before, he had written a remarkable piece on the impeachment process, and *The Times* had devoted a page and a half of space to it.

Now, another long piece — this one a four-page spread on the fall of Richard Nixon — had been put on the press at New Printing House Square. Much of it had been written by Heren, and it had been produced under his direction. The printers now awaited his word to start the presses rolling.

Heren was reluctant, however. It seemed that Nixon had only one option, resignation, but Heren had seen him pull rabbits out of his political hat before. It would be 2 a.m. London time before Nixon went on television, far too late to print an extra four pages. Heren was 95% sure that this was the last full day of the Nixon Presidency, but he needed one more word of confirmation.

To get it, he picked up the phone and dialed directly to the Justice Department in Washington. A highly placed official, who had been a friend of Heren's for a number of years (and whose name Heren still won't reveal), came on the line. Was this the day Nixon was going to resign, Heren asked. Yes, his friend said. Are you sure? Again the answer was yes.

Heren hung up, then placed a call to the press room and told them to start production. The next day *Times* readers had four extra pages of analysis and commentary to supplement the front page story on the resignation of the President of the United States.

The incident is a minor one, but it demonstrates the "special relationship" that many British journalists have with America. One of the most remarkable things about the British press, at least to American readers, is the amount of international news — especially American news — found in the quality papers. Some of the explanations for the British press's international outlook are obvious: the empire mentality that assumes Britain's importance in the world; the fact that Britain, more than any other Western industrialized nation, is dependent on international trade for her livelihood; the large circulations of British newspapers in Europe and many national capitals once part of the empire. The preference for American news may also be explained with the obvious: a common language and heritage, and similar political outlook; political and economic alliances; and a great deal of contact among the private citizens of the two countries.

Yet for a complete understanding of the British press and why it prints what it does, other factors should be taken into account. The facts that the British press structure is a national one, that it operates under a restrictive set of laws, and that its finances are perilous are conditions which in no small way determine the content of the British press today.

A NATIONAL STRUCTURE

Great Britain is one of the few countries in the Western world which can boast of a truly national media structure. At present there are fifteen newspapers -- eight dailies and seven Sundays — which circulate throughout the entire country. The newspaper reader in Edinburgh has much the same choice each morning as the one in Dover, even though these cities are located in different corners of the country.

National newspapers have an almost exclusive hold over the morning newspaper market in Britain. All of the dailies are morning papers, as are the Sundays. Very few regional papers have strong morning circulations. The regional media are confined mostly to the afternoon, leaving them in many instances to repeat only what has already been said by the nationals (especially with regard to news emanating from London).

The rest of the media in Great Britain fall into this pattern. Through a system of regional relay stations, the British Broadcasting Corporation and the commercial Independent Television Authority transmit most of the programming which can be seen on a British television screen. Local stations are allowed to vary their programming some, but their options are very limited. Again, the television viewers in Edinburgh and Dover will have pretty much the same choice of programs to look at.

Radio, periodicals and film distribution are also run on a national basis, although the recent advent of more localized radio stations has introduced a greater variety in some areas. Still, the chances are that, in general, the British, from one end of the country to the other, will on a daily basis have the same choice of what newspapers and periodicals to read, what tele-vision and radio programs to watch and listen to, and what movies to go see.[1]

The reasons for this national structure begin with geography. Britain is a very small nation, an island off the coast of Western Europe. The closest point to Europe is Dover, which is 23 miles from Calais, France, but most of Britain is much further away both physically and psychologically. The size of the island, and the extensive public transportation system through-out, are a help to nationally circulated newspapers.

Another reason for the national press structure is that most Britons, it is argued, want the same sorts of things; their tastes do not vary greatly by region. Just as they buy the same kinds of products in different parts of the country, so they are satisfied to have the same kinds of newspapers.[2]

None of this is to suggest that a national structure means there is no great variety in the British press. The opposite is true. American visitors in London — no doubt used to the greatly homogenized newspapers which circulate in the different regions of their country — are generally struck by the wide variety of papers found on a British newsstand. Some of those papers have a staid, gray appearance resembling the *Wall Street Journal*, others have lively make-ups and a variety of design comparable to many American dailies, and still others look like transatlantic versions of the American gossip tabloids. Depend-ing on taste, a reader may choose from the intellectual enlight-ment of a paper like *The Times* to the snappy gossip and pictures of breasts in the *Mirror* or the *Sun*, and almost any variation in between.

Politically, British papers exhibit some variety, though not as much as many press critics would like. The majority of the nationals support the Conservative Party, with only two or three leaning toward Labour. There is one Communist Party daily, the *Morning Star*, but its circulation is far below all the other nationals.

The British national press is divided into two groups, the "qualities"and the"populars". A brief description of each follows:

Quality dailies

The *Financial Times*: distinguished by the pink paper on which it is printed; goes to the men in the bowler hats who work in "The City", London's financial district; researches subjects in depth with reporters they consider to be experts in the field; executives pride themselves on publishing an "unbiased" paper; also distinguished by the fact that it is making money.

The *Guardian*: doesn't make money; has been called the best newspaper in the world by some (but not everybody); liberal-leftish leanings are evident both in editorials and news columns; read by intellects and intellectual pretenders.

The *Daily Telegraph*: the most "popular" of the qualities; firmly allied with the Conservative Party; mixes a singular brand of politics with tidbits on divorces, murder trials, and some of London's best sports reporting.

The Times: Great Britain's paper of record; leftish-conservative preferring the Tories because they're gentlemen while favoring the Labourites because they have better ideas; often has trouble making up its editorial mind and almost invariably opts for the center; reporters and editors like to use three words when one would suffice.

Popular dailies

The *Daily Express*: the late Lord Beaverbrook's paper; his philosophy of giving the reader what he wants is still alive and thriving; Tory in outlook, the paper makes no pretension to being intellectual but spouts a knee-jerk jingoism instead.

The *Daily Mail*: another of the ultra-conservatives; changed its format from a broadsheet to a tabloid in 1971; filled with articles by, for and about women.

The *Daily Mirror*: the most pro-Labour of any national paper; a tabloid with a punchy editorial style and invariably a picture of a nude girl on page three; one of the largest circulations in the Western world, with more than 4 million copies printed every day.

The *Sun*: Rupert Murdoch, an abrasive Australian, decided to challenge the *Mirror*'s circulation when he took over the

Sun in 1969, so, in the words of one commentary, "Politics went, naked ladies arrived, and the circulation soared".[3] For what it's worth, the paper is pro-Labour.

Quality Sundays

The *Sunday Telegraph*: not quite as conservative as its stablemate, the *Daily Telegraph*, but almost.

The *Observer*: oldest of the surviving Sunday papers; emphasizes foreign news but is looking more and more like its rival, the *Sunday Times*.

The *Sunday Times*: the real heavy of the British press; prides itself in having pioneered "investigative reporting" several years ago and is the only British paper that still makes an attempt at it.

A fourth group is the popular Sundays, which include the *News of the World* (referred to on the street as "news of the screws"), *Sunday Express* (like the *Daily Express*, still giving the reader what he wants), *Sunday Mirror* (more girls, more scandals and more punchy writing), and the *Sunday People* (a happy combination of all of the above). Because of the lack of time, money, and research assistants, this last group does not figure into this study.

An additional paper which is included in this study is the *Evening Standard*, a regional paper circulated in and around London. It is a tabloid with straight news and pictures of girls with more clothes than the ones in the *Mirror*. Just why it was included will be dealt with later in this chapter.

THE BLACK CLOUD OF FINANCES

In today's inflation-plagued Great Britain, no business is more uncertain about its finances than Fleet Street. The death rate of newspapers since World War II has been staggering and depressing. A sudden shortage of newsprint, a wildcat strike by an important union, a breakdown in the transportation system, or any other sudden jolt to the newspaper's normal operation could send several papers toward the brink of financial ruin. Somehow newspapers have survived the most perilous of these conditions, but often it has been a case of Peter paying Paul.

The steady trend of the twentieth century has been away from individual ownership and toward conglomeration of newspaper companies. Many of these companies have outside incomes which helped them survive. The situation is such that in most press groups, the criterion of "profit — or death" is suspended because one newspaper cross-subsidizes another, or the profits from quite different activities subsidize the loss-making newspapers. The *Sunday Telegraph* does not make a profit: it is carried by the *Daily Telegraph*. *The Times* does not make a profit: its losses have been set against profits from other of Lord Thomson's activities, and have built up his moral credit with establishment opinion. The *Daily Mail* does not make a profit: it is cross-subsidized by Associated Newspapers, regional newspapers, and may be later by its North Sea oil interests. The *Guardian* does not make a profit: but the *Manchester Evening News* carries it. The *Daily Express* makes a large loss in some years and is kept alive by other newspapers in the Beaverbrook stable and by its bankers who have the solid security of property in Fleet Street to fall back on. If each newspaper had to stand or fall on its own commercial merits, four out of the eight national dailies in late 1974 would cease publication.[4] Add to that list the *Observer*, which found in late 1975 that the personal fortune of the Astors could no longer carry it.

Just why Fleet Street should be in such trouble is a matter of continuing debate. Owners tend to blame obstinate unions, which have opposed modernization of equipment and any reduction in the work force. Unions blame mismanagement and over-extension by owners. Inflation, circulation wars, and loss of advertising to other media have also played their parts in Fleet Street's financial demise.

It is a fairly good bet that the move toward consolidation of ownership will continue. Of all the solutions for Fleet Street that have been proposed, none has seriously suggested breaking up the conglomerates, though there are many critics of the press who would like to see that happen. Officials of one national daily interviewed by two of the authors said that the day is probably not far off when all the newspapers on Fleet Street will operate out of one or two printing plants. This, they said, seems to be the only solution to the continued high cost of production.

Whatever the reasons for the situation, and whatever the solutions to it, the low financial state of Fleet Street today provides a constant dark backdrop to any discussion of the British press.

TRADITION AND *THE TIMES*

The history of British newspapers is a long and distinguished one. It includes the fights for redress of grievances under Charles I; John Wilkes's battle to open Parliament to public view; the scandals of the British Army during the Crimean War; and many other controversies which have eventually enabled the press to operate more openly in British society.

Traditions have built themselves up around Fleet Street and around individual papers. The most traditional (until 1966 it carried no news on its front page) and the most tradition-laden is *The Times*. For more than a century, "The Thunderer" has been looked upon as expressing the collective opinion of the British ruling class and often government policy itself. As far back as 1856, American philosopher Ralph Waldo Emerson, upon returning from Europe, wrote of that paper:

> No power in England is more felt, more feared, or more obeyed. What you read in the morning in that journal, you shall hear in the evening in all society. It has ears everywhere, and its information is the earliest, completest and surest. It has risen, year by year, and victory by victory, to its present authority. . . .
>
> The influence of the journal is a recognized power in Europe, and, of course, none is more conscious of it than its conductors. The tone of its articles has often been the occasion of comment from the official organs of the continental courts, and sometimes the ground of diplomatic complaint. What would the *"Times"* say?

is a terror in Paris, in Berlin, in Vienna, in Copenhagen and in Nepal. . . .[5]

The importance of *The Times*'s "official voice" should not be lost on observers of the press, especially to Americans who have nothing comparable. The history of *The Times* shows it to be closely aligned with, though often critical of, the British Government. No modern American newspaper could lay claim to such a position, even if it wanted to.

An example of *The Times*'s influence in foreign affairs occurred more than 80 years after Emerson had penned his description. During the delicate negotiations between Britain and Germany over the fate of the Czechoslovakia region in 1938, *The Times* published an editorial saying the Czechs should consider conceding the Sudetenland to Hitler's demand as one of a number of possible outcomes of the negotiations. Since *The Times*'s editor, Geoffrey Dawson, was so close to the then Prime Minister, Neville Chamberlain, and because the paper's editorial policy had been wholly in support of the government's appeasement policy, the capitals of Europe were stunned by the suggestion. It was perceived to be part of the official thinking of the British Government, even though it was denied repeatedly by government officials. The British position in the negotiations never recovered from this blow, and Hitler pressed for, and eventually got, the Sudetenland.[6]

This incident demonstrates one of the subtle differences between the British and American press—government relations. In America, the relationship is generally that of out-and-out adversaries, with newspapers competing not only against themselves but against the government. In Britain, the relationship is one more of cooperation with the government. This is not to say that there is no competition between the government and the media. (The Labour Party could certainly not be persuaded to this point of view.) In individual instances, the government and newspapers often compete and do so vigorously. Yet in Britain, there are more rules to the game than in America, and the British, being the fair-play artists they are, are more likely to observe them.

THE UNOPENED SOCIETY

It is almost axiomatic to say that societies create structures, institutions and laws which reflect their own norms. So it is with Great Britain, her press structure, and the laws governing the media. America — as amply demonstrated by Watergate — is a relatively open society with few laws and conventions restricting newspaper editorial activity. Not so with Great Britain.

Comparatively, the British press has much less freedom in its reportorial approach to government than does the American press. America has formally introduced a "press freedom" clause into her constitution; Britain has no written constitution and a somewhat weaker tradition of press freedom. This weaker tradition manifests itself formally in British law via libel laws, contempt of court laws, parliamentary privilege, and the Official Secrets Acts.

At first glance, British libel laws[7] seem fair, balanced and reasonable to all concerned. Libel is acceptably defined as "a defamatory statement reflecting upon a man's character or reputation, which tends to lower him in the estimation of right thinking members of society; or which tends to bring him into hatred, ridicule, contempt, fear, dislike or disesteem with society generally".[8] A plaintiff does not have to prove loss or damage, though he must prove that the libel refers to him and that the defendant published it.

One defense against libel is justification, or truth. Here the burden of proof is on the defendant. Another defense is privilege, referring to reports of parliamentary and other governmental debates and actions. A third defense is "fair comment", always a tricky one because of its subjective nature. As opposed to libel suits in the U.S., a plaintiff is not required to prove malice on the part of the publisher.

Why, then, should the fear of libel send chills down the nearly frozen spine of Fleet Street? The main reason is money. In Britain, juries are allowed to award damage sums to plaintiffs they judge to have been libelled, and sometimes these sums are astronomical. For example, in 1958 the *Daily Mail* and *Daily Telegraph* ran what appeared to be fairly innocent stories about a police inquiry into a certain London company. The head of the company and his partners sued and were awarded a total of £217,000 by a jury. That amount was later set aside, a new trial ordered, and a different amount settled upon, but the shock waves are still reverberating throughout British news and editorial rooms. A settlement like that could bring any one of a number of newspapers to the head of an open grave. This was no isolated incident either, for juries in Britain have always tended to side heavily with an individual against a corporate power.

In recent years some changes in the libel laws have been proposed with the hope that newspapers may be able to exercise greater editorial freedom. The laws, however, are still perceived as threats, and many newspapers go to great lengths to avoid them. A number of papers have lawyers reading the copy with authority to strike anything they think may get the paper into court. Still, it is doubtful that even lawyers reading copy could have prevented some of the freakish libel suits that have taken place this century, and British journalists cannot help but feel inhibited by them. As Colin Seymour-Ure has written:

> The dangers of the libel laws . . . are not in their impact on day-to-day political reporting and comment but in the inhibiting effect which the application of the law has recently had on exposures in the public interest of inefficiency, corruption and the like. . . . A balance obviously has to be struck in society between the right of free speech and the rights of an individual to protect his reputation . . . at present the balance is uneven and the law protects the scoundrel too easily. . . . "Publish and be damned!" is a fate any editor would be ready to face. When the great journalist Stead went to prison for exposing London prostitution, the *Pall Mall Gazette* prospered. Damnation (and especially memoirs of the damned!) can be a circulation builder. But "Publish and be bankrupt" is more nearly the threat today, and who can blame a newspaper for fearing that?[9]

Contempt of court law also severely handicaps the British press in the coverage of crime and criminal investigations. Once a matter has been taken under investigation by the police, the press can say very little about it. In fact, it can say only what the police allow. When a person is arrested, all comment ceases with the euphemism, "A man is helping police with their inquiries." If that person is charged and brought to trial, only the court action can be covered. A newspaper was recently fined £500 for describing the suit of clothes the defendant wore to his trial because it wasn't considered germane to the case.

Again, the contrast with the situation in America is striking. Newspapers often conduct their own investigations of crime, and, some would argue, accuse, try, and convict their own defendants. The argument over whether a person subjected to tremendous amounts of publicity (such as Lt. Calley or the Watergate conspirators) can receive a fair trial is a continuing one in America. In Great Britain, it never occurs. There, the rule of law is firmly and enforceably on the side of silence before the trial.

Another inhibitor of press coverages of governmental activity is a series of laws known as the Official Secrets Acts. The first of the Official Secrets Acts was enacted in 1889 and was designed to plug information leaks in the Civil Service. From then on, the acts have piled upon one another. In 1911, the act was strengthened as a protection against German espionage. An act was passed in 1920 which dealt a lethal blow to the confidentiality of journalists' sources.

Although the acts have been amended from time to time, sometimes in journalists' favor, they still constitute an ever-present threat to reporters in dealing with government information. Their vague wording lends wide latitude to government prosecutors, and they carry with them the possibilities of stiff jail sentences and fines for offenders. Almost anything the government does can be classified as an official secret.[10]

One of the common characteristics of governments and civil servants everywhere — no matter what form of government — is the desire for secrecy and selective exposure about what they do. Britain's Official Secrets Acts fit this desire ideally. The acts can be used to hide inefficiency, mismanagement and even dishonesty on the part of the government. To assume they do not is to assume that Britain has a set of politicians and civil servants with honesty and integrity far beyond anything the world has ever seen — and that is to assume too much.

Parliamentary privilege is still another way in which the press can be controlled, although its use these days is almost obsolete. Under parliamentary privilege, Parliament has the power to jail or reprimand anyone who has offended it during its sitting. For example, a journalist who might call one or all the Members of Parliament "a drunken coward" could be hauled before Parliament and thrown in jail until the session was ended. Then he could be forced to pay his jailer for his keep, and if he remained sufficiently unrepentant, he could be incarcerated again at the beginning of the next session until his soul had been purged. The parliamentary privilege statute has atrophied with disuse, but it is still present and could be invoked for the discomfort of an offending journalist.

An American, especially an American journalist, might think these laws totally incompatible with his perception of a functioning free press, and he might expect to see British journalists chaffing under them. Such is not the case, however. Most journalists live quite comfortably with most of the laws and desire few changes. Only the Official Secrets Acts and the libel laws come in for much criticism.

Not only do journalists support most of the laws which Americans would find inhibiting, they often carry them further than their letter requires. Several examples of this can be found. On the official level, there are the D-Notices, memos circulated to selected papers from the Ministry of Defence. These provide guidelines on what sort of information may fall under the Official Secrets Acts. The D-Notices have no legal force, so it is up to editors to exercise restraint over themselves about the information contained in the D-Notices. Occasionally, this pact is broken by an editor, but on the whole, it is adhered to and the information in the D-Notices remains secret.

On an unofficial level, British journalists may gather together for their own pacts of censorship. One of the most famous examples of this was the press's self-imposed silence about the romance and marriage plans of King Edward VIII in 1936. The king had fallen in love with a twice-divorced American and could not be dissuaded from thoughts of marriage. Since there was a possibility that he could have his kingdom and his marriage, too, if he negotiated delicately with the members of the Cabinet, Edward asked newspaper proprietors to refrain from saying anything about it. To a man, they did so. At the same time, newspapers in America were having a field day with speculation about the impending marriage, and British journalists were standing mute with a collective stiff upper lip. Their silence was broken only when negotiations were ended and the king had decided to abdicate.

American journalists would have neither made nor adhered to any such agreement. Most American journalists would argue that it is better to inform the public and bring them into the decision-making process, while Britons might say that silence is better than subjecting negotiations to the ebbs and flows of public pressure. Neither view should be seen as wholly right or wrong. What should be recognized is the difference with which journalists understand their roles in the respective societies.

Comprehending this attitude about the role of the press in British society is very important in studying the coverage British newspapers gave to Watergate. A great part of the Watergate story involved the role the American press played in uncovering the secrets of Watergate. British journalists in America at the time had to pass judgment on their American colleagues for doing things they would not or could not have done in their own country. This, as we shall see, presented them with a dilemma which they could only partially overcome.

WATERGATE: A TELEVISION STORY

One of the striking features about the Watergate story is the amount of it that "happened" on television. Senate committee hearings, press conferences and speeches related to the subject, as well as news reports, commentaries and news specials, took up a vast amount of air time both in the United States and

Great Britain. The long-running Watergate story maintained a maximum of political drama and impact, triumph and tragedy, which makes "good television".

This study does not concern itself with the television coverage of Watergate nor with its impact on British viewers, but because there was so much of Watergate on British television — the Senate Committee hearings received nightly coverage — the subject bears a brief consideration. Clear connections between what people watch on television and what they read in their newspapers have not been established in communication theory yet. For our purposes, we may pose two basic questions to keep in mind during the rest of our discussions:

> Do potential newspaper readers turn on their television sets and neglect their newspapers? and
> Do people see something on television news programs and expect to find out more about it in the next day's paper (or vice versa)?

It seems logical to assume that for people who both read newspapers and watch television, the two media at some points supplement information. British readers and viewers received a fairly steady diet of Watergate for more than a year. In such a situation, neither medium could have functioned totally independently of the other.

THE PAPERS IN THIS STUDY

Ideally, the authors would have included each of the national newspapers and at least one or two of the major regionals in this study. Time and resources prevented this, so a selection had to be made. What we hoped for in selecting seven of the fifteen possibilities was to cover as much of the spectrum of political opinion and financial structure of the British press as possible.

The Times, the *Guardian*, the *Daily Telegraph*, and the *Daily Mirror* were selected with this political/financial mix in mind. Here we have the Liberal, Center, Labour and Tory all represented. The *Observer* was selected because of its traditional

Table 2
Circulations of the Papers Chosen

	1973	1974
The *Daily Mirror*	4,261,683	4,192,491
The *Daily Telegraph*	1,423,031	1,472,493
The *Guardian*	344,356	346,635
The Times	345,044	351,203
The *Evening Standard*	519,604	522,000
The *Observer*	794,590	832,283
The *Sunday Times*	1,504,515	1,505,385

Source: Audit Bureau of Circulations.

reputation in covering foreign news. When it came to a choice between the *Sunday Times* and the *Sunday Telegraph*, the *Sunday Times* was selected even though it, like *The Times*, is part of the Thomson chain (of course, the *Sunday Telegraph* is also linked with the *Daily Telegraph*). Tipping the balance toward the *Sunday Times* was Henry Brandon, the paper's correspondent in Washington for 25 years. No study of British comment on America could be complete without him.

The standout in our selection is the *Evening Standard*, which many do not consider a national daily. Technically, it isn't, though it does have some circulation outside Greater London. It was chosen for two reasons. One was our desire to have a Beaverbrook newspaper in the group; and the other, our need for some kind of regional daily. The paper fits into the study more than we had hoped due to the fact that it keeps its own correspondent in Washington and that so many of his reports were devoted to Watergate.

Finally, none of the popular Sundays were chosen because of the expected paucity of their Watergate coverage. For these papers, if it isn't lurid, it probably isn't there.

The remainder of this section is divided into three parts. The first is a separate commentary on how each newspaper selected covered Watergate. The second is the chronological story of Watergate, as told by the British press. This will offer some comparison between what the different newspapers were saying at any particular point. Readers who are unfamiliar with the individual newspapers may want to read the sections as they are presented. Those who are unfamiliar with the Watergate story as a whole may want to read the second part before beginning the first. The third part concerns the Due Process Controversy and should be read last in any case.

A word about the references: to avoid cumbersome footnotes and to give the readers immediate information about when a quote was published, references to this are found in the text. A reference such as (3/13/73 — 3) means that the quote appeared on March 13, 1973 on page three. In other words we are using (month/date/year — page number), the American style, as opposed to the European style of day/month/year. Our European readers will have to bear with us.

The *Daily Mirror*

On its surface the Watergate story was froth with scandal and corruption, abundant with characters representing both good and evil. The *Daily Mirror* — a Labour-oriented tabloid filled with pictures of nude girls, and stories of sex, crime and the general peculiarity of the human condition — specializes in just such stories. Yet the *Daily Mirror*'s coverage of Watergate was sporadic and episodic.

There was a combination of factors which prevented the *Daily Mirror* from giving Watergate anything near complete coverage. First, the story went on too long. A good scandal lasts only a few months at most; Watergate lasted for more than 2 years, and for readers of a paper like the *Daily Mirror* — and for its editors too — Watergate got very old very quickly. Watergate was also too complicated for a paper like the *Daily Mirror*. Campaign financing, bugging, lying, courtroom procedures, plea bargaining — there was too much happening on too many fronts for the punchy style of headlines and writing of this tabloid. Too, there was not much sex in Watergate, which made it, in the eyes of the *Daily Mirror*, a second-rate scandal. What sex there was, namely the letters accusing Jackson and Humphrey of sexual misbehavior, the plot to fix Democratic contenders up with call girls, and CREEP's hiring of a nude girl to walk around in Miami with a Muskie sign, the *Daily Mirror* made the most of, but that sort of thing just could not compete with what the *Daily Mirror* usually gives to its readers.

In the absence of sex, the *Daily Mirror* concentrated on the President's health. The mental state of the President was the paper's major concern during the week after the firing of Archibald Cox as Special Prosecutor. Nixon had put American armed forces on a major alert, a move which the paper found reckless, and he had twice cancelled television addresses to explain himself. Nixon's conduct "has become unpredictable and alarming. . . . How can a man who dare not face up to his own people, after promising twice to do so, face up to the problems of the human race?" And later in that same issue, under a two-page spread entitled "THE BREAKING OF THE PRESIDENT", the *Daily Mirror* asked: How well is the President? "The evidence now lies only in the President's actions and reactions to events" (10/26/73 — 2, 16—17).

Two weeks later the President was no better. Nixon "looked as if he had aged a decade in a year. He seemed to have difficulty coordinating his eye movements. His eyes fluttered and then popped open, and he dragged constantly on an earlobe" (11/8/73 — 4).

The fact that Nixon was really and truly sick when he went to the Mideast the next summer caused even more notice from the *Daily Mirror*. In large front-page headlines on June 26, the *Mirror* announced "NIXON: THE SICK PRESIDENT". Just before Nixon was to return from Moscow, *Mirror* correspondent Anthony Delano wrote that when the President steps off the plane, "the television lenses will be shamelessly zooming in on his left leg. . . . If he is limping, it might be taken as a sign that there could after all be a way out of the long-running national scandal of Watergate."

The last week of the Nixon Presidency gave the *Mirror* ample opportunity to speculate about his mental health. The day before resignation, in bold reverse-type headlines on page one, the *Mirror* quoted an unidentified presidential aide as saying:

"The President won't listen. He's not in touch with reality." In the story that followed, Nixon was said to be "the picture of a man living in a fantasy world, convinced that he had done no wrong . . ." (8/8/74 — 1). The day after Ford's pardon of Nixon, the *Mirror* headlined its story "THE SICK MAN OF AMERICA" and said Nixon was granted a pardon "partly because of President Ford's fear that the humiliation and agony of a Watergate coverup trial could break his health" (9/9/74 — 1).

From both a reporting and editorial point of view, the *Daily Mirror* was anti-Nixon from beginning to end. The day of the 1972 election, John Pilger, the paper's chief international correspondent, wrote, "Today, after a lapse of 196 years, the Monarchy will be restored to America and Richard Milhous Nixon The First will be king . . . never before has a president refused to answer almost daily charges of scandal and corruption and outright crime which can be traced directly to his office" (11/7/72 — 12). When Nixon left office in disgrace via Marine helicopter and Air Force plane nearly 2 years later, the *Mirror* noted: "And true to his 'Tricky Dicky' image to the last, he bummed a free ride. . . . It was a gesture that did not go unnoticed after his 'no climb down, no guilt, no regrets' resignation speech" (8/10/74 — 1).

The *Mirror* had been highly critical editorially of Nixon in other areas, such as the Christmas bombing of Vietnam in 1972, and Watergate did nothing to endear him to the paper. The *Mirror* used the Saturday Night Massacre to call for the President's resignation in the most repulsive terms: "Will Richard Nixon display one single spark of decency and remove himself — or will the U.S. Congress be forced to hand him a loaded revolver?" The editorial quoted what Nixon said in appointing Cox as Special Prosecutor and said, "Those noble, lying words. . . . The sooner America is rid of this man Nixon, the better for her health. . . . Richard Nixon has reduced himself to an historical ruin that can never be restored by political cosmetics or even reincarnation to regain the confidence of his nation or of the world. DEMOCRACY VOMITS" (11/23/73 — 1).

The *Daily Mirror* was quick to be cynical about American politics and overdramatic about the state of the nation. In April 1973, an editorial said, "American politics have always had their shifty, squalid side", as in March 1973, it had said, "Corruption and lying in high place has always been a tragically familiar feature of the American scene. . . ." In June a two-page spread appeared about all the things going wrong in America: the history of political corruption; fuel crisis; veterans with no place to go; dollar in decline; crime; Wounded Knee — all stories laid out around a picture of a haggard Nixon. The *Daily Mirror's* coverage of Watergate then was episodic, sporadic, often erroneous, and heavily tinged with both an anti-Nixon and a more general anti-American bias. The paper added one element to the Watergate story for which it deserves some credit, however. It gave to Nixon's opaque Press Secretary, Ron Zeigler, the nickname of "the White House bongo board".

The *Daily Telegraph*

All during the Watergate crisis, the reaction of Nixon's friends to the searing events was often more interesting than the reactions of his enemies. Such is the case with the *Daily Telegraph*, the Tory-oriented morning paper which became the truest friend Nixon had among the British press. Throughout Watergate the *Daily Telegraph* was the most consistently pro-Nixon and pro-American, two conditions which the paper often tried to equate. The paper supported Nixon's re-election, the Christmas bombing of North Vietnam, the American position in the Mideast war, and Henry Kissinger, especially when he threatened to resign unless people stopped saying nasty things about him.

As a basis for judging the events of Watergate, the *Daily Telegraph* always took a world view: that, as President of the United States, Nixon was the leader of the free world; that he had obtained some notable foreign policy breakthroughs; and that he should be kept on as President solely for these reasons. The editors ignored domestic politics and consistently failed to recognize that credibility begins at home and that unless a statesman — no matter how great — is believed by his own people, he cannot ask for their support to do great things for the world.

Instead, the *Daily Telegraph* decried Nixon's inability to govern because of Watergate and could not understand why Nixon's opponents were threatening world peace by their opposition. When Nixon ordered the world-wide military alert in October 1973, in the middle of the storm created by his firing of Archibald Cox, the paper said:

> The public campaign against Nixon overreached itself in suggesting that he was playing with America's world-wide responsibilities merely as a diversion from his plight. It is time that Congress and the American "media" were less parochial and gave more thought to the United States' crucial responsibilities in the world (10/27/73 — 14).

The *Daily Telegraph* was always willing to give Nixon the benefit of the doubt about his handling of Watergate and about the allegations made against him. On more than one occasion, they were much less willing to give a hard, critical look at the evidence against the President but were content to withhold judgment until more facts were in. For instance, when John Mitchell testified that he told the President nothing about Watergate and that the President never asked, the paper editorialized: "This line may seem difficult to believe . . . but in the context of American politics and the Olympian status accorded to a President, it is creditable" (7/13/73 — 16).

Sometimes the evidence against the President was too overwhelming even for the *Daily Telegraph* to explain away. Consequently, the paper's editors had to resort to ignoring it. When Nixon produced his edited transcripts, they conceded the "serious implication . . .

> as it will appear to some, that the President was at the outset ready to consider finding large amounts of hush money and distributing it perhaps through criminal channels, though after maturer consideration he took a different view. There is continuing uncertainty about when he knew of the cover-up. Moreover, there seems to be no evidence that at any point he was ready to insist on stamping

out the whole thing, root and branch. But it is early days. The House Committee is already split on political lines by Mr. Nixon's move. There lies his hope" (5/2/74 — 16).

The *Telegraph* was consistent in its opposition to Nixon releasing the tapes and transcripts. When the existence of the tapes was first revealed and the hue and cry from all quarters was for Nixon to release them and thus prove his innocence, the *Telegraph*'s was the one lonely voice against it: "Production and publication would be a real betrayal of confidentiality" (7/18/73 –- 18). Nixon's decision to hand over the tapes to Judge Sirica in October was at first sight "inexplicable and irrational" to *Telegraph* editors. Then they proceeded to explain and rationalize it and finally came to the happy conclusion that, once again, Nixon had "certainly acted correctly". But the question they could neither explain nor ignore was why then had Nixon fired Cox? That question was left for the readers to answer themselves (10/25/73 –- 16).

One is hard-pressed to say exactly when the *Daily Telegraph* finally called for Nixon's resignation. Two weeks after Nixon released his transcripts, in a Saturday edition, the paper editorialized about all of Nixon's troubles and ended by saying: "He would now serve it [the world] better if he went" (5/11/ 74 — 16). The paper did not come back to that statement, but within a few days, it was again praising Nixon on foreign policy matters. The real call for him to resign came just one day before he announced his resignation:

> Would not Mr. Nixon's resignation, coupled with a clear confession (most of which has already been made) of the obvious impropriety of his conduct, be the best means of leaving the record straight and proof against controversy or legend? (8/7/74 — 14).

The *Daily Telegraph* was always quite pleased with the British political system where nasty things like Watergate do not happen — or at least are not reported because of stricter press laws. Once the paper suggested it might be good if Americans became a little more like the British:

> ... would it not be a good idea for American parties and politicians to adopt something more like British strict rules under which party

political activities are rigorously separated from Governmental activities . . . ? A change of this kind could be one beneficial result of Watergate (5/2/73 — 18).

In the news columns of the paper, the *Daily Telegraph* correspondents did a more creditable job than their colleagues writing editorials. The coverage they gave during the last year and a half of Watergate was complete and detailed. Almost no argument on either side was left unreported; daily articles kept readers fully informed of events in Washington. Not only was the coverage complete, but for the most part it was accurate, straightforward, and — by American standards — much more objective than that of the other quality British dailies. The news columns contained neither the sharp editorial comments of the correspondents of *The Times* nor the blatant anti-Nixon verbiage interspersed in the reports of *Guardian* journalists.

The *Evening Standard*

Even though a tabloid (moderately conservative by British political standards), the *Evening Standard* offered its readers some of the best of the British coverage and commentary on Watergate. The paper's Washington correspondent, Jeremy Campbell, though he sometimes wrote darkly on the state of the American nation, showed a competent understanding of the American political system and keen insight into reasons behind the fast-breaking events of the crisis. Because of a lack of space, the coverage the *Evening Standard* gave to Watergate was less in quantity than in broadsheet papers, but it was often as complete and thorough. The *Evening Standard* did have the advantage of being an afternoon daily and thus escaping some of the deadline pressures of reporting events the morning after they occurred.

While other correspondents were content to comment from time to time on Nixon's psychological state — and many of the comments were likely to be in the *Daily Mirror* vein — Campbell took the trouble to consult two leading psycho-historians. In a long interview in May 1973, he paraphrased James David

Barber, author of *Presidential Character*, predicting: "He [Nixon] will bring about his own destruction; nobody else will do it for him" (6/16/73 — 23). In September he interviewed Bruce Mazlich, author of *In Search of Nixon*, a long psychological study of the President, as saying that the President presented the self-righteous self image which looks upon challengers as scoundrels — a self image which is projected "by America as a whole" (9/12/73 — 21).

Both Campbell and the *Evening Standard* editorial writers showed some remarkable insight at times. Instead of wishing that Americans could be more like the British (like the *Daily Telegraph*), the *Evening Standard* sometimes hoped that the British system might pick up some items from the Americans, especially with regard to freedom of the press:

> ... the praiseworthy rigour with which the American press has pursued its investigations and the awe-inspiring success with which it has opened the eyes of a sadly abused electorate are bound to exercise an influence far beyond the boundaries of the U.S. (8/20/73 — 17).

On a number of occasions their comments were especially incisive and remarkably predictive of events. Early in the Cox investigations, Campbell discovered that the prosecution team was considering the use of the Nixon Administration's conspiracy law against Watergate defendants — a law written in such a way that it could cast a net around Nixon himself:

> The situation is rich in irony. The Nixon Administration has been so heavy-handed in its use of conspiracy laws against radicals and political dissidents over the last five years that a move is under way to modify them or wipe them off the books (7/18/73 — 21).

Early in 1974, Campbell became perplexed with Nixon attorney James St. Clair's handling of Nixon's legal maneuvers:

> Mr. St. Clair, while smiling as gaily as ever, shows alarming signs that even he does not know the complete story of a case his whole prestige is riding on. ... Mr. Nixon's previous team of attorneys made a shambles of his case because as became increasingly clear, he had not taken them into his confidence. Can it be that St. Clair is now sinking into the same quicksand? (3/20/74 — 19).

And the trend of those who put down Nixon's troubles to

the "isolation of the President" theory was disputed by
Campbell:. "It is not isolation which has brought Mr. Nixon
down so much as a suicidal disregard for those who should be
his natural allies" (8/7/74 — 15).

Like most of the American and British press, the *Evening
Standard* fell into the trap of thinking it would be Senator
Barry Goldwater, acting as a keeper of Republican integrity,
who would tell Nixon that he had to go. The *Evening Standard*
fell deeper into this trap than most, however. In December,
1973, during the congressional recess, Goldwater was described
as the "only elder statesman of the Republican party with
enough independence and integrity to make and unmake kings",
and predicted that if Congress returned still unhappy about
Nixon, the Arizonian would be the one to march down to the
White House and tell Nixon the jig was up (12/19/73 — 15).
Several more times that spring, the *Evening Standard* confidently
reported that Goldwater was about to make his move. The
paper never got around to asking why, if Goldwater was such a
bedrock of integrity, he kept openly and consistently defending
Nixon and criticizing his opponents, especially in the press, all
through the Watergate crisis.

The *Guardian*

The *Guardian*, formerly the *Manchester Guardian*, enjoys
one of the best reputations of any newspaper in the Western
world. It is hailed as a voice of decent liberalism and as an
erudite journal of public affairs. It has a long and distinguished
career, dating back to the 1820's. The *Guardian*'s coverage
of Watergate was, if nothing else, complete — the most complete next to *The Times*'s paper-of-record approach. Every part
of the scandal was reported and analyzed. Unlike *The Times*,
however, the *Guardian* had no inhibitions about commenting
on American domestic affairs and what the reporters and
editors had to say was said in a straightforward tone.

To a person, the *Guardian*'s correspondents in Washington
(Peter Jenkins, Adam Raphael, Simon Winchester, and Hella

Pick) were strongly anti-Nixon. So was the editorial staff, which even went so far as to endorse McGovern's candidacy for President. *Guardian* correspondents anticipated, yea, even hoped, that the Watergate scandal would hurt Nixon's re-election campaign, but, of course, it never did. In August 1972, Raphael wrote, "To the delight of the Democrats, the unmistakable whiff of a major scandal is beginning to haunt the White House and the smell seems unlikely to go away before the election" (8/4/72 — 13), and in September, the *Guardian* talks of the scandal "bubbl[ing] merrily away".

When events of the scandal began to emerge in earnest in 1973, *Guardian* correspondents immediately assumed the worst. It seems as though they had made up their minds about Nixon's guilt and were only awaiting that final piece of proof that would prove them right. Accusations were often talked of as proven facts. In April, Peter Jenkins wrote, "The Administration very nearly succeeded in riding out the scandal. The seven conspirators were bribed and bullied into silence . . ." (4/19/73 — 1). *Guardian* writers were right in the end, of course, but it might be argued that their conclusions at the time were not justified.

The *Guardian*'s best coverage came through at times when the journalist's job in dealing with Watergate was the most difficult — during the first Watergate trial or in the spring when Nixon was daily contradicting himself. There were, however, occasional serious lapses in the reporting, which gave readers erroneous information or impressions. On March 30, 1974, Simon Winchester filed a story saying that Nixon had agreed to give up the tapes and documents. His attorney, James St. Clair, had called the Special Prosecutor, Leon Jaworski, and told him of the decision — a statement to which Winchester gave no attribution. The only apparent reason for the surrender, according to the story, was Senator Mike Mansfield's statement that "the votes are there" for impeachment. There was no follow-up to the story the next day, but within a few days there were more stories about Nixon's continuing refusal to release the tapes. There was, however, no attempt to clear up the confusion by retracting or explaining the March 30 story.

On another occasion, under the headline, "Nixon finds champion on Watergate", Winchester quotes Egil Krogh who "strongly challenged the assertion" that Nixon knew about the cover-up. (This was in January 1974, just after Krogh had turned state's evidence.) Later in the story we read that Krogh had not actually said that but that what he did say "would seem to back up strongly the assertion" that Nixon did not know. The case for Krogh's "championing" of Nixon grew even weaker when Krogh refused to accuse Dean of perjury outright, and finally Winchester had to say that what Krogh had said "tended to confirm Nixon's claim". Consequently, we go from Krogh's "strong challenge" at the beginning to his "tended to confirm" at the end. Winchester was in the unenviable position of having written a lead paragraph that was not backed up with the facts in the rest of his story.

Yet, despite these and other lapses, the *Guardian* distinguished itself in other parts of the Watergate story. Hella Pick did a thorough job in explaining the whys and wherefores of Nixon's tax tangles, and readers of the *Guardian* received much cogent information about campaign financing. And rarely, if ever, was the *Guardian* stodgy about what was happening. When the full text of the transcripts was revealed, the *Guardian* said "deleted expletives" might better be replaced with "excreted expletives":

> Mr. Nixon is clearly fond of lavatorial words, but no more so than he is of religious profanities. God is frequently damned; Christ is called upon often; and many of the Watergate conspirators are considered either illegitimate or sons of female dogs. (7/10/74 — 1).

The Times

The Times of London covered the continuing Watergate story with the most complete reportage of any of the newspapers studied. *Times* reporters covered almost every detail every day from the time of the break-in to the Nixon pardon 27 months later. At certain times when the news of Watergate was coming thick and fast, *The Times* added a special

"WATERGATE" section to its news columns which filled up at least one and sometimes two or three full pages.

The Times gave its readers paraphrased texts of the Senate Watergate hearings, much like it regularly does with Parliamentary proceedings. It also printed the full texts of letters, speeches and some transcripts relevant to the story.

The working reporters for *The Times* were anti-Nixon from the beginning. Their biases shone through in the news columns fairly brightly, yet it could be argued that Watergate was essentially an anti-Nixon story and just to merely report what was happening would be showing a bias against the President. *Times* reporters went a step further, giving us the best example of a basic difference between British and American news reporting. American journalists are haunted by the constant spectre of "objectivity", a spectre which does not bother the British journalist. Consequently, for example, when Nixon was evoking executive privilege to keep John Dean from testifying in March 1973, a *Times* reporter had no inhibitions about inserting in a news story the following paragraph:

> The White House had denied there was any impropriety in Mr. Dean's participation [in the FBI investigation]. If this was the case, it is hard to see why Mr. Dean's appearance might, in the President's words, "harm the public interest". . . . The irony of the President's position is that he is pleading the need to remain silent as Senator Ervin's special committee conducts its study, while denying the committee information it needs to make a significant investigation (3/19/73 — 6).

Times reporters also at times treated the American political scene with a bit of tongue-in-cheek, mixed with a dash of cynicism. When John Mitchell resigned as head of CREEP, Fred Emery wrote of the shock that had hit Washington because of the resignation. "In this atmosphere [of political Washington] it seemed almost inconceivable that anything [in this case Mitchell's family life] could be more important than politics" (7/3/72 — 5).

Editorially, *The Times* was more schizophrenic in its attitude toward Nixon. At first, it looked upon him as a great international leader and with sympathy for his domestic troubles. In all of the accusations, it gave him the benefit of the doubt. When the accusations came, the *Times* editors tended to look upon them as coming from a hostile press rather than having much substance. When their substance later came to light, *The Times* gave due credit to the press but said that now was the time to stop. In June 1973, in the middle of the Senate hearings, *The Times* printed a controversial editorial saying Nixon was unfairly undergoing three trials at once: the hearings, the Grand Jury, and the press. (See the section on the due process controversy.)

The Times's support of the President never snapped; it slowly crumbled. The major blow to its foundation came just a month and a half later when the existence of the tapes was revealed, and the President refused to give them up. Though it tried mightily to understand the President's reasoning — examining every side of the question in a long, wordy editorial — it simply could not side with the President on this one.

> If one accepts President Nixon's letter [to Cox saying he won't give up the tapes], he has embarked on this great constitutional crisis in order to prevent the disclosure of evidence which would not be decisive one way or the other. Even if he is telling the truth, he has decided on an astonishingly dangerous gamble, with the Presidency of the United States as the stake (7/25/73 — 17).

The Times could rarely support the President after that, although it still gave plaudits to his foreign policy ventures. A year later, when the House Judiciary Committee had voted its impeachment articles and the end was drawing near, *The Times* finally came out for resignation. It obviously was not an easy decision for the editors, nor was it an easy editorial for the readers. The pros and cons of resignation were discussed in full, but *The Times* finally came to the tortuous conclusion:

> On the whole, and especially from the point of view of America's foreign allies, the balance comes out in favour of resignation, though subject to certain reservations. In the first place, it should be delayed until the full House of Representatives has voted, probably by August 23. . . . Secondly, Mr. Nixon should find the courage to make a sufficient admission of responsibility to abort the birth of a stab-in-the-back legend. He would have nothing to lose and might

regain a little moral stature by doing so. It is the sort of gesture which would help to compensate for cutting short the slow but deeply impressive procedure on which Congress has now embarked with so much agony (7/31/74 — 17).

Finally with *The Times*, there is the strange case of Bernard Levin, a strongly pro-Nixon columnist. Though he did not say all that much about Watergate, what he did say was said with an air of tutorial instructiveness. On May 8, 1973, he warned his colleagues to be careful not to be overtaken with the mass of accusations against the President. He says there is a "gleeful air of hysteria" in much of the British comment about Watergate, stemming from a latent anti-Americanism, and that Watergate is made to seem more serious than it really is by "the liberal establishment".

Levin was overtaken by his own hysteria a year later when he claimed that Nixon was not getting a fair shake from his enemies. Take, for example, the case of Senator Fulbright, he says. In a pre-primary television appearance the Sunday before, Fulbright had said his campaign had polls showing him just slightly ahead. When Fulbright lost by a landslide, he admitted that there were, in fact, no polls. In other words, Levin said, Fulbright had lied — and yet there was no outcry by those accusing Nixon. He concedes that if Nixon is guilty, he should be removed, but what about Senator Fulbright?

The major strength of the *Times* coverage of Watergate was its thorough understanding of the intricacies of the American political system. Rarely are its editors, reporters or headline writers caught short on this point, and the Watergate story was one which drew heavily on their combined knowledge.

The *Observer*

The *Observer*, as a Sunday newspaper, has the advantage of taking the long view of the week's events, considering and analyzing, and coming to thoughtful conclusions. The *Observer* is also known as a good commentator on foreign news. The newspaper did well in these two areas during the 2 years of

Watergate. The weekly summaries of events in Washington were generally complete and well written. The writers often anticipated events to come and offered novel and intelligent explanations of what was happening; they also displayed a good understanding of the American political system.

Anthony Sampson, author of *The Sovereign State of ITT*, became the *Observer*'s chief correspondent in Washington in September 1973. During the next 2 years he was able to demonstrate his intimate knowledge of American business and political affairs, such as this, written after the Saturday Night Massacre:

> How could Nixon ... not have realized the furore that would result? ... Nixon may have reckoned that resignations on principle are never effective. . . . But Richardson and Ruckelshaus may have dented that tradition ... the principle they stood for was very basic and comprehensible (10/28/73 − 13).

On the White House transcripts Sampson wrote that they made those in the White House sound like they were members of a small ad agency who had been caught fiddling with the books. The impression of weakness they left, however, "may be misleading. No man can be a hero to his tape recorder" (5/5/74 − 10). A week later his column was again about the transcripts, which he called "political pornography". Nixon's opponents, he said, were in shock because "after a year of battering away at the door of the White House, it has flown open to reveal only a few men swearing at one another trying to prop up the façade" (5/12/74 − 13).

The *Observer* hired Mary McCarthy during the Senate Watergate hearings to record her impressions of them. The paper generally gave her the entire front page of the review section and illustrated it with large headshots of the witnesses. McCarthy's reports were impressionistic and short on hard facts, but they did lend a new dimension to a subject which tended to be overcovered. She credited John Mitchell with a "steady dosage of lies" (7/15/73 − 25). "In the Caucus Room, people were arguing whether he [Ehrlichman] or Mitchell was more purely evil. It is hard to decide which of the two should be awarded that particular apple" (7/29/73 − 25). In Haldeman she saw "something almost rabbity about him" (7/5/73 — 21).

Editorially, the *Observer* kept mostly to itself. When the crisis broke into the open in May 1973, the *Observer* simply said that the situation was shaking confidence in Nixon abroad and a 3-year paralysis of the American Presidency would not do the world any good. The domestic situation would be taken care of by the Americans themselves, however, and the paper made no further comments. Even when Nixon resigned, the *Observer* kept its eyes mostly in a world view, praising Nixon's foreign policy achievements. It was also generous to Nixon in saying his trickery was small compared to the international trickery practiced among European leaders in this century.

> Nixon remains an enigma. He may be part crook, but he was part statesman as well. He cannot repeat his malefactions, and it would be unfair if, in the chorus of personal abuse, we were to lose sight of his successful contributions to world peace (8/11/74 — 10).

The *Sunday Times*

No other British newspaper matched the *Sunday Times*'s coverage of Watergate. Being a weekly, of course, allowed it to be more concerned with the general trends rather than the daily flow of news, but the *Sunday Times* added to this advantage by doing the only in-depth investigative work on Watergate produced by the British press. The *Sunday Times* invested the efforts of several reporters in digging behind the Watergate events and bringing to light facts all their own.

In early October 1972, Stephen Fay and Philip Jacobson looked into the political disruption carried on by the Republican Party and concluded that the Watergate raid was "merely the culmination of a sustained operation which ranged from petty disruption of primary campaigning to full-blown sabotage, spying and phone-tapping" (10/5/72 — 13).

During the next spring there were long pieces on the Ellsburg trial and the Vesco connection and campaign financing:

> The extent to which many of Nixon's closest advisors were directly involved in soliciting, concealing, and ultimately directing the misuse

of contributions like Vesco's has become abundantly clear. There is no question of it being simply a few instances of influence peddling by unscrupulous fund raisers. What emerges in the case of Vesco and others . . . bears the hallmarks of a coldly conceived strategy (4/29/ 73 — 8).

In a remarkable piece of reporting, *Sunday Times* correspondents took apart, paragraph by paragraph, Nixon's May 22 (1973) statement and showed contradiction after contradiction of the President's words and deeds. They delved into the connection between McCord and the CIA in June 1973, and came up with the theory that a rift between Nixon and the CIA — caused when Nixon told the agency to investigate campus radicals, and the agency concluded, much against Nixon's own feelings, that they were acting from conviction rather than subversive design — had led to Nixon's plumbers' unit. McCord might then be a counter-agent for the CIA, still working for the agency to plot Nixon's downfall. The *Sunday Times* was also the only British newspaper to go deeply into the background of the Agnew investigation.

Another major asset of the *Sunday Times* was its chief Washington correspondent, Henry Brandon, who had been in the American capital for 22 years when Watergate began. Brandon was distinguished enough to have had his telephone tapped:

> The *New York Times* last week reported that my telephone had been tapped. I was not the only one thus honoured — one fellow reporter suggests that having your telephone tapped is the next best thing to getting a Pulitzer Prize (5/13/73 — 1).

Brandon's credibility was soiled, however, when he failed to make the enemies list.

The *Sunday Times* combined all these advantages to produce some very good editorials and commentary about Watergate. For instance, when Nixon took to the television screen in August 1973, to concede little and admit nothing, the *Sunday Times* wrote that it was a "dismaying performance".

> . . . [Nixon is] incapable of appreciating the foulness of the actions done in his name. . . . Leadership of a kind may still come out of Washington: but international initiatives will be hampered by a

broken-backed presidency for the next three years. That is the measure of Mr. Nixon's tragedy: he has allowed mortal damage to be inflicted on his own dearest hopes, and he cannot even see that he has done it (8/19/73 — 12).

And after the dizzying events of that incredible week in October, the *Sunday Times* wrote: "The crisis of the Presidency is a crisis for the world. . . . It is in the end the actions and attributes of Mr. Nixon himself which have destroyed the moral authority of the President" (10/28/73 — 12).

THE GOSPEL ACCORDING TO THE BRITISH NATIONAL PRESS

Even though it lasted more than 2 years, Watergate became part of the regular diet for British newspaper readers. Rarely did the story die down; there was little respite from it for either journalists or readers. More often, the events that made up the story took place at a breakneck pace. Scandal piled upon scandal. One sensational event had hardly finished before another was taking place.

Just how did the British press cover all of these events? And what picture of America did British readers gain from this coverage? This section will attempt, in an abbreviated way, to relate the story of Watergate, as told by the British press.

In the beginning . . .

The original break-in at the Watergate office building was given at least cursory coverage by most of the British press. It was not the break-in that British journalists were interested in so much as the political effects it might have on the upcoming presidential elections. "The episode is showing signs of being treated as a major political issue in the presidential election campaign", said the *Daily Telegraph* (6/20/72 — 4). But the first reaction of the press was to imply that activities of this type were nothing new to American politics, such as the *Guardian*'s statement: "Bugging for political purposes is an ancient and well tried practice in this country. . . ." (6/20/72 — 1)

With the upcoming political conventions, however, the break-in soon became a secondary, and often submerged, issue. It resurfaced occasionally during the campaign, but never often and never for very long. There were those among the British press who wished that something would indeed come of it — namely the *Guardian* — but these hopes were in vain. In mid-September a *Daily Telegraph* correspondent wrote that the bugging and break-in might obscure the more important issue "about the movements of campaign contributions which wound up in the bank account of one of the 'bugging' burglars, Mr. Bernard Barker" (9/15/72 — 4), but that did not seem to worry *Daily Telegraph* editorials, who could be found flailing McGovern the next month for "droning on endlessly about the Watergate 'bugging' affair, in which the great majority of Americans stubbornly refuse to be interested" (10/16/72 — 16).

On the whole, British journalists were content to quote the charges published in the *Washington Post*, but they did little else. Only the *Sunday Times* tried to follow up some of the questions raised by the *Post*, but they produced little more information than *Post* reporters had done.

The Watergate affair showed some staying power when, just after the Nixon landslide, the pro-Nixon *Daily Telegraph* thought that the President would be "under strong political pressure to purge his staff of any taint of the 'Watergate bugging' scandal". No such purge occurred then, however, and the scandal disappeared from the pages of the British press.

The word made flesh

In January the men caught in the Democratic National Headquarters went on trial, constituting the first open inquiry into the Watergate affair. While other papers were more concerned with the Vietnam peace negotiations, the Christmas bombing, the inauguration of Nixon and the death of Lyndon Johnson, *The Times* and the *Guardian* produced almost daily reports of the courtroom scene from reporters who did not like what they saw. Simon Winchester of the *Guardian* wrote:

> The most significant aspect of Mr. Silbert's [the prosecutor] opening

statement is the conscious absence of detailed reference to senior
officers in President Nixon's reelection campaign organization —
the men who presumably gave Mr. Liddy his alleged orders
(1/11/73 — 1).

And when the trial ended, the *Guardian* still found most of the
Watergate questions unanswered. The trial "added little to
public knowledge of the affair in spite of the judge's honest
efforts to save it from being a show trial". The prosecutor made
no attempt to get out the facts, and "the judge had to do his
job for him" (2/3/73 — 3).

Times correspondents, too, were struck by this: "Neither the
prosecution nor the defence during the trial had any interest
in going into the related political questions such as who hired
the spies and financed them" (2/1/73 — 5).

The first indications that Watergate might turn out to be
more than just the trial of seven men came from Capitol Hill,
where the Senate had voted to set up an investigative committee,
headed by North Carolinian Sam Ervin, and where Nixon's
nominee to the FBI directorship, Patrick Gray, was beginning
to twist ever so slowly in the wind. One by one, British journalists appeared on the Hill to see what was happening. Of the
Gray hearings, *Observer* correspondent William Millinship
wrote:

> From his [Gray's] own evidence, it is clear that his anxiety to get
> to the bottom of the Watergate affair weakened the closer it came
> to the White House and to the key question of who was ultimately
> responsible for the political espionage operation against the Demo-
> cratic Party (3/25/73 — 8).

Something was up. Just what became a little clearer when
James McCord, one of the seven defendants, wrote to Judge
Sirica saying that a cover-up was taking place. Suddenly, the
British press began to take it all much more seriously, as indicated by the *Daily Telegraph*'s telling its readers it should *not*
be taken seriously. If Jack Anderson can steal state secrets and
print them, ". . . why should political party secrets be sacro-
sanct? Mr. Nixon's enemies, and their name is legion, having
failed in their efforts to damage him on so many other counts,

have renewed hopes of getting him on this one" (3/28/73 -- 18). The *Daily Telegraph*, as it did so much during Watergate, showed a split in thinking between its editorial writers and its correspondents in the field when Stephen Barber's piece appeared a week later:

> The loudest laments about its tragic potentialities and about President Nixon's oddly inept handling of it have lately come not from his enemies so much as from his staunch admirers — although his critics are certainly relishing each new allegation. . . . As Senator Weicker put it, the issue of Watergate is whether the American people would or should accept new and cleaner standards for Presidential elections or that lies, sabotage and spying are to be accepted as a way of life (4/6/73 — 18).

By the end of April, when Nixon could stay hidden from the scandal no longer, the British press correspondents were sending back daily dispatches on new allegations and the state of the besieged President. The *Sunday Times*'s Henry Brandon summed up the feelings of many when he wrote, "For the first time in 23 years, I sense a fear that the government may be rotten at the core" (4/29/73 -- 9). Nixon's behavior was still dismaying the long-suffering but ever-forgiving *Daily Telegraph:*

> His own behaviour as the crisis mounted has been such as increasingly to undermine faith not only in his own competence but also, however hesitantly, in his own integrity. . . . Could they [his subordinates] . . . have shielded him from the sordid details and the increasingly reckless cover-up campaign? Even if all this is so, Mr. Nixon, at best, stands condemned of having picked a lot of very unsuitable people for positions of particular trust. . . . If his faults, as we assume, are at worst no greater than misjudgments or indiscretions, the American people will bear in mind what they owe him — and so will the free world (4/30/73 — 18).

The day that editorial appeared Nixon went on television and gave the first of his many explanations of his non-part in the Watergate affair. He also announced that four key men, including two of his closest aides, Robert Haldeman and John Ehrlichman, were no longer part of his administration. The leave-taking of these two was mourned by none of the British press, but the rest of Nixon's speech failed to satisfy. Wrote a *Times* reporter: "A national audience hungry for reassurance was treated to a string of humble and occasionally nervously delivered protestations and assertions. The President provided hardly any new material" (5/2/73 — 1). Jeremy Campbell of the *Evening Standard* said, "Watergate cries out for answers, and all Mr. Nixon gave us were more questions" (5/2/73 — 21). Predictably, the *Daily Telegraph* took a different view; this time it was their correspondent Barber who wrote that the speech was "super-Checkers", a reference to Nixon's masterful political speech of 20 years before which kept him on Eisenhower's presidential ticket. "To be sure, it will not satisfy everybody — nothing could — but given that most Americans would far rather believe in their President than not, even if they didn't vote for him, it will surely placate a majority" (5/2/73 — 18).

Barber's placated majority was nowhere in sight when the Senate Watergate hearings began later that month. On May 22, Nixon again tried to stem the tide by issuing a long statement giving more details of the scandal and what he didn't know about it. With this one not even the *Daily Telegraph* was convinced. The White Paper, it said, "does not do much to reassure those most included so far to give him the benefit of the doubt". But the *Telegraph* was certainly not willing to give up on Nixon. "American commentators . . . in their fever to destroy Mr. Nixon, and having tasted blood . . . appear to have lost all sense of proportion" (5/24/73 — 18).

John Dean's testimony before the Senate Committee received double and sometimes triple coverage in the British and American press. The week before he was scheduled to testify, much of what he planned to say was leaked to the press. His testimony was then postponed for a week when the hearings adjourned for Brezhnev's visit to Washington. Finally, the next week, Dean went before the Senators and the television cameras delivered, in fascinating detail, an account of life and mentality in the Nixon White House. The one item that gained most coverage in the British press was the White House enemies list. The list included a wide variety of people — everyone from film stars for the *Daily Mirror* to scholars for *The Times*.

The July testimony that Nixon had taped all of his own conversations (as well as many between other people) was a little difficult even for the now-hardened British press to take. "What President in his right mind" would record incriminating conversations? the *Guardian* asked (7/18/73 — 2). The only sense they could make of it was that possibly Nixon — that sly old fox — was holding them back as a "second strike" weapon. The *Evening Standard* was forced to the same conclusion: "The only credible answer is that Mr. Nixon was saving up the tapes for a time when he could crush his accusers with maximum effect — a dangerous ploy, if so, since his standing has already been irreparably damaged" (7/19/73 — 19).

The Times, in its first real break with the President, said Nixon should stop the delay and turn the relevant tapes in for examination. When Nixon made it clear that was the last thing he had in mind for the tapes, *The Times* editorialized: "When an accused man refuses to produce evidence which would decide the matter, the natural inference is that he does not do it because he dare not do it. . . . The inference will be drawn almost universally" (7/25/73 — 17).

The Times was right to put on that last qualifier. The *Daily Telegraph* certainly didn't draw that inference; on the contrary, they too argued against disclosure saying, "Production and publication would be a real betrayal of confidentiality" (7/18/73 — 18).

When it became clear that the tapes were not a second strike weapon which Nixon had poised for release right at the precise moment, the British press began to speculate on why he was not going to give them up. Brandon wrote in the *Sunday Times:*

> Probably he has convinced himself in the de Gaulle manner, that it does not matter whether people believe him or not, because he must perform the duties for which he has been elected and that the damage Watergate has done will wear off (7/22/73 — 11).

A sea of troubles

The forces contending against Nixon continued to add new ammunition to their stocks. Besides the clamor for the tapes, there were unanswered questions about Nixon's homes, taxes and finances. Among the British press, *Guardian* correspondent Hella Pick delved into these tangled matters and went a long way toward sorting them out for her readers.

The major blow to Nixon during the month of August came from a completely unexpected source. In an extraordinary press conference, Nixon's Vice-President, Spiro Agnew, revealed that he was under investigation in Maryland on charges of bribery and extortion. For the first time in history, a holder of the second highest office in the U.S. was the object of a criminal investigation.

The significance of that was not lost on British journalists. Although the Agnew investigation had nothing to do with Watergate, it quickly became an integral part of the Watergate story because of the effect it was having on Nixon's crumbling credibility. Its most profound effect, however, was that it threw the matter of succession into question. The British press, in covering the Agnew affair, often speculated that as long as Agnew was in this position, Nixon was safe in office. If Agnew were thrown over, Nixon would be more vulnerable than ever because the one stumbling-block that most of his opponents had to impeachment — the succession of Agnew — would be out of the way.

Except for the *Sunday Times,* which went into great detail about the charges against Agnew, the British press generally refrained from commenting too much about the investigation. Journalists were probably reflecting the habit they had picked up in their own country about not writing about a criminal investigation while it is in progress. Certainly, of course, this restraint was self-imposed since they were under no legal compulsion to do this in America.

The comment about Agnew remained political and personal, and in some quarters of the British press it was surprisingly sympathetic. In summing up Agnew's performance as Vice-President, Louis Heren of *The Times* wrote: "On balance, and despite his attacks against the press and television, he was probably a power for good." Agnew, he said, had helped stop Wallace and had given working-class people a voice. "The liberal intellectuals never understood this", he said, in a rather bewildering conclusion (9/27/73 — 20).

Agnew vociferously denied the accusations against him and vowed never to resign right up until the day he pleaded guilty to a minor charge and sent a letter of resignation to the Secretary of State. The British press was taken completely by surprise. Anthony Sampson in the *Observer* commented: "Like the last chapter of whodunnit . . . it makes all the chapters before it look different" (10/14/73 — 29).

Little was said about Agnew after he left office; it was almost as if the man had dropped out of sight and was never heard from again, with only the occasional rumor of a reappearance now and again. Instead, speculation turned to Agnew's successor, and when the name of Gerald Ford was put forth, the reaction among British newspapers was decidedly cool. The *Evening Standard* called him a "political hack, a party wheelhorse, so bereft of intellectual sparkle or creative drive that even fellow Congressmen don't think he would make a good President" (10/17/73 — 21). *The Times* simply said he was "unlikely to be a disaster" (10/15/73 — 16), but Henry Brandon of the *Sunday Times* was incensed:

> Gerry Ford's mediocrity is likely to become more obvious in the White House than on Capitol Hill. The old cliché therefore that the Vice-President ought to be the best qualified man to take over the Presidency if necessary does not seem to have been the President's primary consideration in his deliberations with himself (10/14/73 — 3).

When the Agnew investigations were announced in August, Nixon's sea of troubles did not recede. If anything, he came under increasing fire as more facts about the scandal came to light. Haldeman's testimony was not well received either at the Senate Committee hearing or in the press. A *Sunday Times* editorial said:

> His concern was not so much to deny that dreadful deeds were done as to distract attention from them by claiming that they were not the issue. Two themes have been used to this end. The first is that the President himself did not know what happened. The second is that even if these things happened, they could be

justified by reference to national security. But as the horrors unfold, it is becoming ever harder to be seduced by these contentions (8/5/73 — 12).

Nixon went on television in mid-August and in "blunt, uncompromising tones" (*Guardian* 8/16/73 — 1) refused to give up the tapes. Here again we find a split between reporter and editorialist in the *Daily Telegraph*. Richard Beeston reported that the speech "did little to rebut any of the allegations made at the hearings" (8/16/73 — 1), but an editorial the next day said, "To the average American . . . this downbeat approach is likely to make more sense than would have done any attempted point-by-point refutation" (8/17/73 — 16). To the *Sunday Times* the speech was a "dismaying performance" in which Nixon seemed "incapable of appreciating the foulness of the actions done in his name" (8/19/73 — 12).

The press conference the next week was a rough and tumble affair between reporters and Nixon. The *Guardian* said it was "pitched with a display of press ferocity rarely seen in this country" (8/23/73 — 1), while *The Times*, in a classic understatement, said, "Some of the questions were of an extreme directness" (8/23/73 — 1). The *Daily Telegraph* again heralded it as putting Nixon back on the road to recovery: "America's well-wishers and protégés throughout the world have good reason to feel that Mr. Nixon is back in business again in home and foreign affairs" (8/23/73 — 16).

The week that was

The war in the Middle East and the resignation of Spiro Agnew were the two major stories which occupied Washington journalists during the first half of October, but nothing could have prepared them for the searing events of the third week of that month and the reverberations which continued throughout the fourth. The catalyst for it was the Saturday Night Massacre. In order to stop Special Prosecutor Archibald Cox from taking him to court over the release of the White House tapes, Nixon dismissed him — but not before his Attorney General, Elliot Richardson, and his deputy, William Ruckelshaus, had resigned. That all happened on a Saturday evening, October 20. Within a week, Nixon had surrendered some of the tapes to Judge Sirica (capitulating on the very issue over which he fired Cox); he placed U.S. military forces on top alert because he perceived a threat of Russian forces moving into the Middle East; he scheduled and then cancelled television appearances twice, and finally had a vicious televised tangle with the press the next Friday night. It had, indeed, been a week unlike any other.

Comment about the Saturday Night Massacre was uniformly bad in the British press. Nixon "has bankrupted all his moral reserves", said *The Times* (10/22/73 — 1). Editorially, the *Guardian* demanded "the quickest possible transaction . . . to a trustworthy Presidency" (10/22/73 -- 10). The *Daily Mirror* called on Nixon to "display a single spark of decency and remove himself" (10/23/73 — 1), and the *Sunday Times* said Nixon had "destroyed the moral authority of the Presidency" (10/28/73 -- 16). Even the *Daily Telegraph* was shocked: "Now this high-handed use of personal power to prevent this [Cox taking the case to the Supreme Court] not only shocks but increases the impression that he is still covering-up." Yet the *Telegraph* managed to find some merit in even these actions! He had put the issue squarely before Congress, the editorial concluded, either impeach or put up with a paralyzed Presidency (10/22/73 — 18).

In some of the most lucid comment to come from the British press that week, Jeremy Campbell of the *Evening Standard* said it was "highly unlikely that Cox was dismissed for the sole reason that he opposed the compromise on the secret tape recordings or that he refused to desist from demanding the surrender of certain White House papers and memoranda" (10/24/73 — 21). Campbell stayed on the mark in describing the Friday press conference:

> But for all the rowdy behavior, the Press did not come to grips with any of the central questions of the Watergate and related scandals or follow up an evasive answer with another question. The President was not even asked the obvious question, namely why he had dismissed Special Prosecutor Archibald Cox for urging

him to hand over his tapes and then three days later surrendered the
tapes in the very manner advocated by Cox (10/27/73 — 1).

There were more shocks to come. Within a week it became
known that some of the tapes Nixon handed over to the judge
had gaps in them and that others did not exist at all. Knowledge
of this "shattered an incredulous Washington" (*Guardian*
11/1/73 — 1), and added a "sensational new twist" (*Daily
Mirror* 11/1/73 — 1) to the whole story.

The tape gaps also provoked a special hearing in Judge
Sirica's court during the month of November that had its own
straining effect on credulity. Finally, "credibility snapped"
(*The Times* 11/29/73 — 18) when Nixon's secretary, Rose
Mary Woods, tried to show how she might have erased part of
one of the tapes. The *Observer* said that the nation was being
treated to "the tragic story of two loyal servants of the President
[Ms. Woods and lawyer J. Fred Buzhardt] fighting for their
lives to defend an indefensible position" (12/2/73 — 6), and
even Stephen Barber of the *Daily Telegraph* had his doubts:
"It will require much additional explanation to persuade
already incredulous Americans that none of them [Nixon's
lawyers] had ever listened to the tapes" (11/29/73 — 4).

The crisis fermented through the month of December and
came bubbling back to the surface in January, though not with
the force that it had gathered by the end of October. There
were daily stories about the tapes, impeachment, Nixon's taxes
and land deals, and speculation on Nixon's possible resignation
throughout the British press.

Nixon's claim in his State of the Union address that "a year
of Watergate is enough" found symphathetic hearing with the
Daily Telegraph. "Mr. Nixon must surely have echoed the
feelings of a majority in saying that the time had come to bring
the Watergate investigation to an end", an editorial said (2/1/
74 — 16). But the next day the *Telegraph* was forced to report:
"Despite Mr. Nixon's pleas, Watergate refuses to be buried"
(2/2/74 — 6).

Not even the British general election campaign in February
could bury the Watergate story completely. While the *Daily*

Mirror and the *Observer* were almost exclusively concerned with the election, the other papers continued to give fairly full coverage to the events in Washington. The Mitchell—Stans trial in New York was opening, the tapes hearing continued, the House Judiciary Committee was beginning its impeachment work, and the House seat that Gerald Ford had held for 25 years was captured by a Democrat. And when nothing else was going on, Nixon could always be counted on to say he wasn't going to resign.

I know what I meant

Nixon's I-know-what-I-meant-I-know-what-I-said press conference in March drew a variety of descriptions from British journalists. The *Observer* reporter noted that Nixon "sweated profusely" (3/10/74 — 6), while *The Times* also pointed out his perspiration problem: "sweating heavily", Nixon was "visibly shaken by some questions" (3/7/74 — 1). Meanwhile, the *Guardian* was content to remark that Nixon came out "looking noticeably tense and nervous" (3/7/74 — 1).

However much Nixon sweated, his press conference did nothing to stem the ever-increasing tide against him. His troubles mounted and continued to mount during the next two months. The announcement that he would pay nearly a half million dollars in back taxes caused hardly any special comment in the British press. By this time it was just another in a series of events for which journalists on both sides of the Atlantic had lost their ability to say anything new. It was like bad science fiction where one incredible thing after another keeps happening, and the author soon runs short of superlatives.

It took Nixon's edited version of the tape transcripts at the end of April to start the words flowing again. For the *Daily Mirror*, the transcripts were "a last desperate gamble", doomed to failure before it began (5/1/74 — 5). The *Daily Mirror* tried to seal Nixon's fate with a series of headlines throughout the month reading: "THE NET IS CLOSING AROUND NIXON" (5/10/74); "NIXON: THE LAST DAYS" (5/11/74 — 1); "NIXON THE AVENGER" (5/17/74). When Nixon would not lie down and die, the *Mirror* asked with its own sense of desperation: "How much longer can Mr. Nixon continue to brazen it out?" (5/13/74 — 2).

The transcripts were taken a little more calmly by the other papers, but they invoked no less strong reactions. Each paper printed at least a part of the transcripts, with the *Daily Telegraph* publishing five pages of excerpts. That paper's correspondents were forced to the conclusion: "Far from supporting Mr. Nixon's claim of utter innocence . . . it lends support in a number of instances to the interpretation that the President tried hard to find ways of stopping the whole truth from coming out" (5/1/74 — 2).

The *Times* reporter felt the same way. "The transcripts simply do not correspond to the President's claims of the night before — let alone with his solemn statements of a year ago" (5/2/74 — 14). And an *Evening Standard* editorial said:

> Despite Mr. Nixon's confident assertion . . . that the transcripts would vindicate him, the unfortunate "ambiguities" . . . are, in fact, a good deal less ambiguous than he had indicated . . . to many it must seem that since these new revelations, the [unintelligible], to borrow the transcripts' style, has really hit the fan (5/1/74 — 21).

The attention of the press was soon diverted to the legal battle between James St. Clair, Nixon's new attorney, and Leon Jaworski, the new Special Prosecutor. What Nixon had tried to stop in October — a hearing on the tapes before the Supreme Court — was now almost certain to take place. There were also the hearings of the Judiciary Committee, which, even though secret, were almost daily producing some sensational pieces of news. It was found that the transcripts were much more heavily edited than Nixon had indicated and consequently much more damaging. The fact that Nixon had been named by the Federal Grand Jury as an unindicted co-conspirator in the Watergate conspiracy case was buried in the deluge of other news.

Nixon's trips to the Mideast and Moscow in June did little to shift the limelight away from his Watergate troubles. Still his tumultuous welcome in Cairo was duly reported, and the *Daily Telegraph* saw nothing wrong with his foreign trips if "there are genuine policy achievements at hand or readily attainable" (6/6/74 — 18). The Mideast trip did succeed in refracting the view of at least one British journalist. Hella Pick of the *Guardian* had travelled with Nixon throughout the Middle East. She returned to Washington and was assigned to covering the unglamorous Senate confirmation hearings of Earl Silbert, the original Watergate prosecutor, who had been nominated for the federal district attorney's job. Silbert was undergoing some rough questions, and Pick was shocked that the mood in Washington had turned so "petty, vindictive and extremely sour" (6/21/74 — 2).

The Supreme Court hearing on the tapes on July 8 provoked some very different images from British journalists, who were well-represented in the courtroom. The Sunday before the hearing, Michael Davie wrote in the *Observer* that Nixon was coming to the case "wounded and trailing blood but still on his feet and still defiant" (7/7/74 — 7). Simon Winchester, however, let himself get carried away with his own words in the lead paragraph of his description of the hearing:

> Not since its birth two summers ago has the shoddy mess of scandal in Mr. Nixon's ruling machine ever seemed anything other than just that — shoddy, messy and scandalous. Today, for 185 minutes all that changed: and Watergate blossomed like a butterfly into a thing of dignity, precision and majesty (7/9/74 — 1).

Well, hardly.

Most of the British press, in one way or another, predicted that Nixon would lose. Some journalists resorted to their own expertise while others consulted members of the legal profession. But what if Nixon lost and was ordered to hand over his tapes? Would he obey the High Court's ruling? That question dominated the speculation in the intermission between the hearing and the decision, and British journalists became increasingly impatient with the ways James St. Clair found of evading it. St. Clair's press conference on July 23 provoked these comments from the *Daily Telegraph*:

> . . . sweating profusely . . . the lawyer saw immediately that he had gone too far [in answering a question about Nixon's compliance].

Sweat trickling all over his face, he flashed a nervous smile, ran his finger under his collar and answered: "I think I have said all I'm going to say on the subject" (7/24/74 — 5)

and *The Times*: "Most dismaying to the public . . . was Mr. St. Clair's repeated refusal to answer the simple question whether President Nixon would abide by a Supreme Court ruling ordering him to turn over tape recordings . . ." (7/24/74 — 5).

The Court's ruling that Nixon must, indeed, release the tapes was praised by the *Evening Standard* as representing "a triumph and a vindication of the American Constitution" (7/25/74 — 19). But no sooner had journalists digested the Supreme Court's decision than they were made to sit down to another full course of editorial meat with the impeachment evidence, charges and hearings. The hearings were covered in detail, and the first vote to impeach provoked images of King Charles I from the *Observer*'s Michael Davie:

English history, indeed, has been rather prominent in these proceedings. Any Englishman sitting in the committee room, hearing the angry accusation that the supreme but absent "he" was violating the rights of the representatives of the people . . . must have sensed spine-tingling echoes of the Parliament of Charles I (7/28/74 — 1).

To the *Evening Standard*, the quality of the debate said something about the American people:

The American people may be less cynical than we suppose. They are showing a new kind of trust in their representatives, a confidence that they will act in the best interests of the country and in the general spirit of a Constitution which still exerts its magic powers (7/31/74 — 17).

And the *Daily Telegraph* sadly conceded that few who had followed the tapes battle

. . . with their intensely suspect erasures, omissions, and garblings, together with the examinations of Mr. Nixon's leading associates, will question Saturday's first decision by the House committee [to impeach]. The accumulation of circumstantial evidence already seems overwhelming — and there are still 64 tapes to come (7/29/74 — 12).

There was only one tape which the *Daily Telegraph* need

have worried about, and after an agonizing weekend at Camp David, Nixon produced it. It clearly showed that he had actively participated in the cover-up and had repeatedly lied about his involvement. The *Daily Telegraph* called the admission "appalling" (8/6/74 − 1), the *Evening Standard* said Nixon, "stands on the brink of ruin" (8/6/74 − 1), and the *Guardian* said, "Mr. Nixon has virtually committed political suicide" (8/6/74 − 1).

Nixon refused to be buried just then, however. On Wednesday the *Daily Mirror* labeled him "THE OUTCAST" (8/7/74 − 1), and the *Times* correspondent just could not believe that he was still hanging on: "His contorted claim that whatever he ordered and however he conspired, it all came out right in the end because the 'guilty', as he calls them, were prosecuted simply will not wash. The Nixon Presidency is dying with a whimper" (8/7/74 − 14). The *Daily Telegraph* argued for a little common sense from Nixon:

> This [his refusal to go] may be a credit to his toughness, and, in a sense, there is something to be admired about his refusal to submit. It is not, however, any service to the world. . . . Would not Mr. Nixon's resignation, coupled with a clear confession (most of which has already been made) of the obvious impropriety of his conduct, be the best means of leaving the record straight and proof against controversy or legend? (8/7/74 − 14).

Nixon's resignation speech did not come until after 2 a.m. on Friday morning London time, but all of the a.m. dailies in London held their last editions for it. Hella Pick looked upon it as a "personal tragedy", and wrote dramatically, "it will be hard, if not impossible, for him to face the bleak life ahead" (*Guardian* 8/9/74 − 1). The *Times* reporter, Fred Emery, was dissatisfied with the speech and said Nixon "made a most cursory apology for the scandals . . . his one admission of wrong struck an incongruous and paltry note" (8/9/74 − 1).

Editorially, several papers felt the need to reassure readers that America was still strong. The *Daily Mirror* said the U.S. was a proud nation, "quick to bounce back" (8/9/74 − 3); the *Daily Telegraph* said Americans "may well be surprised and proud that they came through it as well as they did"

(8/9/74 — 16); and the *Evening Standard* commented:

> ... in a curious and heartening way, Watergate has not been just a
> one-theme story of corruption and deceit in high places. The long
> agony of President Nixon caused Congress to rediscover its authority,
> reaffirmed America's traditional confidence in the judiciary and
> rule of law, and reestablished the need for a bold and unfettered
> press (8/9/74 — 21).

Descriptions of the President's final speech to the White
House staff were ripe in the British press. Simon Winchester
wrote of those last few moments:

> The last we saw of him as President was his limp right hand flapping
> occasionally like a dying fish, trying to wave a laconic farewell . . .
> expressed the utter dejection and humiliation of a man who now
> passes into the most public kind of obscurity . . . [during his speech]
> he sobbed violently, his tears somehow eluding the gravitational
> pull and remaining shining in his eyes . . . even to the end Mr.
> Nixon was not coming clean . . . (*Guardian* 8/10/74 — 1).

Another view of it was taken by *The Times:*

> Much of his going was studied, as he has always controlled every
> reaction toward outsiders. Only a Nixon could have released the
> poignantly emotional photo of his family and his daughters, in
> their moment of anguish. . . . He obviously couldn't bear to leave
> (8/10/74 — 1).

The *Daily Telegraph* said: ". . . [he] walked proudly, almost
defiantly but was fighting back the tears" (8/10/74 — 1).
British readers who took in all these accounts might have
formed a picture of Nixon, walking away defiantly but waving
limply with a public manner so controlled that he cried but
refused to let the tears roll down his cheeks.

The British press followed the goings-on at San Clemente
for a few days, but before long Nixon dropped out of sight
much as Agnew had done. During the month of August there
were occasional stories about his health.

When President Ford announced that he was pardoning
Nixon, the *Guardian* was upset, especially since it had warned
Ford against that very thing just after he took office. Hella
Pick led off her story of the pardon announcement with,
"Deliberately choosing Sunday, fortified by Holy Communion,

emphasizing his role as a servant of God, and stressing the quality of mercy, President Ford . . ." (9/9/74 — 1), and the lead editorial strongly condemned.

In taking this stand, however, the *Guardian* was alone among the British press. The *Evening Standard* did not comment on it, and *The Times* wrote one of its typical editorials in which it examined all sides of the issue and came to the astounding conclusion that Ford had taken a "bold and difficult step" (9/9/74 — 13). The *Telegraph* thought the pardon justified but added, "It seems manifestly unjust that the underlings should suffer while the chief — if guilty — should go free" (9/9/74 — 12). The major surprise was the *Daily Mirror*'s attitude: "President Ford can claim that he acted with humanity. Not to say generosity. Mr. Nixon can count himself lucky. . . If it is right for President Ford to pardon the man at the top, he should surely be equally merciful to those lower down the ladder" (9/10/74 — 2).

THE DUE PROCESS CONTROVERSY

The Watergate scandals were in full swing by June 1973. The *Washington Post* had been given due credit for its initial exposures, the Senate Investigation Committee was showing daily televised hearings, and the Federal Grand Jury was interviewing the principal witnesses. The investigative role, once shouldered by the press (namely the *Post*) alone, had been taken over by the three branches of government. Even though these "official" investigations were underway, the press did not give up its investigative role. On the contrary, the press was doing more investigation now than at any other time in the Watergate story. New allegations were being made almost daily against the President and his men in different newspapers and newsmagazines.

The Times grew increasingly disturbed about this, fearing a "trial by the press" situation. In a long editorial headed "Due Process of Law", written by editor William Rees-Mogg, *The Times* said the *Post* should be given credit for what it had done, but:

... now we have a simultaneous process of trial by newspaper allegation, beside the Senate hearings and the Grand Jury. The American press, and particularly the *Washington Post*, deserve their full credit for forcing the Watergate affair into the open. They are however now publishing vast quantities of prejudicial matter that would be contempt under British law, which again must tend to prejudice the fair trial of any accused, or, if it came to that, of the President.

The Times went on to criticize the *Post* and the *New York Times* for printing the Grand Jury testimony of John Dean:

Of course the American law of contempt is very different from ours, but the principles of fair trial are the same. How can one justify the decision to publish the Dean leak? Here is a real piece of hanging evidence, the missing element — if it is believed — in a chain of proof. Here is a piece of wholly suspect evidence unsworn, unverified, not cross-examined, contradicting previous evidence, subject to none of the safeguards of due process, given by a man who may be bargaining for his freedom. How can the newspapers defend themselves from the very charge they are bringing against the President, the charge of making a fair trial impossible, if they are now publishing evidence so damning and so doubtful with all the weight of authority that their publication gives? (6/5/73 — 17).

The editorial caused quite a stir in the U.S. It was largely seen as an untimely defense of President Nixon, and Tom Wicker, columnist for the *New York Times*, said that no newspaper could back off from a breaking story "of substantial importance" and rely instead on official sources. "That is what too much of the American press did from June, 1972 until early this year" (*Times* 6/11/73 — 6).

The *Washington Post* printed most of the editorial, with an editorial of its own refuting it:

For how long would a British Government remain in office if it had lied systematically to the press, and by extension to Congress and the public, for ten months.... Would *The Times* of London in such circumstances be talking about due process for the Prime Minister? This is the heart of what is wrong with the *Times* argument. We are not in Britain; we have a different set of checks and balances .... (*Times* 6/14/73 — 6).

Rees-Mogg was invited to address the National Press Club in Washington the next week, and he did not back off from his criticism. In fact, he went further with it. He said that the press in America had always been unfair to Nixon; that publication of the Pentagon Papers had indicated their disregard for state secrecy; and that they were behaving like a "hunting pack", especially with the "uncritical" handling of Dean's testimony (6/16/73 — 5).

Two days after Rees-Mogg's speech, however, the *Sunday Times*, in a long editorial entitled "What due process?", put up a spirited defense of what was happening in America. It conceded that in Britain, once an investigation had begun, publication about it would cease. But things are done differently in America: "The argument that Senator Ervin should now suspend operations, and that the American Press should suddenly embrace the British law of contempt of court, is couched in the high language of due process." The argument rests on two false assumptions. One is that what Ervin and the press were doing was in contempt of judicial proceedings.

> The President's role in Watergate and his future in the job are not matters for legal and judicial assessment. . . . Mr. Nixon does not face trial. What is happening to him is political not judicial in character.

> The second false assumption is that the political crucible in which the President's future will be resolved should somehow exclude the Press and Congress, or at least restrict their function more narrowly than it is restricted by the Constitution. . . . It may be that the Ervin hearings will affect the future trials of men yet uncharged. But, as far as the President himself is concerned, they remain not only a justifiable but a vital undertaking. There is no case for abandoning them. Nor will any but the most occasional charges of inaccuracy or imbalance stick against the press.

> We believe that the rescue of President Nixon, if it can be accomplished, must come from greater not less disclosure. If British practice has anything to teach it is not in the law of contempt, but in the tradition which insists that the Prime Minister cannot remain silent in the face of damaging allegations. . . . it is right that the search for truth goes on in a way fitting the American system (6/17/73 — 16).

The *Evening Standard* waded into the fray ten days later on the side of the *Sunday Times*:

> . . . to decry the unfairness of the Watergate hearings is to misunderstand the nature of the American system of government and of the offences allegedly committed. . . . This is . . . a political inquiry: in

a sense it is only incidental that the offences were criminal. The real point is to discover whether the American electorate has been misled and misgoverned by their President and his chosen lieutenants, and with total disregard for the law (6/26/73 — 21).

REFERENCES AND NOTES

1. Winston Fletcher, "Britain's National Media Pattern," in J. Tunstall (ed.), *Media Sociology*, London, Constable, 1970.
2. Fletcher, p. 256.
3. Fred Hirsch and David Gordon, *Newspaper Money*, London, Hutchison, 1975, p. 67.
4. Hirsch and Gordon, pp. 116—17.
5. Quoted in Claude-Jean Bertrand, *The British Press*, Paris, O.C.D.L., 1969, p. 108.
6. For excellent analyses of these events, see Colin Seymour-Ure, *The Political Impact of the Mass Media*, London, Constable, 1974, and Franklin Reed Gammon, *The British Press and Germany, 1936—1939*, Oxford, 1971.
7. Much of this section is taken from Colin Seymour-Ure, *The Press, Politics and the Public*, London, Methuen, 1968.
8. Seymour-Ure, 1968, p. 129.
9. Seymour-Ure, 1968, p. 149.
10. The *Sunday Times* has recently been involved with a controversy over the printing of the diaries of a former Labour Cabinet member, the late Richard Crossman. The information contained in these diaries is, by most accounts, fairly mild stuff, but Harold Wilson's government has fought tooth and nail to keep it from coming to light.

3. The French Press

All these papers are the fodder of the ignorant, the resource of those who want to speak and judge without reading, the scourge and disgust of those who work. They never resulted in the creation of a good line by a good mind, nor prevented a bad author from creating a bad work.

Diderot

In America, as in France, [the press] constitutes a singular power, so strangely composed of mingled good and evil that liberty could not live without it, and public order can hardly be maintained against it.

Alexis de Tocqueville

AN OVERVIEW

Strasbourg, 1438. Some 50 years before Christopher Columbus set foot on dry land in the western hemisphere, German inventor Johannes Gutenberg revolutionized the nature of communication and the future of society by introducing a printing machine capable of reproducing written texts. Although the French cannot claim credit for that milestone — since, unlike today, Strasbourg wasn't then part of France — they have never been far from major breakthroughs in the history of the press.

Indeed, during almost three and a half centuries since its first publication appeared in 1631, the French press has contributed substantially to the development of modern "American-style" journalism:

— The first "modern" magazine, *Le Journal des Scavans*, hit Paris streets in 1665. Written in French rather than Latin, its varied contents focused on philology, history and sciences with an international perspective.[1]

— Charles Havas laid groundwork for the first press agency in 1832. L'Agence Havas's initial success owed much to rapid transmission of financial information from the London Stock Exchange by carrier pigeon.[2] Although Agence France-Presse (AFP) replaced it as the country's national wire service in 1944, L'Agence Havas continues to thrive as France's largest advertising agency.[3]

— Two Frenchmen launched a 10-centime newspaper, precursor to the "Penny Press", in 1836.

— *Le Petit Journal* followed in 1863 as the first popular tabloid, selling at 5 centimes to an audience of 400,000 which, by 1898, surpassed 1 million.

— *Excelsior*, founded in 1910, set precedent as the first daily in the world to accord photography a major role.[4]

Though these and several other contributions indicate the strength and importance accorded the printed word in France, the French press has by no means enjoyed a steady or easy evolution. The "Fourth Power's" development has reflected the social turbulence and political convolutions of France's history, with press freedom variously granted, suspended, redefined, or totally obliterated depending on the regime in power. Only the French people's dogged insistence on freedom of expression has allowed their press to repeatedly overcome political repression and emerge as one of the world's most vigorous and independent voices.

The first weekly publication in France appeared in January 1631 under the catchy title, "Ordinary News from Various Places". Setting precedent for a long history of press concentration, a more powerful and permanent publication called the *Gazette* absorbed Louis Vendosme's "Ordinary News" 5 months later.[5]

The unmitigated scorn of France's influential men of letters presented some resistance thwarting the periodical press's growth. Several *belle-lettrists* added condescendingly snide tidbits to Diderot's comment: Rousseau in 1775 labelled the periodical "an ephemeral work without merit or usefulness", while Voltaire found newspapers "narratives of nonsense".

Compared to their Anglo-Saxon counterparts, French publications generally adopted a more literary and less newsy orientation. Even so, leading intellectuals never stooped so low as to contribute to them.[6]

Intellectual snobbery proved a trifling nuisance compared to the authoritarian control exercised by various monarchs and emperors who viewed the press not as a voice of and for the people, but rather as a propaganda tool for amassing political power and currying favor among their subjects. Thus a major advance toward press freedom accompanied the French Revolution of 1789, from which evolved Article XI of the Declaration of the Rights of Man:

> Free communication of thoughts and opinions is one of the most precious rights of Man: all citizens may thus speak, write, and freely print, except that they shall be answerable for abuses of this liberty in those cases determined by the law.[7] *

This newfound press liberation and the flourishing expansion accompanying it proved shortlived, however, when the revolutionary government 3 years later suspended freedom of the press due to hazards it posed to the regime.

Once the revolutionary government had curtailed press freedom, succeeding regimes, whether monarchies or republics, showed little inclination to remove the muzzle. Not notorious for enacting libertarian measures, Napoleon saw no use for an independent press. As one of his first acts (January 17, 1800) following the coup d'état he seized control of the press, limited publication to thirteen closely watched newspapers in Paris, imposed prior restraint, and finally established *Le Moniteur* as his — thus the French Empire's — official organ.[8]

The French press labored under one repressive government after another for roughly 100 years following the revolution. This trend climaxed in 1877 when the republican press suffered formidable oppression — including more than 2,000 press trials within a few weeks — engineered by monarchist leader Albert *duc de* Broglie during a crisis within the Third Republic. Broglie's campaign to silence the press failed miserably, however,

* All translations from the French by Jim Trezise.

demonstrating that it had grown too powerful to be felled by political maneuvering. The republican victors, eager to abandon a politically dysfunctional policy of press suppression, and convinced that the press's diversity no longer permitted the mass mobilization of public opinion which had previously helped to spark revolutions, liberalized the press with its law of July 19, 1881.

Consisting of some 300 articles, it legislated everything from journalism to the printing process to distribution, tolerated attacks on the government and pleas for civil disobedience, and prohibited prior restraint by the government. In essence, this law granted freedom from government control, but offered no guarantees from other kinds of interference such as market forces.

Renewed press freedom ushered in the *belle époque* of French journalism, which lasted until the onset of World War I in 1914. An ever-expanding market and a monopoly on the means for collective information created this "golden age" for most of the Western press, but for France it proved even more so. In terms of the number of publications, their distribution, their political power and public opinion influence, this era marked the French press's finest hour. Though weak in foreign news and always small in size, the papers treated internal political issues such as the Dreyfuss affair extensively, influentially, and with uncharacteristically violent controversy. Between 1870 and 1914 the French press reached its saturation point, with daily distribution mushrooming from 1 to 5 million in Paris and from 300,000 to 4 million in the provinces.[9] In 1914 *Le Petit Parisien*, with a daily circulation of 1.5 million, boasted the largest press enterprise in the world.[10]

World War I brought the *belle époque* to an abrupt halt. Whereas in the United States and England the war triggered a newspaper boom due to reader interest, in France it only presented some insurmountable problems. Advertising resources withered. Paper shortages limited many newspapers to only 4 — and, after 1917, two — pages. Distribution declined sharply as military transport burdened the railway network. The price of newspapers rose and thus their readerships, centime-wise during the lean wartime years, plummeted. Within a few months of August 1914, more than thirty daily newspapers folded in Paris. The crowning blow arrived with censorship, an obvious friction producer between journalists and the government, the main cause of newspaper mediocrity which weakened reader interest during the war, and a persistent wound to newspaper credibility in its aftermath.[11]

Drawing on its hard-times experience during the first conflict, the French press approached World War II with relative fatalism. Even before the official declaration of war on September 3, 1939, several repressive measures had been instituted to silence the press: on August 26, prohibition of Communist publications; 2 days later, implementation of censorship. Compared with the First World War few newspapers disappeared, however, and the press's relationship with censorship officials caused much less difficulty during the "phoney war" (*la drôle de guerre*) from August 1939 to June 1940. Then France's military collapse buried many papers, while several other Parisian publications fled south. During the Vichy government (1940—44) most of the press which survived degenerated into Pétain's propagandistic pap, opposed only by a small but influential clandestine press. In the end, this war further scarred the press's credibility due to its mediocrity and especially its collaboration, aggravated by a vastly increased radio audience emerging from the war years.

The war's close brought profound changes to the structure and operation of the French press. Following liberation by the Allies, all publications which had continued functioning — thus collaborated — during Nazi occupation were summarily suspended and their material assets seized by the new regime for later redistribution among authorized newspapers and magazines. Resistance teams or heads of political parties initially directed the new press, and close coordination between government officials and media professionals ensured that all authorized publications began with an equal chance of survival and success.[12]

In a formal sense, then, the contemporary French press's

history dates only to this fundamental transformation following World War II. However, the major characteristics of today's
press — concentration, depoliticization, regionalism, the importance of the periodical press, and the underdevelopment of
advertising — share interwoven roots extending back to World
War I.

Concentration

Increased costs of putting out a publication, the formidable
investment required to launch a new one, and the effects of
advertising demands toward monopolizing an audience and
simplifying publicity campaigns have combined to pressure
much of the contemporary Western press toward steadily growing concentration.

The first major move toward press concentration in France
occurred during World War I. While small circulation newspapers collapsed under wartime economic stress, those publications large enough to weather the financial slump scavenged the
abandoned readerships and created cooperative agreements
to undercut competition. The five major Parisian dailies struck
accords for common advertising and distribution in collaboration with L'Agence Havas and Les Massageries Hachette, precursor to the Consortium which would attempt to monopolize
the market after 1918.

This trend slowed temporarily during the post-war years,
only to be refueled by the Depression of 1929—30. Technical
changes in newspaper production required enormous invest-
ments during an era of devalued money. Prices for primary
materials escalated and increasingly powerful printers' unions
pressured for higher wages. Increased production costs upped
the price of newspapers, which decreased sales in a bread-line
economy, which dried up advertising money. Small publications
folded, large ones grew.[13]

At the 1914 curtain to French newspapers' *belle époque*,
sixty Parisian dailies circulated. A scant 25 years later that
number had been nearly halved, to thirty-two in 1939. Twenty-

eight emerged after the second war. Thirty years later there remain only eleven. Within 60 years the Parisian press has lost five-sixths of its newspapers while losing only about one-third of its readership. All attempts to establish general information dailies in Paris during the past 20 years have resoundingly failed. It is foreseen that in 5 years only four daily newspapers — two morning, two evening — will survive.[14] The same pattern, though less pronounced, holds true for the provincial press: today's number of publications totals roughly one-third of the 1914 count, while circulation has remained relatively constant throughout the period.[15]

Press concentration in France has assumed a "vertical" form whereby one newspaper dominates a particular region, as opposed to the "horizontal" variation typified by American chains or news syndicates publishing in various places under various titles.[16] Since 1966, territorial agreements among major provincial papers designed to end costly frontier wars have drastically altered the regional market. These accords have virtually assured each region a monopoly within its specified territory. More importantly, collaborative advertising among several papers has spurred concentration by driving up the cost of advertising space in those excluded from the group. Shrinkage in the number of regional dailies from roughly seventy-five today to thirty within 10 years lurks as a distinct possibility. Already in several cities — Besançon, Bordeaux, Lyon, Saint-Étienne — recent agreements have ended newspaper competition by granting one publication a monopoly.

One rather amusing impediment to blatant concentration stems from the *habitude* of the French readership. Any alteration in style, format, layout or logo disorients — thus invariably loses — readers accustomed to their newspaper as one steady, predictable part of their lives. A major regional which has absorbed numerous smaller publications must often distribute several editions to please the local folk: *Le Dauphiné Libéré* in the Grenoble area runs sixty-four editions: *Le Progrès*, headquartered in Lyon, prints forty-seven.[17]

Frequently these are actually identical newspapers weakly

camouflaged by different names. In Besançon, for instance, the reader can choose between the native *Le Comtois* (circulation 11,000) or *L'Est Républicain* (published in Nancy with thirteen editions) which appear side by side on the newsstand and are identical — word for word, picture for picture — except for their titles. Editions for other cities within *L'Est*'s sphere of influence require different local news, however, necessitating separate page layouts. So whereas the typical thirty-two-page Parisian daily prints thirty-two page layouts, a major regional paper often runs from seventy to one hundred and seventy layouts in order to offer its various sub-readerships a sixteen- to twenty-page newspaper.[18]

Depoliticization

Concentration has catalyzed depoliticization of the French press. As publications absorb others or merge, several voices yield to one and, with the financial necessity of attracting the largest possible audience, newspapers cannot safely advocate extremely partisan positions.

> A political press flourishes in many West European countries, particularly in the Scandinavian countries, Belgium, Italy, Finland, Greece, and the Netherlands, where almost half of all newspapers are affiliated to a political party. In France and the Federal Republic of Germany, on the other hand, the thriving pre-war political press has almost ceased to exist. All large and almost all small circulation papers are politically independent.[19]

Following World War II, the revolutionized press flourished despite paper shortages. Twenty-eight new dailies surfaced in Paris and 175 in the provinces by 1946, with the political slant everywhere tilting heavily leftward due largely to the Communists' active role in the Resistance. This proved an over-abundance of publications during a time of continued economic strain. As a result, most of the political press lost its readership to more moderate newspapers such as *France-Soir* or *Le Figaro* or to political periodicals like *L'Observateur*, launched in 1950 by journalists abandoning the floundering leftist daily *Combat*.[20]

Depoliticization of the press does not necessarily reflect

depoliticization of the population, however. Communist dailies like *L'Humanité* have shrunk to about one-fifth their 1946 circulation (1,500,000). But ironically the French Communist Party, particularly in the Paris area, draws most of its electoral support from readers of anti-Communist newspapers like *Le Parisien Libéré*. Today *L'Humanité* thus functions less as a propaganda weapon for wooing the masses than as a doctrinal organ designed to inform and instruct a militant core and provide cohesion within party ranks.[21]

It deserves note that depoliticization of the contemporary French press is relative to its past and *not* relative to the American press. Indeed, one of the first things an American notices is the obvious political slant in most French publications. With the exception of newsmagazines which have adopted the American formula, an American journalist — dedicated to or hung up on the ideal of "objectivity", depending on one's view — blushes at the blatantly evaluative comments in "news" articles contributed by France's top writers in highly respected and respectable publications. Political commentary appears frequently in many non-news media as well: a typical issue of a popular monthly film magazine contained a special section (supposedly) treating Super-8 film technique and suggestions. One part of this three-part article, subheaded "Super 8 and Capitalism," permitted the interviewees to dutifully lament the unavoidability of prostituting their artistic endeavors by contributing to capitalist film enterprises like Kodak and Agfa.[22]

Traditional expectations regarding the press's role in French society and the population's political diversity largely explain this politicization vis à vis the American press. Many of today's French newspapers remain more literary — both in terms of convoluted writing style and presentation of philosophical ideas — than their Anglo-Saxon counterparts. Contemporary intellectuals like the late Albert Camus (*Combat*) and Jean-Paul Sartre (*Libération*) have abandoned their predecessors' boycott of the periodical press since it represents such an effective outlet for spreading their philosophical viewpoints. Much of the

French press, particularly in Paris, remains an "idea" press interpreting news events through a specific conceptual filter. Different shades of the liberal—radical political spectrum account for a majority of this idea-logical press, and the gaps between liberal and conservative publications in France dwarfs that in the U.S.

Similarly, political orientations of the French population cover a considerably broader range than in the United States. Incumbent President Valéry Giscard d'Estaing, a moderate compared with Gaullist predecessor Georges Pompidou but conservative next to Socialist opponent François Mitterand, squeaked by the 1974 election with only 50.8% of the vote. Again, the left in particular includes numerous and often divisive sub-positions, ranging from moderate Socialists to militant Communists to those still further to the left. The more politicized press in France provides ideologically correct reading material for various political subgroups.

Regionalism

The French press is neither strictly a national nor a regional press. If anything it leans heavily toward regional, with Paris considered one of the regions while dominating national and international news. Paris-based national dailies like *Le Figaro* and *Le Monde* provide in-depth coverage of French and world events, whereas regional papers such as *L'Est Républicain* in the northeast or *Ouest France* in Brittany concentrate on local affairs.

Again events during World War I set a trend. Since provincial distribution of the Parisian press proved so difficult, the regional press grew in size and influence — particularly because the motorcar facilitated distribution in small villages and rural areas.

Despite this beginning, the regional press's predominance in France is largely a post-World War II phenomenon. Increasingly powerful regional presses, weekly newsmagazines, radio and television have steadily eroded a Parisian press whose power and influence had previously gone unchallenged. Reduced from about 60% (1939) to 30% of national circulation,[23] the Parisian press now essentially serves the Île-de-France, distributing only a quarter of its copies to the provinces — and then normally as complementary reading to regional papers.

A potential danger lurks in this regionalization since provincial papers devote relatively little attention to national affairs, and less yet to international events. In abandoning these fields of information, they are relegating to the Paris-based dailies — and their largely Parisian readership — surveillance of these environments and thus relinquishing an essential part of their role as a "Fourth Power".

Regional newspapers feature local/provincial news while devoting less than half their news surface to national and international matters. Each major regional runs several editions carrying local news submitted by correspondents from various communities. Roughly 420 daily newspapers circulate in some 220 districts, including local editions of the large regionals and some smaller community papers. Almost all regional papers appear in the morning, while roughly 40% of Parisian dailies' circulation comprises afternoon/evening papers which, like *Le Monde*, often include national distribution.

Politically, most regional papers appear (by French standards) timid and boring except in cities where two papers battle issues editorially. Generally balanced articles presenting various sides of an issue stay relatively noncommittal. A mere three Communist dailies survive in the provinces, with a combined circulation reaching only about 150,000.

The French press presents difficulties for categorization into "quality" and "popular" newspapers. Although the French introduced the popular press, they never carried it to the yellow journalism excesses of Pulitzer or Hearst in the United States. Several popular illustrated magazines like *Paris-Match* exist, but *France-Soir* (circulation 725,000) remains the only quasi-popular newspaper. If anything, "quality" and "popular" labels describe the Parisian and regional newspapers, respectively. The former, more politicized than the provincial, offers readers several serious newspapers covering the entire political spectrum. Regional newspapers compensate for their bland political neutrality by luring readers with oversized, semi-sensational headlines and photographs accompanied by shallow copy.[24]

Periodical

Since 1914 the daily press in France has suffered a steady decline. Great strides made in radio during World War I provided newspapers with tough competition as information brokers. Emergence of weekly illustrated magazines forced radical changes in the daily press's function and content.

No longer monopolizing the information market, dailies became obliged to consider audience appeal which, in essence, forced diversification of content to attract the widest possible readership. Crossword puzzles, cartoons, women's pages, cultural sections and similar features usurped space previously devoted to politics. What politics remained normally suffered dilution to avoid offending a more politically heterogeneous audience, and loyalty to a newspaper gradually shifted from its political stance to its serial cartoons. In addition, many French readers had become disaffected with daily newspapers which had prostituted themselves as propaganda organs during the war.

Financial woes between the two wars further weakened daily newspapers while the periodical press expanded in size and influence. Then, with the daily press re-compromised into propaganda sheets for the Vichy government, radio's influence soared during World War II. Later, the advent of television further cornered the printed word. Suddenly just a complementary medium to radio and television news broadcasts, print journalism evolved toward either news commentary and analysis or, as an important boon to the regional press, presentation of local news which national electronic media cannot regularly cover.[25]

Since 1946 more than 100 daily newspapers — or about half

the daily press — have folded, while circulation has levelled off at roughly 15 million (1972) despite a population explosion which doubled the 1939 census figure.[26] In 1967, daily newspapers accounted for only 47% of the paper used in all French publications and produced only 51% of all copies.[27] For every 1,000 inhabitants in 1970, 460 copies of daily newspapers were available in England, 302 in the U.S., and 233 in France. Ninety-nine daily newspapers survived in France in 1972. In the United States, 1,750 dailies circulated among roughly 200 million people. The same ratio of dailies-to-population in France would require 400 papers.[28]

An incredibly inefficient distribution system exacerbated the dailies' decline. A daily newspaper comprises a blend of intellectual creation and industrial product which acts as a public service in providing news, practical information and diversions, fulfilling certain psychological needs, and integrating the reader into his or her culture. As a business, its sales organization should reflect the product's nature as a marketable entity: the newspaper resembles a timeless industrial product much less than a perishable agricultural commodity which must be sold while still usable. Yesterday's news is no news.

Reader subscriptions guaranteeing income represent the core sales technique in most media distribution systems. Yet nearly 70% of France's daily newspapers are sold on a non-subscription basis. Periodicals, on the other hand, wisely rely on subscriptions: weekly newsmagazine *L'Express* distributes over 60% of its copies through subscription; technical and specialized publications, or "class media", the largest single category comprising some 7,000 titles, average a 70% subscription rate.[29]

This high percentage of non-subscription newspaper sales — and the relatively high price of a newspaper due to distribution costs and losses on unsold copies — results from a relative lack of choice. Postal subscriptions remain unpopular because the newspaper arrives after commuters have downed their *café au lait* and left for work. With few regional exceptions like Alsace where home delivery accomplishes 80% of total distribution, the newspaperboy awaits discovery. *Crieurs* hawk papers at cafes and on the street, and France abounds with media outlets — press stores, kiosks, *tabacs* on virtually every block in the center of most cities — but fickle reading habits and bad weather often counteract trumped-up headlines from luring customers to the newsstands. Individual sales fall miserably short of filling the subscription gap, so in France the press owns the dubious distinction as the industrial sector in which distribution cost runs highest.[30]

The same factors steadily eroding the daily press have simultaneously strengthened periodicals, at least indirectly. The periodical press enjoys much more importance in France than in most other Western countries, and an American first wandering into a press outlet immediately notices the number and diversity of magazines available in a country smaller than the state of Texas. In 1970 more than 10,000 periodicals existed in France, ranging from highly specialized journals to newsmagazines to opinion sheets, women's magazines, youth magazines, sports, culture, etc. Even in most pop-specialization areas such as cinemaphotography or handcrafts the reader can choose from among several competitors.

Lack of "the Sunday papers" has catalyzed the emergence of periodicals in France. Of roughly ninety week-day papers, only twenty run *journaux du septième jour* whose subscription sales (20% of total circulation) represent the lowest rate. Unlike the mammoth Sunday newspapers in the United States and England, these appear in their standard size and format with additional space normally devoted to sports, horse racing results, and cartoons. "Seventh day papers" owe much of their readership to track results, but still drop in the provinces to about 60% of weekday circulation, and to less than 25% in Paris.[31]

Traditionally the French have envisioned weekly publications as primarily a political press. Not so concerned with "scoops", with more time to reflect and project, weekly magazines were expected to present well-thought-out, reasoned, convincing pre-packaged opinions. The press's evolution has radically altered that situation: most surviving opinion sheets find themselves floundering while newsmagazines and general information weeklies — much less politicized while still presenting political, economic and social news and information — are flourishing.[32]

Paris-Match, a profusely illustrated weekly similar to *Life* in the U.S. with a circulation approaching 650,000, has suffered somewhat from television but is in no immediate danger of going under. *L'Express*, founded in 1953 as a politically charged weekly but converted in 1964 to the *Time* magazine formula, continues to thrive with circulation surpassing 60,000. The 1972 appearance of *L'Express*'s only newsmagazine competition, *Le Point* (160,000), only served to expand that market.[33]

A more national distribution has also increased the periodical press's dominance in France. The Parisian dailies remain essentially a Paris-region press, with 1972 provincial distribution accounting for anywhere from 12% (*Combat*) to 32% (*France-Soir*) to 53% (*Le Monde*). Weekly general information magazines, most of which are also based in Paris, attract a considerably larger provincial audience: from 55% (*Le Nouvel Observateur*) to 67% (*L'Express*) to 80% for the pop illustrated *Paris-Match*.[34]

Underdevelopment of Advertising

Perhaps more than any other European country except Italy, France continues to grope for a definitive political-economic identity, torn among Capitalism, Socialism and Communism while laboring under an uneasy mixture of the three. Most members of the printed press also grapple with this conflict, jealously guarding their hard-won independence from the government — sparked by the daily reminder of government-controlled radio and television — and yet deeply suspicious of "the rut of the commercial press":[35]

The relationships of clients and their agents, the advertising agencies, with the press are very complex and rest on a fundamental ambiguity: for the reader the value of a publication depends on its editorial contents while for the advertiser it depends uniquely on the quality of its readership.[36]

This ambivalence has hindered development of advertising. French media average less than a quarter the advertising in American media. Whereas publicity harvests about 60% of all press revenues in the U.S., it accounts for only 40% of the French press's receipts. Few local merchants indulge in newspaper advertising, and the regional press structure discourages national publicity. The relative amount of advertising also determines a publication's characteristics — and vice versa: French Communist Party organ *L'Humanité* averages ten pages while the independent *Le Figaro* runs thirty; these figures reflect their percentages of advertising receipts (10% and 78%, respectively).[37]

Still, the financing — and political slant — of contemporary media increasingly depend on advertising. Multiplication of the field of information and the range of cultural and personal interests has forced publications to diversify their contents. Contrary to the *belle époque* when newspapers unilaterally decided what to offer their passive readerships, today the audience determines what it wants to read — thus what will sell — so marketing has assumed a primary role.[38]

This trend has weakened dailies while contributing to the periodical press's boom, since periodicals lend themselves more readily to simplified and efficient advertising campaigns. Publicity had also provoked concentration by favoring media with larger and more consumer-oriented readerships, and encouraging collective advertising campaigns among publications in order to cut corners on preparation. Such cooperative advertising schemes have flourished in the provinces since 1965 and account for much of today's regional concentration.[39]

Predictably, the high price of inefficient media economics falls onto the consumer. In August 1974 a regional daily newspaper in France cost the reader 1 franc (or 100 centimes), whereas the Britisher paid only 40 centimes and the American 78. By October 1975 the price had climbed to 120 centimes for a regional daily and 130 for *Le Monde*, with fully 60% of that price devoted to covering distribution costs: getting the newspaper to the reader.[40] Even the more financially efficient periodicals are relatively expensive: *L'Express* sells for 5 francs on the newsstand while *Time* magazine, its imported English-language equivalent, goes for only 4 (1975). Further compounding the cost of French media is the fact that the average Parisian's buying power represents only about half of the average New Yorker's. Due to higher prices and lower salaries, a Frenchperson must work nearly twice the hours as his or her American counterpart in order to buy the same commodity.[41]

Still, according to a 1963 survey by ten major regional dailies, 79% of the French population above 15 years old manage to read newspapers, with 64% perusing them daily and the others at least three times a week. Men spend nearly an hour with their paper, women about 45 minutes. Nine out of ten readers consider their daily ritual a time of *détente* or winding down and prefer the activity at home, normally in the evening (36%), but also over breakfast (24%) and during the 2-hour French lunch break (26%). Eighty-five percent regularly read local news, 62% national and international affairs, and about one-third attend to cartoons, radio and TV programming, classified ads, and sports.[42]

The average French reader approaches printed media with considerably more skepticism than his or her American counterpart, notwithstanding the decline in recent years of Americans' confidence in institutions, including the press.

> Each country creates a myth of journalism which is very revealing of its national temperament: thus, seen from American literature and films, the journalist appears as an incorruptible redresser of wrongs, an ardent defender of the public interest and of the truth, while French literature since Balzac in *Les Illusions Perdus* and Maupassant in *Bel Ami* presents rather for the public an image of an unscrupulous opportunist.[43]

More than 13,000 professional journalists, including some 2,500 women, labor under this dubious image. In recent years the profession has spurted in popularity with a 55% increase in numbers between 1960 and 1972.[44] Journalism requires a specialized education in France, traditionally obtained at *L'École Supérieure de Journalisme* in Lille or the *Centre de Formation des Journalistes*. More recently the Universities of Bordeaux and Strasbourg have developed journalism programs.[45]

A 1935 press law contains, among other protections, a Clause of Conscience guaranteeing the professional journalist's right to leave a publication with indemnity when its character or orientation evolves beyond a point consistent with his or her moral conscience.[46] One lingering fear among French journalists, however, involves the publishers' financially-based control of media. In recent years, increasingly powerful writers' unions have been pressuring management for guarantees of editorial independence and a greater voice in direction of the publication. With the notable exception of *Le Monde*, which will be discussed later, most such attempts have failed to yield definitive results, but writers' unions remain a force for management to consider.[47]

The Fifth Republic's 1958 Constitution legally guarantees "freedom of the press" in France. Censorship and unreasonable government demands for restraint due to national security are prohibited. Press freedom translates into the right to publish whatever one wishes *plus*: name and address of the publisher; information which judiciary authorities demand must be included; the response of any person cited in an article.

This "freedom of the press," like others, remains subject to various internal and external pressures, both governmental and not:

— judiciary: seizures, legal prosecution;
— fiscal: threat of money measures against journalists;
— financial: fines, retraction of state publicity and support (national lottery, loans, refusal of nationalized banking access);
— professional: no access to sources, information;
— flattery: awards, invitations, solicitations;[48]
— strikes: powerful printers' unions have exercised considerable conservative influence in preventing technological evolution of the French press;[49]
— commercial: market forces; advertising, concentration.

Finally, a word about French television. Since 1959 the *Office de Radiodiffusion-Télévision Française* (ORTF) has directed the state monopoly on television, whose relative importance as a news source remains low. With one TV set for every four people (versus one for two in the U.S.) and only 55% of French homes equipped with "the blue light", viewing opportunities are limited. Roughly one-third of TV1's audience watches the half-hour 8 o'clock news broadcast, while only 12% of TV2's viewers stay tuned.[50]

A lingering credibility gap further hinders television news's influence. The Gaullist Party, which retained the Presidency from 1958 to 1974 and shifted control of the electronic media from the Post Office to ORTF, notoriously exploited television news as a political weapon. Blatant manipulation has largely disappeared in recent years, but bitter memories keep the viewing public skeptical of TV news.[51]

The nature of television news also lessens its influence as a source of in-depth information. In France, as in the U.S., the broadcast covering national and international events lasts a mere half hour, grossly insufficient time to provide background and analysis of the day's news. This "headline" approach creates a gap requiring supplementary information obtainable only through printed media. So TV's sketchy presentation often serves to increase newspaper and magazine sales by whetting the public's news appetite.

Sample Survey

The extraordinary sequence of events collectively referred to as "Watergate" covered a period of more than 2 years. Roughly ninety daily papers and a handful of weekly magazines comprise the French "news" media. Leafing through 2 years' worth of 100 publications would require an enormous team of bilingual media researchers. Obviously, a full survey of French publications was not feasible. Nor, fortunately, was it really necessary since the structural characteristics of today's French press provide for highly representative sampling.

The publications surveyed in this analysis were selected specifically to reflect this overriding structure. *L'Est Républicain* typifies the large and influential regional newspapers, featuring provincial news within a quasi-popular format to a largely captive audience due to its territorial monopoly. The major newsmagazine *L'Express* provides a good example of the powerful periodical press, heavily laden with publicity and reaping a 60% subscription rate from a more nationally distributed readership. Internationally reputed *Le Monde* represents a serious, quasi-political Parisian daily attracting a heterogeneous readership which extends to the provinces and abroad. The combined audience of these three publications totals more than one and a half million people covering a broad geographical, political, and socio-economic range. Each publication will be introduced more intimately below.

WATERGATE COVERAGE

> Since the beginning of Watergate, I have tried to explain to my
> European friends what this affair has meant to Americans.
> Without much success. Apparently, they don't understand what
> it involves. We're not talking about the same thing.
>
> Pierre Salinger

L'Est Républicain

Founded in 1889, *L'Est* has grown into one of France's major regional dailies (including Sunday), covering the northeastern section of the country. Its logo occasionally trumpets: "From Belgium to Switzerland". *L'Est* harvested much of its current influence only since 1967 when it formed the core for a common advertising program with — and virtually absorbed — seven other provincial dailies.

The paper's circulation statistics are somewhat misleading: technically, the thirteen regional editions of *L'Est Républicain* comprise a distribution of about 250,000 (1972).[52] But this figure ignores several identical newspapers merely appearing under different names — such as *Le Comtois* in Besançon —

whose inclusion more than doubles circulation to about 550,000.[53]

Headquartered in Nancy with a staff of 182 journalists, *L'Est*'s twenty-five agencies and 3,000 local correspondents submit community news for various editions. National and international news remain the same in all editions so, if roughly 60% of the provincial audience still reads these sections, some 330,000 French people followed *L'Est*'s account of Watergate.

By French standards, *L'Est* leans slightly to the right politically. It runs from fourteen to twenty-two pages in full format, with national news usually dominating the front page, and most international tidbits on the back. Regional news and sports occupy roughly 75% of its daily news surface. Most by-lined international stories appear toward the back under the standing columns "News in Brief" or "Reflections of the World".

Three- to five-column photos often splash over a quarter of the front page; immense headlines — sometimes with a midword change in type size to squeeze them in — are the rule; and copy is generally short. Typical daily fare included: a large, front-page photo of a newsmaker (Nixon, Pompidou, Brezhnev) or personality (Brigitte Bardot, Jean-Paul Belmondo, Liz Taylor and/or Richard Burton) with a short boxed caption; one gory crime — "STABBED FOR REFUSING A DANCE: Drama at the Prytanée Ball"; one gruesome death — "THREE BROTHERS AND SISTER BURNED ALIVE"; one bizarre accident — "ASPHYXIATED IN HIS BATHTUB"; one chilling murder — "CHILDREN MASSACRED AND IMPALED: Horror in England"; one *scandale* — "BORDEAUX WINE ALTERED"; one story of government excess — "TOPLESS BATHERS BANNED AT CANNES: Severe Repression on the Beaches"; one article covering food resources — "SNAILS PROTECTED FROM OVERHARVESTING"; and extensive sports coverage which, particularly during soccer or cycling seasons, comprises the largest single section of the paper. Local news appears by village or city, and *L'Est* fulfills an important social role by announcing various rites of passage — births, weddings, deaths — occurring among its audience.

L'Est Républicain's coverage of American-related news fell into four major categories: American foreign policy; U.S. presidential elections; Watergate; and, particularly in relation to the last two, Pierre and Renée Gosset.

American foreign policy was presented by *L'Est* — before, during, and after Watergate — with the same overall view it received in most French publications, though less rhetorically and acerbicly than by left-wing papers like Jean-Paul Sartre's *Libération* or Communist Party organ *L'Humanité*, and less subtly than in the sophisticated *Le Monde*.

General orientations: the imperialist United States is constantly seeking to establish hegemony over Western Europe *à la* Soviet Union and its East-bloc satellite states; the U.S. thus seizes every opportunity to quash nascent European unity; cooperation with the U.S. and formation of a United Europe are mutually exclusive; since the other "docile allies" in Europe manifestly lack the courage, France must assume the lonely role of adversary to a superpower.

France officialized this role in 1958 when Charles de Gaulle decided to withdraw his country from NATO and develop an "independent" military force including a nuclear *"force de frappe"*, a symbol of great pride among most French people. Indeed, it is little more than a symbol, today (1975) representing only 1/15,000th of Soviet nuclear strength, while the Russians could raze France with less than 1% of their nuclear capability.[54] The true nature of France's military "independence" becomes evident each time the U.S. threatens to withdraw its military presence from Europe: almost invariably, France — which expelled American troops in its show of independence from NATO — protests first and loudest.

France's main bargaining power lies in an accident of geopolitics: centrally located in Western Europe, bridging the gap between the Common Market's Latin and Germanic peoples, surrounded by NATO countries, France can thus freely criticize U.S. policies and disrupt European unity with relative impunity. In this regard, France's overall policy of non-cooperation is not limited to the U.S., but also emerges within the European

Economic Community (E.E.C.) as well. Again, Charles de Gaulle, notorious for his profound hatred of supranationality, threw a persistent kink into the works by intransigently insisting that E.E.C. policies be instituted by unanimous (versus majority) vote, thus in effect granting veto power to any one dissenting country — a power which has been exercised almost exclusively by France. The French conception of European unity, as seen from a non-French perspective of E.E.C. behavior, essentially involves a community of equals, with some members being more equal than others, and France being the most equal of all. A recent example of French striving for European unity occurred during the 1973—74 oil crisis when, despite pleas for a common European stance, France insisted on a "go-it-alone" policy.

The French fear of American domination borders on paranoia, and the view most news media take toward American foreign policy is not, to say the least, favorable or complimentary. The U.S. is often put in a no-win position: following strident complaints that the U.S. had long been ignoring Europe in favor of Israel, Vietnam, and détente, Henry Kissinger's "Year of Europe" elicited only bitter mockery and his proposed "New Atlantic Charter" drew righteous indignation as the latest attempt at hegemony; incessant self-righteous charges of American imperialism for its role in supporting South Vietnam (where the French would still be, had they not lost *their* war there) turned into equally recriminating accusations of American irresponsibility, unreliability as an ally, and neo-isolationism following the American evacuation.

Such constant criticism of the United States, and its relative absence in regard to the Soviet Union, creates the impression that France greatly favors — and does not fear — the U.S.S.R. A more probable explanation, however, is that French carping about U.S. policies stems from a combination of romanticism regarding the role of lonely adversary to a superpower; lingering nostalgia for France's own heyday as an empire and resentment of America's dominant position in today's world; and — perhaps most significant — the luxury of being able to freely criticize within the security of knowing that, in case of emergency, the U.S. would surely rally to France's defense after her limpid *force de frappe* was depleted.

Except for U.S. presidential elections (which carry international consequences), little American domestic political news appears in *L'Est*. Occasional exceptions involve the Kennedy family, for whom the French bear a special fondness and curiosity — perhaps in part because they are Catholic. Otherwise, U.S. domestic news usually includes only prominent personalities (Jackie Onassis, Marlon Brando, Liz/Richard) or sensational crime stories like the Manson Murders, the Houston, Texas slayings, or the Patricia Hearst kidnapping, which fit neatly into *L'Est*'s daily menu.

The 1972 presidential race between George McGovern and Richard Nixon received considerable coverage in terms of number of articles, if not their depth. Reportage fell into two main categories: relatively straight accounts of public opinion polls, political strategies, presidential platforms, choice of running mates, the Eagleton affair, etc., mostly from uncredited sources; secondly, the extremely slanted reporting of Pierre and Renée Gosset.

Similarly, Watergate drew extensive coverage which fluctuated in both frequency of appearance and depth of articles with the unrolling of events in Washington. Here again the straight/Gosset dichotomy came into play.

Pierre and Renée Gosset are (apparently) a husband/wife journalist team acting as stringers for *L'Est* as well as *Nice Matin* (circulation 268,000)[55] in the south of France. During the presidential campaign and Watergate, they lived in Potomac, Maryland (a suburb of Washington) where they were neighbors of convicted Watergate burglar E. Howard Hunt (*L'Est Républicain*, May 14, 1973).

Their by-lined articles, usually appearing in the paper's interior pages under "News in Brief" or "Reflections of the World", typically ran much longer than other *L'Est* pieces, often extending to twenty or thirty paragraphs and usually accompanied by a photo reflecting the article's tone. This tone, beginning with the campaign, was blatantly pro-Nixon, pro-Republican, anti-Democrat and, in general, anti-American. As the Watergate scandal began intensifying, they adamantly flew to Nixon's side, presenting him as a great — at times, almost European — President; a righteously persevering martyr being senselessly and mercilessly persecuted by his traditional political enemies in Congress, the Eastern Intellectual Establishment, and the Eastern press; all the while being ignored — and sometimes even attacked — by the politically innocent American public he had so nobly represented. From the Gossets' perspective, the American press is scandalously irresponsible and inordinately powerful, Daniel Ellsburg is a traitor and well-known Soviet spy, political enemies abound and were determined to oust Nixon after he humiliated them with his landslide victory, the American public is incredibly naive, and Richard Nixon is a saint. The Gossets, who mounted their campaign rather subtly at first and gradually reached near-hysteria toward The End, will be quoted at length in the summary which follows.

L'Est Républicain clearly endorsed Richard Nixon for the 1972 presidential contest, even without help from the Gossets. The paper's fondness for Nixon was equalled by a strong distaste for George McGovern, typified by a front-page editorial titled "America: The Ill-at-ease Man" which dubbed his politics naive, his policies unworkable, and added several unkind personal barbs — like he would never be mistaken for a movie star (7/13/72 — 1).

The Gossets multiplied this tendency with coverage of the political conventions. "FOUR DAYS OF CIRCUS IN MIAMI: For McGovern, Victory of the Sorcerer's Apprentice" headlined their three-column article describing the Democratic National Convention (7/14/72 — 12). "Sorcerer's Apprentice" alludes to McGovern forces' triumph over traditional convention politiking *à la* Mayor Richard Daley by what the Gossets harrumphingly labelled " a majority of minorities". They found it inexcusable, for instance, that "15% of the convention delegates were black, when only 10% of the American population is", and that women, who had "just recently discovered politics", accounted for such a large percentage of the delegation.

"HE GAVE THEM THE MOON . . . Nixon 'The Magician' Elected by His Own" occupied four front-page columns 2 days before the Republican National Convention nominated Nixon for a second term (8/21/72 — 1, 10). McGovern had promised Americans the moon, the Gossets snickered, but even if he could deliver it would be too little too late since Nixon had already *given* it to them. "One of the greatest Presidents", Nixon had virtually eliminated racism, poverty, unemployment, is the best friend Israel ever had and, like all true patriots, stands categorically opposed to amnesty for traitorous draft dodgers and deserters. His enormous popularity and esteem among Americans, and McGovern's lack thereof, has triggered formation of a "Democrats for Nixon" committee boasting such prominent politicos as John Connally. A photo of Nixon in the woods with his dog accompanied this article.

Between these two convention pieces the Gossets wedged in two other campaign articles. The first hailed Spiro Agnew as "Hero of the Middle American", explaining — and praising — his role as Nixon's mouthpiece for (justified) verbal attacks aimed at students, welfare recipients, the press, and the Eastern Intellectual Establishment (7/29/72 — 12). Two days after Senator Thomas Eagleton's resignation from the Democratic ticket due to his past health record, the Gossets fired off their first anti-press diatribe ("THE REAL LOSER OF THE EAGLETON AFFAIR", 8/4/72 — 14) maintaining that the *New York Times* had politically assassinated McGovern's ex-running mate.

An October 5 (p. 16) "Gossett" asserted that the American presidential elections had been defused of their excitement because people were no longer impressed with McGovern, loved Nixon, and saw no real contest. This theme reappeared on election day, November 7 (p. 12) when the Gossets assured a no-contest landslide between "a professional" and a "prairie preacher". Two days later, after he had been officially re-elected, the Gossets let it all hang out with five columns of unabashed adoration for Richard Nixon. This article included a short, Horatio Alger-riddled biographical sketch, a subtitle "Ferociously Pacifist" heading a column which credited Nixon's Quaker origins for his intrinsically peace-loving nature, and praise for his "European" tastes and character: he often listens to classical music and reads biographies at the end of a day, cherishes solitude and time for reflection, and remains more old-world and solid than most "gregarious" Americans (11/9/72 − 12).

Regardless of *L'Est*'s and the Gossets' unshakable conviction that Nixon was right for America and Americans, his Administration continued as a prime target for foreign policy criticism. While headlining Nixon as "SPOKESMAN FOR THE 'SILENT MAJORITY' " during the campaign (8/25/72 − 1), *L'Est* ran a two-column piece, "UNITED STATES AND JAPAN UNIFIED AGAINST EUROPE", complaining that a recent U.S.–Japanese meeting had produced trade and fiscal measures designed to undermine Europe's economy (9/2/72 − 15). "NIXON RELAUNCHES WAR ON NORTH VIETNAM" (12/19/72 − 1) and "HANOI ACCUSES NIXON OF NEW HIROSHIMA" (12/26/72 − 1) typified front-page headlines appearing within two months after *L'Est* had toasted Nixon's re-election and explained his ferocious pacifism. Similarly, American behavior at the onset of the international monetary crisis in March 1973 incurred *L'Est*'s editorial wrath. Once again the interpretation pitted the U.S. − which refuses to cooperate − against Europe.

The Gossets slipped in a bubbling piece between the Vietnam and monetary crisis harangues. "FOUR-DAY FESTIVAL FOR AN ENTIRE NATION: The New 'Crowning' of Richard Nixon" described America as exuberantly awaiting Nixon's inauguration. Since he is a President of the People, the festivities will include soul food, rock music, etc., and now there will be "Peace, finally" (1/19/73 − 13).

For roughly 9 months following the Watergate burglary attempt, *L'Est* virtually ignored the story. Watergate received mention only twice: announcement of the burglary and a suggestion that the Republicans might also have some "skeletons in their closet" were buried near the end of a campaign article (8/14/72 — 14); four back-page paragraphs cited a *Time* magazine story about Donald Segretti's political sabotage and Howard Hunt's link to Maurice Stans (10/16/72 — 16).

L'Est began picking up on the Watergate story in April 1973, however, and from April 25 to May 22, almost daily, in-depth articles recounted new Watergate developments. One major story almost totally ignored was the April 30 resignations of top White House staffers H. R. Haldeman, John Ehrlichman, and lesser figure John Dean. Since May 1 is a French national workers' holiday, no paper was printed, but even in subsequent editions with extensive Watergate coverage, no conspicuous mention of this event appeared; one paragraph on p. 20 (5/5/73) noted Nixon's selection of General Alexander Haig to replace Haldeman as chief of staff.

The Gossets did not have a total monopoly on opinion within *L'Est*'s pages, and often they were at variance with others who submitted views. For example, a four-column update of Watergate events by Jean-François Kahn concluded with: "All that, let's not forget, because a free press did its work, seconded by an independent judiciary" (5/3/73 — 18). A few days later Ben Bradlee, executive editor of the Watergate-scooping *Washington Post*, was quoted as asserting that if Watergate had happened in France, the government would have fallen by now. This remark sparked an editorial by Georges Mamy, "AND IF IT HAD HAPPENED IN FRANCE . . .", which took issue with Bradlee. If it had happened in France (as it well could have, since there had been concurrent scandals, including wiretapping) the same kind of justice would most likely *not* be attained because there does not exist the same freedom of the press, political independence of the judiciary (specifically the grand jury system), nor the close liaison between the two. Overall, an article complimentary to the United States (5/7/73 — 1).

Enter the Gossets. On May 14 a three-column article, accompanied by a three-column photo of McGovern and Kennedy, appeared on p. 14. Excerpts:

> The true dimension of this affair, as exaggerated today by the President's enemies as it was stifled during the November elections by his confidence men. . . .

> But the error was in thinking that, after the election, the Watergate affair would fade away. . . . The obstinancy of the opposition press and a judge named Sirica, furious to see justice scoffed at in the name of the State, would prevent that from happening.

> The "plumbers" are not ordinary skilled laborers. Howard Hunt, one of our neighbors in Potomac, lives in an enviable $125,000 villa. He is the author of several spy stories — maybe he read too many?

> Today, rather than asking if Watergate will force Nixon to abandon his functions — which is pure sensationalism — the question is, how is he going to change things so that he can govern his country effectively for the remaining three years?

Another part of this article contained the Gossets' first allegation that Daniel Ellsburg had supplied the Pentagon Papers to the Russian Embassy well before he gave them to the *New York Times*.

The following day another large Gosset piece appeared (p. 14): "AMERICANS STILL INDULGENT TOWARD 'MISTAKES' OF THEIR PRESIDENTS". Most Americans (77% according to the latest poll), many of whom think Nixon is not being frank and honest about Watergate, still believe resignation is out of the question: "There is great innocence in this ambivalence of the American people toward their president. Rather, toward the Presidency." Curiously enough, Americans have a great tolerance for "Political Man", can accept routine political corruption like influence peddling, but will not accept:

> the smallest suggestion of these secretive spy operations, common to all governments; the simple notion of state secrecy revolts the average American.
> This is a sentiment totally exploited by the American press when it defends the citizens' "right to know all".
> Never before, in two centuries of controversial history surrounding the U.S. Presidency, has anything like this taken place. And, on the other side of this undertaking from a part of the press which, like a Samson, is attacking the columns of the White House in blind

furor, it is the Senate, which [the press] calls upon to dishonor
Nixon, which is the first to take into account: it's not the President,
but the institution of the Presidency itself which is in danger. . . .
But the American press remains so obstinately vowed and determined to rummage through wastebaskets that it doesn't even notice
the behind-the-scenes bargaining between the White House and
influential senators who are going to ensure the rescue of Richard
Nixon and prevent the Watergate affair from degenerating into an
institutional crisis.

Modern Monarch

A good number of cool heads are taking into account: the issues
on which the American press's vendetta is overflowing amount to
the arraignment of the inherent vices of democracies. The destruction of Richard Nixon risks being the destruction of the System
itself. . . . This is the true significance of Watergate: the defeat of
the modern monarch which Richard Nixon is, in his struggle against
the Congress, the condemnation of a government of technocrats
which he had assembled to short-circuit Congressional power.

The Gossets conclude their article by asking rhetorically whether
Nixon will still be able to govern effectively, and respond by
assuring that in at least one domain — foreign policy, "the
most important" — he retains his efficacity because Henry
Kissinger has gone unscathed from Watergate.

As a brief intermission from Watergate, a short May 16
article deserves note in exemplifying France's self-appointed
adversary role in relation to the Common Market and the U.S.
The international monetary crisis provided the issue; specifically, preparation for the "Nixon Round" of talks. The mouthpiece was French Foreign Minister Michel Jobert, who would
later rise to national stardom for his actions — or lack thereof —
during the Washington Energy Conference in February 1974.

NIXON ROUND: PARIS PREACHES FIRMNESS

The Minister of Foreign Affairs, Mr. Michel Jobert, yesterday
took the contrary view to proposals presented by the Brussels
Commission in preparation for the next multilateral negotiations.
Reminding the council of ministers of the "Nine" that the European
Community had not been the party to request these negotiations,
Mr. Jobert reproached the Community for giving the impression
that they were losing their reasoning abilities.

"The Community", Mr. Jobert said, "must make it clear that
commercial negotiations make sense only if perspectives exist

for a return to the convertibility of the dollar. We must refute
the idea that the object of these negotiations is reestablishment of
the American commercial balance."

One of few articles counterbalancing the Gossets' Watergate
slant appeared on May 21 (p. 16). "CAN NIXON STILL
GOVERN?" presented a fifteen-paragraph, relatively sophisticated analysis of Watergate's effect on Nixon's influence in both
domestic (budget battle with Congress) and foreign (Vietnam
and Soviet Summit) arenas. It described the Watergate affair
as a complex, bipartisan domestic political crisis, with Nixon's
various friends and foes hailing from both parties.

In late May and most of June, Watergate was upstaged by
summitry — first the Nixon—Pompidou meeting in Iceland,
then Brezhnev's visit to the U.S. Some time before the former,
a front-page headline blared that the Franco-American summit
would occur in neither Paris nor Washington, but on neutral
ground — as if the countries were more enemies than allies.
Three articles covering this summit deserve mention.

The first, a two-column piece by Yves Rouault on May 29
(p. 18) headlined "POMPIDOU—NIXON: STRAINED DISCUS-
SIONS", sulked that the French felt slighted since Henry
Kissinger had spent 4 full days in Moscow arranging the upcoming Brezhnev visit, while devoting only an hour and a
half in Paris for the Icelandic summit. Strained talks are predicted because France is no longer a "docile ally" but rather
has a spirit of "national independence". Pompidou (apparently
by self-appointment) would be speaking for other European
countries as well. The article's central thrust reiterated the
hegemony theme:

> But what does America want? Apparently to put Europe back in
> ranks. A French politician remarked the other day that a Common
> Market of six members was undoubtedly the maximum that the
> U.S. could tolerate.

"POMPIDOU: AMERICAN TROOPS MUST STAY IN
EUROPE: French Firmness Toward Nixon in Iceland" (6/1/
73 -- 20) flaunted Pompidou's tactical coup in opening the
summit with the outright demand that the U.S. retain its military

presence in Western Europe (a seemingly strange position for a country boasting an "independent" military). This brilliant opener, the article bubbled, caught Nixon off guard and assured that he wouldn't use threats of U.S. troop withdrawals as a bargaining chip in negotiations.

The final Nixon—Pompidou piece (6/2/73 — 1) pictured the summit as having been virtually useless. "It was more like a conception than a birth", quipped Pompidou, "but after all, a conception is far more pleasant." Nixon was quoted as saying that, before he took office in 1969, Americans had attributed U.S.—French tensions to Charles de Gaulle, when in reality they were attributable to previous U.S. Administrations. "I've tried to improve this situation", Nixon said, "and some people say I'm becoming more and more Gaullist."

The Nixon—Brezhnev summit received similar coverage. First a short article posited that Nixon and Brezhnev needed each other and their summitry: as a Watergate counterbalance for the former; and to increase the Russian leader's political leverage for stifling internal Soviet squabbles concerning détente (6/19/73 — 16). The next day an article (p. 16) announced that John Dean's potentially explosive Watergate testimony would be postponed until after Brezhnev's departure to avoid hindering Nixon in the summit talks. "NIXON AND BREZHNEV DETERMINED TO 'SUCCEED' " briefly described a relaxed atmosphere in which "serious discussions" were taking place (6/21/73 — 18).

On June 22 (p. 15) the Gossets contributed "JOVIAL LEONID AT HIS AMERICAN COUSIN'S : A Masterpiece in Public Relations", their six-column analysis with a photo of Brezhnev spilling his champagne and Nixon laughing. In their quasi-paranoid piece covering U.S.—Soviet détente in general and this summit in particular, the writers contended that since Henry Kissinger's proposed New Atlantic Charter had withered into a dismal failure, the U.S. had now resorted to making tacit solidarity agreements with Moscow in order to establish combined *world* hegemony. After all, the Gossets mused, what else could they have been talking about during all those long walks in secluded Camp David and on deserted San Clemente beaches? The final section:

De Gaulle Was Right

This acceleration [in U.S.—Soviet deténte] can be measured by two numbers: of the 108 accords between these two countries during the last half-century, 48 were created by Richard Nixon and Leonid Brezhnev.

"When you get to the bottom of things", said a Soviet minister this week while, it is true, leaving a White House banquet including plenty to drink, "you are the only country that matters to us. Not only because you are the other superpower, but because we feel a common heritage."

This reconciliation of estranged cousins was prophetically predicted by General de Gaulle.

If it had to be accomplished at the expense of an ever-divided Europe, one would find even less admirable an [American] political policy which, having slackened its transatlantic ties, has done everything to prevent the creation of that Europe. . . .

Following a handful of short articles covering government "security" expenditures on Nixon's various residences, John Dean's testimony, and a Nixon family weekend at Camp David, *L'Est* threw in a little spice on July 11. "CALL-GIRL WANTS TO TALK ABOUT WATERGATE", on the front page, related pseudonymned Faye Martin's story about how she became a political call-girl, often worked the Watergate apartment building, had shared beds with Democrats at Republicans' request and vice versa in order to gather information, compromise people, etc. She obviously wants to achieve instant celebrity status by testifying before the Senate Watergate Committee, *L'Est* chuckled, but she probably won't be summoned since it's questionable whether the Committee really wants to hear "the naked truth".

The Gossets resurfaced on July 16 (p. 14) with a three-column defense of John Mitchell. "NIXON'S BEST FRIEND RISKS IMPRISONMENT", accompanied by a photo of Mitchell cutlined "Because of loyalty to the President", led off with the following separate introduction:

What is he going to do in this parliamentary gallery before this commission of inquest into the Watergate affair where he follows these secret agents or these little proto-fascists, Dean, Magruder, avowed perjurers with the exaggerated good behavior of choirboys recovering their innocence by confession after having sneaked a swig of the altar wine, what is he going to do here, this paragon of honor who is likely to be dishonored?

John Mitchell, the Gossets plead, comes across as a "cold fish" in public appearances, but those who really know him offer a diametrically opposed description: he is a "lawyer of great integrity, a model husband, loyal friend, extroverted, human and full of humor". Known as one of New York's foremost lawyers, he teamed up with Richard Nixon and, out of loyalty, left the "good life" to direct his 1968 campaign. He further sacrificed by accepting the Attorney General's post during Nixon's first term. Following Nixon's re-election, Mitchell had planned on returning to his New York law practice.

But alas, implicated — because of his loyalty to the President and his image of the Presidency — in the Watergate cover-up and half a dozen other affairs, inherent to political morality, this would be for him the beginning of a dizzying fall.

Not only will he probably lose his law practice, but he may even go to prison. This man, they lament, is a classic victim of a Greek tragedy.

In reality, this is a less exalted contemporary drama in which, opposite those who consider it a publicly cathartic exercise in democracy, many Americans see only sordid accounting practices during the 1972 election campaign.

It is difficult for a European journalist, thinking he understands America and accepting this image of it as a *Country-not-like-the-others* [italics theirs], to be shocked by such deplorable practices which support, with a good dose of hypocrisy, a press latching onto the smallest thing and whose power has gone to its head.

And the "Father Virtue" personage that these Senators posing as judges assume lacks just as much plausibility. Few would not be shamed if someone stuck their nose into their electoral kitchens.

The Gossets' house-painter mumbled "All our leaders . . . all of them . . ." while watching the televised **Watergate Follies** [heavy type theirs]. Generalizing from one random comment to a population of over 200 million, they then ask rhetorically:

Should we deplore or find refreshing this cynicism of the American on the street?

In any case, it exists. Sociologists will probably say one day that the American public was immunized against lies by the commercial publicity to which it has been daily subjected during so many years. But the latest public opinion poll taken this week across the U.S. weakens this position:

71% of Americans believe, rightly or wrongly, that their President is lying, that at the very least he was aware of efforts to cover up the Watergate burglary.

Only 18% think that, because of this, he should resign or be deposed.

Those who exploit this scandal beyond the limits of elementary decency are doing so against the current of this public opinion . . . [of people] who are today thinking only about their vacations.

A couple of weeks and a few articles after the Spiro Agnew scandal hit *L'Est*'s pages (8/8/73 — 1), the Gossets launched their preliminary defense of the American Vice-President. Agnew suffers a crude appearance in the eyes of most Americans because of his speeches, but:

politicians in the Senate (where he presides) have learned to gauge his vigorous personality, his real culturedness and finesse, unknown to the public, of this provincial wandering in the capital who has made himself a force.

The Veep would have been unbeatable in the 1976 presidential elections. He was "Mister Clean", unsullied by Watergate, but is now involved in a scandal of his own.

It was almost inevitable if you consider the passion which has possessed hundreds of petty judges and even more journalists. A federal attorney of Maryland is thus sticking his nose into the affairs of the Vice-President and opening an inquest into his relations, from the time he was governor of that state, with Baltimore construction companies.

The Gossets conclude their defense with a snippet of old-world wisdom:

"It would be naive to think", said Spiro Agnew to some journalists, "that companies sharing my political ideas didn't contribute to the financing of my electoral campaign."

It would be even more naive to think that they did so in a totally disinterested fashion.

In September 1973, the French indulged in a little semantic juggling to christen one of their own *scandales* "Winegate".

The Bordeaux-based scandal, which later had a videotape replay (*Newsweek*, 11/17/75), involved the falsification of wine labelling: *vin ordinaire* and cheap sugared wines were passed off as fine *Bordeaux*. Roughly comparable in effect to the U.S.—Soviet wheat bargain, the affair hit both French dinner tables and pocketbooks. France has the highest per capita alcohol consumption rate in the world: less than 2% of its population, the French imbibe 30% of the world's total alcohol. And as the world's largest wine exporter, France relies on its *bons vins* as the single most valuable agricultural export, having harvested 3 billion dollars' worth of foreign currency in 1973.[56] Thus this scandal drew extensive press coverage and public outcry.

Vice-President Agnew's resignation received surprisingly small coverage — four front-page paragraphs on October 11 — probably because two other issues took priority: the outbreak of war in the Middle East; and the "Lip" affair. The latter involved mismanagement and resultant bankruptcy of a major Besançon watch factory (Lip), its subsequent occupation and operation by workers determined not to lose their jobs, and its gradual escalation into a major French political issue receiving national press coverage at its peak intensity in early October.

The short Agnew blurb simply stated that he had resigned and been fined $10,000 following a no-contest plea to fiscal fraud; that the White House had pointedly ignored Agnew during the past few weeks; and that Nixon must now select a new Vice-President who will undoubtedly become the Republican presidential candidate in 1976.

The following day (p. 16), the Gossets unleashed their unmitigated wrath in "THE MISFORTUNES OF 'SPIRO-THE-GAFFE': His Resignation Makes Watergate Forgotten." Accompanied by a photo of Nixon and Agnew walking together and smiling, the complete text follows.

> [Introduction]: The resignation and especially the admission of guilt by Vice-President Agnew surprised Americans, who thought that the spokesman for the "silent majority" was more combative. On the other hand, they help Nixon in relegating Watergate to the background.

"I am innocent. Even if indicted, I will not resign." Thunde-
rous applause in this auditorium sheltering the congress of California
Republicans' wives to whom, a little while ago, the Vice-President
of the United States — with fixed gaze, determined expression,
carrying voice — gave an address.

Empty promise: he resigned yesterday.

Several days of travelling in America convinced us, however,
that even yesterday a good portion of public opinion, like these
women, was still, sentimentally, behind Spiro Agnew, prematurely
nicknamed "Spiro the Gaffe" since, in reality, his excessive out-
bursts had been made in the name of the "silent majority" of
America, of which he had become the spokesman.

[Agnew enjoyed] Popular enthusiasm such as Richard Nixon
never knew during all his ups and downs. . . .

But first of all, what did this concern? An investigation led by
a zealous — or "encouraged"? — Baltimore prosecutor into under-
the-table kickbacks and other "contributions" by Maryland construction companies in order to obtain important public works' contracts
during the time when, before becoming Vice-President, Spiro Agnew
was governor of that State.

A Moral Lynching

Some of the testimony seems overpowering. But then, corruption is standard practice, notorious, a quasi-traditional institution —
if not a respectable one — in the State of Maryland, which is one
of the most venal in the U.S.A. And how difficult it is to distinguish,
sometimes, between an envelope slipped to the commissioner and
legitimate electoral contributions, even those not for political
favors.

Spiro Agnew admits this himself: "It would be naive to imagine
that, among many others, some large contractors sharing my political
ideas didn't contribute to the financing of my electoral campaigns."

In short, a situation simultaneously clear and ambiguous. By
contrast, there is no doubt about the exploitation of this affair.
A veritable moral lynching. Nixon's ex-dauphin wasn't wrong in
asserting that he could no longer be judged impartially. He was
declared guilty even before knowing whether or not he would be
indicted.

"I am", he ascertained today, "a man completely destroyed,
my political future is zero."

His career is indeed ruined, he who just a few weeks ago was the
Republican Party's quasi-designated candidate for the Presidency
in 1976.

Minimobilization

Normally, America has little sympathy for the defeated. So why
is there this minimobilization of public opinion in his favor which we
mentioned at the beginning of this article? Because it is the support

of females, who admire the man who fights? Because in comparison
to the corruption of power, exposed in the tale of Watergate, financial corruption appears to be practically innocent? Most probably
because this time the political maneuvering was so crudely apparent
in the Agnew affair.

Where did this maneuvering come from? Spiro Agnew, who never
minces his words, accused the Justice Department — up to its
highest level — of having inspired, in flagrant violation of its secret
inquiry, this assassination campaign which would result in his
condemnation for fiscal fraud.

Indeed, the very famous and very ambitious Attorney General,
Elliot Richardson, who has an eye on the Presidency, has never
been known as a friend [of Agnew]. Spiro Agnew's elimination is
that of an obstacle in the path.

But, in the final analysis, isn't the White House the real benefi-
ciary of the Agnew affair? Ever since it exploded, Watergate has
disappeared from newspaper headlines. Only one question on this
explosive subject, at the end of 25 minutes, during President Nixon's
latest press conference.

Sacrificed for Connally?

As for [Nixon], he has seemed to maintain until now an almost
ostentatious official neutrality: "The Vice-President", a White
House spokesman recently told some journalists, "is entitled to
the same presumption of innocence as any other citizen". That
was no news.

Ever since the Watergate scandal, Richard Nixon's freedom of
action has obviously been reduced. But everyone in [Nixon's]
entourage is aware that after a four-hour interview, it was he who
authorized his Attorney General to have the accusations held against
his Vice-President presented before a Baltimore grand jury.

Without too much regret, apparently. Relations between him
and Spiro Agnew had become icy. During the latest White House
reception in honor of Pakistani President Bhutto, he was seen
turning his back on his Vice-President.

"Hold on, Baby!"

This loss of affection dates back to the day when Richard Nixon
became infatuated with the Texan John Connally, a recent deserter
from the Democratic Party, in whom he suddenly saw the best
chance of keeping the Republican Party in the White House in 1976,
after his own departure.

The opportune resignation of Vice-President Agnew will perhaps
permit the President to name John Connally as successor during the
rest of his term in office, thereby making him first in line before the
elections.

[This is] An operation which won't be easy. The aggressive
neophyte displeases many people at the heart of his new party.

Recently in this regard, a very diverse group of men symbolically rushed to the aid of Spiro Agnew. Eighty-six members of Congress dedicated to him a humorous photo of a cat clinging to a telephone cord with the caption "Hold on, baby!" Even Senator Edward Kennedy, probably [Agnew's] worst enemy, but quick to drive his wedge into this fissure in the Republican Party, was righteously indignant.

The worst possible complication would have been if Spiro Agnew had repulsed this presidential scenario. He finished by surrendering through resignation.

It is now up to Richard Nixon to find a successor. For the moment — and for the 17th time in their history — the Americans do not have a Vice-President. But this is the first time in the history of the White House that a Vice-President has resigned.

An eight-paragraph article announcing Nixon's nomination of Gerald Ford to succeed Agnew included a brief political biography describing Ford as a "constructive conservative, international realist, a team man and", according to Washington gossip, having "played football too long without a helmet" (10/14/73 — 20).

"POLITICAL HARI-KARI FOR NIXON" (front page, 10/22/73) led off a series of eight articles within 4 days recounting the "Saturday Night Massacre" and its various political, legal and public opinion repercussions. Nixon's firing of Special Prosecutor Archibald Cox and the top-level Administration resignations it triggered had grossly backfired by arousing strong bipartisan opposition for the first time. His decision to obey a Supreme Court ruling that he turn over certain tape recordings to Judge John Sirica did little to mollify public sentiment toward impeachment (44% for) or resignation (48%). Nor did Nixon gain popularity or public confidence by calling an atomic alert during the Middle East crisis.

Then, a mere 15 days after the Gossets had acidly castigated Nixon for his role in the anti-Agnew conspiracy, they regrouped to the President's defense against the Cox conspiracy. This article (below) included a photo of Archibald Cox, cutlined "a very special prosecutor" (10/27/73 — 18).

The Greatness and Weakness of Richard Nixon
AN UNGOVERNABLE AMERICA?

[Introduction]: When Richard Nixon, President of the United

States, sets in motion an atomic alert, the U.S.S.R. backs off. And the world holds its breath. But a simple tape recording can cause the fall of a man this powerful. General astonishment: is America ungovernable? Pierre and Renée Gosset attempt to answer.

If we must believe the experts, America finds itself shaken by a crisis "without precedent". Once again.

But must we believe these experts, for whom, sensationalism being a means of bread-winning, every crisis is greater than preceding ones in the United States?

"The Watergate burglary is a greater tragedy than the Civil War", said Senator Ervin, chairman of the Senate investigatory committee whose hearings are being televised.

An even greater tragedy for him, if people quit talking about it. . . .

Is America really shaken to its foundation today by the latest rebound of Watergate involving the White House while Nixon distracts their attention with his firmness in regard to the Middle East? Maybe. That which is excessive isn't necessarily without importance here. . . .

But how difficult it is to believe. The fundamental placidity of this country is disconcerting for a European. During the most explosive era of the Vietnam war, we drove 10,000 kilometers across the continent without hearing any mention of it en route.

Football First

It appears to us that, even more than big smiles, what raises spirits in the United States is the football season which, for three days each week, draws crowds of 70,000 to 80,000 spectators from Buffalo to San Diego and from Minneapolis to Miami.

And tens of millions of television watchers everywhere else. There were more people in front of their little screens to watch the "Redskins" of Washington battle the "Cowboys" of Dallas than there were listening to President Nixon addressing the nation.

Official America remains upside down. And, because of that fact, this crisis, after so many others, indeed threatens to paralyze the system a little more.

At the bottom lies this wretched Watergate affair: sinister and scandalous electoral practices systematically formulated but certainly not without precedent, an affair exaggerated by the hatred of Richard Nixon's enemies.

It all ended up with the investigation's focusing on tape recordings of conversations between the President and his advisors. These tapes, which can prove his innocence or cause him more problems, he refused to deliver to a panel of judges or to Senate investigators.

Magistracy and Reputation

"A President could no longer govern if he was obliged to submit his private documents at the slightest request." To avoid the constitutional crisis which threatens him in the midst of the Middle East conflict, in order to not, as he says "paralyzed, submerged by events, find myself incapable of controlling them", he nevertheless decided, reluctantly, with remorse for betraying his successors by setting this precedent, [to make'] what he considers a major concession to Congress.

The venerable Senator Stennis, a member of the opposition Democratic Party whose integrity has never been questioned, offered to listen to the tapes in private and transcribe those parts which are related to the Watergate investigation, without revealing those passages which could endanger national security or national interests. Speaking for his committee, Senator Ervin agreed [to this proposal].

But that was without taking into account a judiciary system which considered itself dispossessed. Above all a legal fraternity also which, deprived of its bone, revolts.

There are some magistrates who are accommodating to power: this Baltimore judge who, yielding for the good of the country, abandoned the case against Vice-President Agnew in exchange for his resignation.

Some others had no such intention. The obscure Judge Sirica, for example, who by a simple chance of jurisdiction was put in charge of Watergate. Considered incompetent by his peers, vindictive and vainglorious, he is the one, of 400 United States District Court president judges, whose decisions have most often been overruled by Appeals Courts.

How could he [be expected to] give up the publicity spotlight which has made him a celebrity?

But it was another jurist who truly set this new crisis in motion.

Archibald Cox is an ambiguous personage. As a sign of good faith to his accusers, President Nixon allowed his Attorney General to name this "Special Prosecutor" furnished with exceptional powers, and hardly suspected of sympathy for Nixon.

Well-known Harvard law professor, beneath the façade of amiable detachment from current events, Archibald Cox is in reality very politically involved. He has lobbied and served for several years in preceding Democratic Adminstrations. He would undoubtedly be Edward Kennedy's Attorney General if Kennedy became president in 1976.

Loyal Students

In assuming office, Cox proclaimed his intention: "To restore honor and integrity to the government of this country."

At the very least that is admission of prejudice. In addition, he surrounded himself with 80 young lawyers whose sole purpose immediately seemed to be to shed light on Watergate only for illuminating some scandal which would implicate President Nixon and thus provoke his fall.

At the very least that's how Archibald Cox's investigation appeared to the White House.

When they publicly rebelled this week by holding a boisterous press conference to oppose the Stennis compromise proposed by President Nixon, the latter seized the opportunity to dismiss this unmanageable high official at that very moment.

"To accept the defiance of one of his employees", he said, "would be for the American government to acknowledge its weakness during this Middle East crisis period, in the eyes of the world and particularly to the Soviet Union."

This was the conflict. Attorney General Elliot Richardson, who had named Cox [as Special Prosecutor] was now supposed to fire him, but he preferred instead to resign himself: [Richardson] had been [Cox's] student at Harvard and had promised him independent power similar to that of the Senate.

The Big Word

And within two days this conflict reached such proportions that after having watched his afternoon football game on television, like everyone else, and telephoned the coach of the winning team with his congratulations, the President of the United States admitted defeat:

A White House lawyer announced to Judge Sirica that [Nixon] would hand over the infamous tapes in their entirety.

Why this surrender? Because the wolfpack of his political enemies unleashed the big word "Impeachment". They will propose this as soon as Congress reconvenes. So the question becomes: Is the United States still a governable country? The President still possesses, according to the Constitution, extraordinary powers worthy of a monarch of yesteryear. But as soon as he exercises them, everyone cries dictatorship. . . .

The same thing happened to Truman when he summarily dismissed his Korean Commander, General McArthur, and forced his retirement. At that time, like today, the press called for "Impeachment".

Living on this side of the Atlantic, we sometimes ask ourselves if the exclusive vocation of this press given to iconoclasm and which, having broken Lyndon Johnson and attempting to ruin Richard Nixon, isn't to settle its account of power [with] whatever may be constraining it.

In "RICHARD NIXON CLEARLY SHIPWRECKED" Jean-François Kahn explained that "Watergate" involved much more than a mere burglary and detailed the business aspects of the scandal: ITT, the milk fund, the Vesco affair, Nixon's illicit tax deductions, etc. Nixon, like many French politicians, had tried to benefit from legal finesse and tax loopholes, some very questionable. Concludes Kahn: "Decidedly, America is a country where it's better to be a real estate agent or insurance

salesman than Head of State: it's safer" (11/7/73 — 16).
Around this time, a government investigation of wiretapping practices in France drew moderate press coverage. The issue exploded, however, on December 5 when headlines blared that *Le Canard Enchaîné* ("The Chained Duck"), a satirical weekly newspaper, had uncovered a bungled government attempt to eavesdrop its offices. This sparked a *L'Est* article, "AL CAPONE RIGHT HERE," by Philippe Marcovici, which expressed outrage at such practices, chided the French for self-righteously thinking that such things happened only in the U.S., and lamentingly predicted that, although much newsprint and rhetoric would be devoted to the affair, in the end nothing would really come of it because the French press doesn't wield the power and independence (vis à vis the government) that the American press does. His prediction proved accurate (12/10/73 — 16).

Following a January lull, *L'Est* ran a short, front-page article carrying a definite pro-Nixon slant followed by a Gosset tract inside its February 1 issue. The former mentioned that adversity had always fired Nixon's adrenalin so now, facing the energy crisis and the Watergate scandal, he was more determined than ever to remain in the post to which the American people had elected him. He could be assured, the article said, by the warm response Congress had given his State of the Union message.

"THE IMPROBABLE IMPEACHMENT OF RICHARD NIXON" (p. 15) replayed several of the Gossets' pet themes: the American press is vicious and irresponsible; Daniel Ellsburg is a well-known Soviet spy; the White House "plumbers" caught burglarizing Watergate had been recruited to plug up alarming national security leaks. They then gush sympathy for the American President:

Secret and Solitary

This is the drama of Richard Nixon. Not able nor willing to reveal anything, he defends himself poorly and awkwardly. He is by nature a secret and solitary man, characteristics which are intolerable for many Americans.

Very soon, a terrifying campaign will rage against him, led by his political enemies beating war drums, by the so-called liberal press of the Eastern part of the country which detests him. Also by all those — politicians, men of law — until now unknown. Or journalists who find this an unprecedented opportunity for flashy publicity or personal profit.

But, with regard to him it's a vendetta. The list of alleged misdeeds of the President, a most varied assortment, sometimes most extravagant for a European mind and without any connection to Watergate, does not cease to increase from week to week.

After listing a handful of Nixon's most innocuous misdeeds and minimizing their significance, the Gossets conclude:

Richard Nixon is perhaps not without reproach. But who is? Finally, we see Senator Goldwater, the model of integrity, throw up his hands in despair: "If investigators persisted in examining every one of us in identical fashion, not one single member of the 535 in Congress would come out of it unscathed."

Everything said — let's forget Watergate for a minute — as much in foreign policy as in the domestic administration of a prosperous, peaceful country, disengaged from Vietnam, its racial quarrels calmed, Richard Nixon remains a remarkable President of the United States. But a frightening climate has been artificially created around him in America.

Watergate was eclipsed during the first half of February by the Washington Energy Conference, which transformed French Foreign Minister Michel Jobert from a spunky Gaullist politician into a national folk hero. Sponsored by the U.S. as a forum for coordinating policy and thereby increasing the bargaining power of oil-consuming nations, the meeting was perceived by France as just another American ploy to annex Europe as the fifty-first state. Predictably — and ostentatiously — taking the adversary position and assuming that other European countries were following his lead, Jobert appeared shocked and appalled at their general agreement and cooperation with the U.S., and considered their actions nothing short of treason. Thus he graduated from "Jobert versus America" to "Jobert versus the World" and, via his knee-jerk negativism, emerged as the new symbol of French nationalism: a small but fiercely proud David having battled Goliath, or several of them, and returning home — if not clearly the victor, at least not vanquished.

Major Watergate news reappeared on April 13 (p. 16) with a

Gosset article, "NIXON'S TAX RETURNS UNDER MAGNI-
FYING GLASS." They elaborated on four main themes: pity
for Nixon ("I'm scraping along", said Richard Nixon. "I'll
borrow to pay [these taxes]"); Nixon's innocence (it was his
tax lawyer, being overzealous for a client, who had caused the
problem); the tax investigation was an "underhanded campaign";
this latest scandal was just another manifestation of the widespread political conspiracy to dethrone Nixon. The Gossets
maintain that Nixon, who voluntarily asked Congress to audit
his taxes, was then sabotaged by "political enemy" Wilbur
Mills who assembled an anonymous team of biased experts to
implicate the President. "The systematic persistence to close
in on the weakened prey . . . would be comical if it didn't
involve the deliberate destruction of the first person of the
State." In a section subtitled "An Unmerciful Hunt," the
writers say that Nixon is being viciously and unjustifiably
attacked, that Lyndon Johnson had similarly reaped tax deductions from his vice-presidential papers for even more profit,
and: "In fact, since the time of George Washington who notoriously cheated on his financial affairs, no one in two centuries
has had the bad taste to stick their nose into the tax returns
of presidents." Quoting Article II of the U.S. Constitution, the
Gossets explain that the President can only be impeached for
"high treason, corruption, or other major criminal actions",
and assure their readers that "Nothing like this has happened
until now from Watergate as far as Richard Nixon is concerned."

Following a smattering of articles recounting Watergate-
related miscellany, the Gossets resumed their offensive on
May 10 (p. 16). "NIXON DECIDES NOT TO IMITATE
BRANDT: Less Afraid of Scandal than the Chancellor" featured
a photo of Nixon pointing proudly to the published tape transcripts which "will establish my total innocence". Alluding to
West German Chancellor Willy Brandt's resignation following
revelation that one of his top aides moonlighted as an East
German spy, the Gossets back-slap Nixon for far greater courage
and righteous perseverance than Brandt. Other points: Egyptian
President Anwar Sadat warns that "Nixon's departure would be

a tragedy for the world"; Mitchell and Stans were acquitted; John Dean is a no-good turncoat; in 1964 Barry Goldwater rightly said: "if we could cut off the east coast of the United States and let it drift off into the Atlantic, the country would be much better off"; the published transcripts' contents aren't as important as the fact that Nixon released them in "Operation Sincerity", an effective counter-coup against critical senators; the congressional investigatory committees are stacked with Nixon's political enemies; this summer the House of Representatives will probably adopt their Judiciary Committee's recommendation and, "playing Pontius Pilate", impeach Nixon, thereby laying final responsibility on the Senate; Nixon remains convinced that his "trial by the press" with "thousands of miles of editorials" will be overruled by true justice; he will be saved by the west, south, and midwest who will ensure that the President they elected does not fall "victim to a political cabal centered in Washington, New York and Boston".

Taking a break from Watergate, one week later the Gossets fired off an article about French presidential elections (Independent Valéry Giscard d'Estaing against Socialist François Mitterand) following Georges Pompidou's death, as seen from the United States. Clearly piqued that French elections drew so little attention, their introduction scolded:

> Communists in the Paris government? A traumatic idea for Americans. Submerged in Watergate by the press and television which hardly tells them of anything else, this shock was required before they finally discovered the French presidential election (5/17/74 — 14.)

"UNITED STATES OF AMERICA VERSUS RICHARD NIXON," describing in six paragraphs the Supreme Court's hearing of the tapes controversy, led off with this introduction:

> Just back from the Middle East and USSR, Richard Nixon finds himself once again in the United States dealing with the interminable political comedy of "Watergate." A performance more serious because it is taking place in the neo-grande décor of the Supreme Court (7/8/74 — 14.)

"NIXON'S FATE DECIDED THIS WEEK: Arraignment

Probable" said that Nixon would abide by the Supreme Court's decision and yield the tapes. This move will probably rally some public support but may also incriminate him. If he had only had the "cleverness" to provide just those tapes favorable to him and proving his innocence, the article moaned, he surely wouldn't be impeached. But now the House Judiciary Committee is expected to recommend impeachment and the House to follow suit (7/26/74, p 1 eight paragraphs).

The next day, five columns carried the Gossets' last stand (p. 14). "NIXON: FROM BURGLARY TO THE JUDGEMENT OF HISTORY: Two More Days of Suspense" included a photo of Nixon smiling and George Meany clapping ("Nixon applauded by his enemy number one: George Meany, president of powerful AFL-CIO unions"). Excerpts:

> Never has such a tragedy been produced from such a banal news item:
> On the night of June 17, 1972, a conscientious night watchman surprised five burglars in a deluxe apartment building in the American capital: Watergate.

The burglars' bungled wiretapping, explain the Gossets, was for stopping "security leaks", and once again they contend that Daniel Ellsburg is a Soviet secret agent. Nixon was re-elected by a landslide, but has been victim of an orchestrated press and television campaign in Washington and New York:

> "I've never been their pin-up", said Nixon. "Their ideological vendetta has lasted for 15 years. If it hadn't been Watergate, they would have found something else."

This campaign has led to a "veritable massacre of all collaborators":

> Did the President himself order the break-in? A very implausible question. In our old country it would elicit a simple shrugging of the shoulders. But the formidable American innocence must be taken into account. . . .
> In the meantime, the anti-Nixon campaign has assumed immeasurable proportions, in quest of other scandals, none of which are new or original in American politics: shady electoral contributions, the buying of ambassadorships. . . .
> Finally, in the face of an America weary to the point of nausea, the press campaign is becoming obsessive.

132 Watergate: A Crisis for the World

In a section subtitled "A Dubious Commission," the Gossets claim that House Judiciary Committee Chairman Peter Rodino is financially supported by union czar George Meany, who has sworn to get Nixon ejected from office. They wrap up their diatribe with a Nixon quote:

> "History will judge me", said President Nixon philosophically, "not the *New York Times* or *Washington Post.*"

Significantly, the Gossets disappeared from *L'Est*'s pages as the full impact of the tapes and inevitability of Nixon's fall became apparent. Perhaps they were on vacation.

As The End approached, headlines came fast and furious: NIXON: PESSIMISM AT THE WHITE HOUSE (8/4/74); WAR COUNCIL AROUND NIXON: The President Prepares His Defense (8/6); NIXON: THE END APPROACHES: Even His Supporters Are Leaving Him After His Stupefying Avowals (8/7); SIX DAYS AFTER, HE KNEW EVERYTHING (8/7); NIXON: RESIGNATION IMMINENT (8/8); then, on August 9:

His Refusal to Resign Couldn't Withstand the Scandal
NIXON SURRENDERS

This front-page banner headline was accompanied by photos of Nixon and Ford, and a six-paragraph article describing the resignation, including Haig's and Kissinger's roles in prompting it. "AN ALL-POWERFUL CONSTITUTION," an editorial by Guy Chaisse, also appeared on p. 1. This entire affair was a shame in regard to Richard Nixon, he said, but the country will survive and even be better off. Americans are not traumatized, but rather relieved that it's over and are still proud of their country and its institutions — especially the press, the courts, and Congress. The Presidency will not be appreciably damaged because the power lies in the office and not the man. This article provided a general explanation of the American system, with several notes of admiration for its functioning during Watergate.

Six follow-up articles appeared on p. 12. "FIRST

RESIGNATION OF AN AMERICAN PRESIDENT" provided brief biographies of Nixon and Ford and noted that not only was this the first presidential resignation, but also the first time a president (Ford) had not been elected, due to Agnew's previous resignation. Short mention was made of Senator Edward Brooke's sponsorship of a bill to grant Nixon immunity in exchange for a full confession. A third, eight-paragraph article recounted Ford's political career and personal characteristics. "CROOK AND STATESMAN" spouted the man-on-the-street's opinion that maybe Nixon was a crook but he was also a great president. A two-column piece, " 'DOCTOR JEKYLL AND MR. HYDE': 'Tricky Dicky' Victim of his Love of Power", offered an in-depth personality profile of Nixon as a notorious loner surrounding himself with authoritarian yes-men, a believer in absolute power and the absolute separation of powers, amazingly persevering, but in the end letting his lust for power precipitate his fall. The final article, "AMERICA READY FOR POST-NIXON ERA," by Bernard Hartman, dealt mostly with (positive) financial repercussions of Nixon's resignation.

"AMERICA GOES ON: President Ford Keeps Kissinger as his Right Arm" headlined the front page on August 10, with a four-column photo of Ford being sworn in, another of Nixon hugging daughter, then waving goodbye to his White House staff in front of the helicopter. The transition of power was covered on page 14, including articles on Ford and his family. Kissinger's continued presence, and "A VICTORY FOR THE FOURTH POWER" complimentary to the American press.

The next day, "SMOOTH TRANSITION IN THE UNITED STATES: Americans Reassured by Ford's Activities" virtually marked the end of *L'Est*'s Watergate coverage. One notable exception (8/12): "Nixon ousted . . . even from the museum" captioned a front-page, four-column photo of Nixon's wax head being carried out of Madame Tussaud's museum because he was no longer "an eminent contemporary personage".

Summary

Watergate first began appearing regularly in *L'Est Républicain* at the beginning of April 1973. Between that time and Nixon's resignation in August 1974 (approximately 460 days), 126 editions of *L'Est* carried one or more Watergate-related articles averaging 10.8 paragraphs in length. The ten Gosset-Watergate articles averaged 28 paragraphs. Discounting Gosset articles, average article length was 9.3 paragraphs. The highest frequency of coverage for 1 month (17 days) occurred in May 1973 following the resignations of Haldeman, Ehrlichman and Dean. The Agnew resignation and Saturday Night Massacre in October 1973 drew 13 days of coverage. The tapes controversy in May 1974 merited 12 days, and Nixon's resignation in the first half of August, 10. The amount of space devoted to Watergate followed a similar pattern (250 paragraphs in May 1973; 150 in October 1973; 77 in May 1974) with the notable exception of 325 paragraphs covering the resignation era.

During this period, two Watergate editorials, identified as such, appeared ("AND IF IT HAD HAPPENED IN FRANCE . . .", and "AN ALL-POWERFUL CONSTITUTION") with tones generally favorable to the American system's functioning in regard to Watergate. Occasional editorial comments (e.g. ". . . the interminable political comedy of 'Watergate' "; "All that, let's not forget, because a free press did its job, seconded by an independent judiciary") surfaced in news articles, but these were rare, usually inconspicuous, and counterbalancing. For the most part, *L'Est*'s day-to-day Watergate reportage comprised short, relatively straight accounts, often from secondary sources, describing major revelations and events in Washington, public opinion polls, media stories, government reports, etc. Almost none of these articles were identified by source.

Pierre and Renée Gosset were clearly considered *L'Est*'s specialists in American domestic politics: their by-lined articles, appearing during crisis periods, provided the most in-depth coverage of Watergate events and ran three times as long as the standard *L'Est* fare. Though they silently slithered away before the final tapes bomb exploded in August, their final defense of Nixon occupied about two-thirds of all the news surface *L'Est* devoted to Watergate during July 1974. Appearing under the standing columns "News in Brief" or "Reflections of the World" inside the paper, Gosset articles were never identified as editorials.

What, then, did these experts on the United States offer as "news" to their provincial French readers? What "pictures in our heads" did they pass on — and multiply — by their Watergate reportage? The best way to analyze this problem is by treating separate subjects: Nixon, the press, the Judiciary system, Congress, the Office of the Presidency, Americans, Corruption, and Conspiracy.

The Gossets adored Richard Nixon long before they flew to his defense during the Watergate scandal. "A professional", a "modern monarch", "Nixon 'the Magician' " with a four-year wave of his wand had invoked a vanishing act on all the festering social problems in the United States. His "new crowning" created near-hysterical mobs of loyal subjects partaking in the "four-day festival for an entire nation". The Gossets clung to King Richard throughout the various battles in the Watergate war, staving off press attacks, exposing political enemies, banishing conspirators lurking in the shadows. They unflinchingly supported Nixon in every Watergate-related article except one: the Agnew piece depicting the President as a co-conspirator — if not the ringleader — in the plot to depose his luckless Vice-President. He also sparked Gosset wrath for his summit conspiracy with Brezhnev to take over the world. Otherwise, Nixon was a tragically misunderstood king, a martyr, almost a saint.

And the press was the devil. Of all American institutions, the press most often incurred the Gossets' unmitigated anger: it drew negative comment at least once in every article that these "journalists" wrote, was lambasted six times in one article, and never merited anything faintly resembling praise. The American press, "latching onto the smallest thing and whose power has gone to its head", is "like a Samson, attacking the columns of the White House in blind furor". "Obstinately vowed and determined to rummage through wastebaskets", the press irresponsibly ignores the fact that "the issues on which

[its] vendetta is overflowing amount to the indictment of the inherent vices of democracies", so their attempted destruction of Richard Nixon risks causing "the destruction of the System itself". "Journalists who find Watergate an unprecedented opportunity for flashy publicity or personal profit" are "leading a terrifying campaign against Nixon", persisting obsessively "in the face of an America weary to the point of nausea". Its "exclusive vocation" seems to be "to settle its account of power with whatever may be constraining it". Etc. . . .

The American Judiciary system (including the Special Prosecutor's office) similarly suffered several Gosset attacks, with specially poisoned barbs fired at Judge John Sirica for incompetence, vindictiveness, vanity, and opportunism, and at Archibald Cox for insolence and a thinly veiled conspiracy. Mentioned in five articles and receiving special attention following the Saturday Night Massacre, the legal system drew unanimously negative comment except for a Baltimore judge whom the Gossets commended for being "accommodating to power" in the Agnew case.

Congress and/or its individual members made all but two Gosset articles. As an institution, Congress came under attack, though less severely than the press and judiciary, as a sinister body of plotting, self-righteous, corrupt politicos. Senate and House Watergate committees within this "opposition Congress" overflowed with Nixon's political enemies financed or otherwise motivated by even more enemies. However, some politicians like Senator Barry Goldwater, a Gosset favorite for quotable quotes, received numerous kudos for their noble stands and wise words.

The Presidency *is* the government. In five of their Watergate articles, these correspondents directly stated or implied at least thirteen times that the Office of the Presidency is sacred and, more generally, that the executive branch of the American government is clearly superior to the others and above investigation. Of the four major institutions — press, the Courts, Congress, and the Presidency — only the latter drew unqualified praise while the others received almost total criticism. Also, other than during Nixon's anti-Agnew caper (and excepting Cox, whose functions — if not job security — were more judiciary than executive), all individuals within the executive branch were consistently touted as the good guys.

No love was lost on Americans. In seven articles, the Gossets defamed the American national character no fewer than fifteen times. "Gregarious" Americans with "big smiles" and "football season to raise their spirits, unable to tolerate a person who is by nature secret and solitary", were not as actively involved in the anti-Nixon conspiracy, but still warrant guilt by passivity for their "disconcerting fundamental placidity" and "formidable innocence". Americans, for whom "that which is excessive isn't necessarily without importance", supported "with a good dose of hypocrisy, deplorable practices" in the handling of Watergate, and have "little sympathy for the defeated". Combining Gosset attitudes toward American institutions and Americans yields a good indication of their opinion of the country they were living in — and representing to their audience: overwhelmingly unfavorable.

It would be an exaggeration to say that the Gossets unqualifyingly advocated corruption, a subject appearing in nine of their ten articles. Rather, their attitudes were: corruption exists; it has existed for a long time; it will continue to exist for a long time; it is human nature; it is an inherent vice of democracies; it exists at all levels of society and government; you're corrupt, I'm corrupt, everybody's corrupt; you know this, I know this, everybody knows this: so what's all the fuss about? These correspondents, like others from the "old country", would offer a "simple shrugging of the shoulders" at government corruption, so they find the American attitude "formidably innocent".

At times, Gosset reportage appears rather schizophrenic: John Connally, lauded for his role in the Democrats for Nixon committee, degenerated into "a recent deserter from the Democratic Party" during the Agnew coup. Nixon, worshipped and defended throughout Watergate, drew harsh criticism for his summit with Brezhnev and an even more biting diatribe for

throwing Agnew to the wolves. "Conspiracy" ties all the loose
ends and apparent contradictions together. The Gossets are
addicted to conspiracy theories: a direct mention or implication of some sort of conspiracy appeared in each of their
articles no less than twice and, at their paranoid peak, ten times
in one article, with a grand total exceeding fifty. The particular
conspirators and conspiratees depended on the times and situation, and some conspiratees (like Nixon, above) could meta-
morphose into conspirators, exchanging their haloes for horns.
Other forces — such as the American press, the Judiciary system,
certain individuals, and Congress — were by nature conspira-
torial and could be counted on to support any conspiracy
because that is how they make their living. In short, for the
Gossets, a conspiracy always exists and once the victim is
defined, it becomes easy to identify the conspirators: everybody else.

The Agnew "investigation led by a zealous — or 'encouraged'?
— Baltimore prosecutor" enabled Nixon to "relegate Watergate
to the background" and culminated in a "veritable moral
lynching" attributable to "political maneuvering so crudely
apparent". He "was declared guilty even before knowing
whether or not he would be indicted" and his "elimination is
that of an obstacle in the path" of Elliot Richardson's ascension
to the Presidency. Or perhaps he was "sacrificed for Connally?"
in this "presidential scenario".

"A very special prosecutor", Archibald Cox, "beneath the
façade of amiable detachment from current events, is in reality
very politically involved" with the opposition party and has
recruited eighty young lawyers "whose sole purpose immediately seemed to be to shed light on Watergate only for illuminating some scandal which would implicate President Nixon
and thus provoke his fall".

"The wolfpack of [Nixon's] political enemies unleashed the
big word 'Impeachment', [and] very soon, a terrifying campaign
will rage against him, led by his political enemies beating war
drums, by the so-called liberal press of the Eastern part of
the country which detests him." This "unmerciful hunt" has

led to "a veritable massacre of his collaborators", and "the anti-Nixon campaign has assumed immeasurable proportions" which makes him the "victim of a political cabal centered in Washington, New York, and Boston".

Ad nauseam.

Timothy Crouse has described France as "a nation that suffers from an obsession with conspiracies and a craving for saviors".[57] Though clearly a gross generalization, this label fits the Gossets like glove on hand.

L'Express

L'Express newsmagazine strikingly resembles America's *Time* in terms of cover style, interior format, slick tone and homogenized writing. One immediately noticeable difference is *L'Express*'s greater thickness — normally running 125 to 150 pages and at times more than 200 — due to considerably more advertising. Also, unlike *Time*, most *L'Express* articles are by-lined and a quote appears at the bottom of each week's cover.

Launched in 1953 by several prominent journalists under the patronage of ubiquitous public figure Pierre Mendès-France, *L'Express* experimented unsuccessfully for 6 months as a daily publication before returning to its weekly format. It emerged as a politically activist journal, peaking in combative advocacy journalism during the French-Algerian war.

One of its most vociferous and influential reporters during that era, Jean-Jacques Servan-Schreiber, eventually rose to publisher of the magazine. A prominent and controversial Frenchman reputed for his fierce individualism, political independence and outspokenness, he was recruited for a cabinet post (Minister for Reform) in President Valéry Giscard d'Estaing's government. Shortly thereafter, "J-J S-S" publicly criticized France's *force de frappe* Pacific Ocean testing and became an ex-Cabinet member in record time (June 9, 1974). Giscard had better luck with another ex-*L'Express* power, Françoise Giroud, who in July 1974 swapped the magazine's editorial directorship for the newly created post of Minister for the Condition of Women, highly flaunted by France as the first such position in the world.

L'Express officialized a gradual depoliticization when it hired the Havas advertising agency to increase its early 1960s circulation of 100,000. The repackaged magazine emerged in September 1964, and within 10 years Havas's marketing scheme harvested another half-million customers. In the process, however, *L'Express* sacrificed several of its original and more influential journalists, who fled to — or founded — more politically activist publications. In some cases a cascading effect occurred: some disillusioned *L'Express* writers opted for *Le Nouvel Observateur* until that magazine yielded to advertising, then moved on to *Politique Hebdo.* . . .

Havas's transformation of *L'Express* wrought fundamental changes in the magazine's circulation, audience, contents, and reporting.

Its circulation soared from 100,000 in 1964 to 600,000 in 1974, with an estimated 3.5 million readers sharing these copies each week. More men than women read *L'Express*; the largest age group (31%) falls between 35 and 50 years old; 46% have had university educations, representing the largest percentage among all weekly publications. *L'Express* remains the "establishment" newsmagazine, only weakly challenged by *Le Point* which surfaced in 1972 with a team of former *L'Express* journalists unable or unwilling to cope with Servan-Schreiber. In contrast to the regionalism of daily newspapers, *L'Express* wields a more national influence, with fully two-thirds of its circulation going to the provinces. Again in contrast, it thrives on a financially sound 60% subscription sales rate.

The magazine carries substantial advertising, accounting for roughly 75% of its revenues, in a variety of forms. Normally, the first 30 to 50 pages advertise consumer products (cigarettes, cognacs, perfumes) with occasional non-ad copy breaking in (cinema listings, television schedules). The table of contents follows this heavy advertising. Most of the magazine's middle covers national and international news, including two pink pages headed "Equipment Notes" and "Business Notes". Then "Businesses Offer You . . .", usually running 10 to 15 pages, presents a want-ads department for young and not-so-young executives. *L'Express* thus provides an important market for the French business community, which accounts for a good percentage of its readership.[58]

Compared to other French printed media, *L'Express*'s reporting appears strikingly neutral and balanced. In relation to American news publications, it contains subtle slants — again very much like *Time* — created with occasional evaluative nuances, snide remarks, slick formula writing, and the seeming inability to end an article without some useless, pseudo-heavy sentence ("Where all this will lead remains open to question").

The great majority of *L'Express*'s Watergate coverage was contributed by Pierre Salinger, former press secretary for President John F. Kennedy and director of communications for George McGovern's 1972 presidential campaign. Though his well-known political leanings rendered him suspect for journalistic bias, Salinger's Watergate reportage remained admirably neutral, analytical, thorough, and potentially very educational for a French audience interested in American domestic political affairs. Unlike *Time*, *L'Express* runs weekly "issue" editorials, but these and most other evaluative comments on Watergate and the American system of government were submitted by French writers. Salinger's only quasi-editorial writing appeared in an open letter to Nixon.

It should be remembered, however, that Salinger enjoyed the advantages of writing for a weekly, rather than a daily, publication. Rarely able to "scoop" stories, newsmagazines typically concentrate on news summaries and analyses. Their reporting thus often seems more complete, reliable, and sophisticated than that which must battle the daily deadline. On the liabilities side, Salinger had to interpret (least importantly in terms of language) an American domestic political crisis to a foreign — specifically and importantly, French — audience.

L'Express's news coverage normally appears under seven standing departments: France, The World, Modern Living, Arts

and Entertainment, Books, Interview, and Cover Story. Watergate reporting usually occupied part of "The World" section,
but also merited six *L'Express* covers. Between April 2, 1973
when Watergate made its first appearance and the end of
August 1974, the magazine devoted roughly sixty articles and
100 pages to the crisis. A summary and analysis of this coverage
follows.

Three weeks after Salinger first revealed "SCANDALS IN
WASHINGTON" (ITT, the Watergate break-in and cover-up
— 4/12/73 — 120, 121) to his French audience, *L'Express*
ran its first Watergate cover (4/23/73). "THE SCANDAL
WHICH SHAKES AMERICA" featured a photo of Nixon
surrounded by drawings of the Watergate apartment complex,
burglars in action, a wiretap installation, and similar episodes.
Below stood a Montesquieu quote: "Espionage would perhaps
be tolerable if it were practiced by honest men."

Inside, three articles elaborated on the cover theme. A
full-page editorial (p. 57) by Jean François Revel titled "THE
TWO STUDENTS" examined a contemporary political problem
in all democracies: where does legitimate presidential authority end and tyranny begin? Nixon and French President
Pompidou, he maintains, were both protégés of the late Charles
de Gaulle, Nixon having studied and applied the General's
autocratic political style — "profoundly contrary to the American tradition" — to the American Presidency. The Watergate
affair and a current French political scandal, says Revel, involve
essentially the same issue — executive abuse of power — and are
equally serious. But there the similarity ends: while America
is pursuing justice primarily because of a true balance of powers
and a strong Congress, the French scandal, characteristically,
will just fade away.

A cartoon by Tim, a regular *L'Express* contributor and
renowned French political cartoonist, accompanied Salinger's
first article in that issue. The drawing depicted Nixon listening
to headphones whose numerous wires were plugged into the
stars on an American flag. "SENATE DECLARES WAR ON
NIXON" (p. 104) described the Watergate burglary and other

events, but focused on Senator Sam Ervin ("He has only one religion: the Constitution") and the emerging congressional role in the overall Watergate investigation.

Salinger's second piece, with the cover's title, ran six full pages and almost 100 paragraphs, with eight photos of Watergate figures and places. Salinger thoroughly explained the developing scandal under five categories: Political Espionage, Campaign Financing, Political Sabotage, Investigations, and Public Opinion. Under the latter, he noted that American public opinion had been slow in developing and was still somewhat nebulous because of a general cynicism toward politics and because, until now, there had been no clearcut, earth-shaking revelations. The article left no doubt, however, that more news would soon be coming from Washington.

"THE WEEK OF THE LONG KNIVES" appeared the next week (pp. 118, 119) with the heavy-type introduction, "The Watergate scandal today threatens Mr. Nixon. And, more seriously, maybe even the Presidency." Nixon's White House staff, "the Germans", are beginning to crack under the pressure of accusations hurled at them by other witnesses, and now it's "every man for himself". More accusations and some resignations appear imminent, the scandal is leading to the door of the Oval Office, 42% of Americans think Nixon knew about Watergate, and Alice Longworth Roosevelt opines: "We'll be able to save either the President, or the Presidency. But not both."

In the same issue, American humorist Art Buchwald made his first of several appearances with a column apparently written specially for *L'Express* since no other copyright was cited. "THE SINKING OF THE 'WATERGATE' " (p. 119), parodying Nixon's White House team and its information system, ended by asking Captain Nixon how he felt about losing so many members of his crew. The response: "That was very painful for me. But it was every man for himself."

Washington Post executive editor Ben Bradlee became the first journalist ever to rate a *L'Express* cover (May 7). Hailed as a "SPECIAL EDITION: THE DRAMA OF THE WHITE

HOUSE", the cover pictured Bradlee against a background of the *Post* edition headlining the resignations of Nixon's top aides, with a Thomas Jefferson quote below: "If I had to choose between government without newspapers and newspapers without government, I would not hesitate to choose the latter."

Inside, Jean-Jacques Servan-Schreiber and Françoise Giroud combined forces on a full-page editorial entitled "20 YEARS" (p. 77). This largest-ever (236 pages) edition of *L'Express* marked the magazine's twentieth anniversary and, by sheer coincidence, most of its contents were devoted to demonstrating, via Watergate, the indispensability of a free press to counterbalance government tyranny. "The moral health and creative capacity of a society are measured very precisely by the true freedom of expression of its press." In this "victory of America over itself", they praise Bradlee's (and the *Post*'s) persistent search for "the truth" of "the crime: espionage, burglary, blackmail, deceit, and corruption at the highest levels", and also indulge in a little anniversary toasting.

Above Salinger's cover article (pp. 150—54), two adjacent pictures of Nixon appeared, one while giving his 1952 "Checkers" speech (cutline: "America was moved to tears") and the other during his 1973 Watergate discourse ("America listened without conviction"). "Watergate appears less and less to be an accident, but rather the culmination of a campaign of political sabotage which has lasted 15 years", announced the heavy-type introduction. The article cited evidence: the 1960 burglary of John Kennedy's physician's office to verify that J.F.K. had Addison's disease and would thus be unfit for the Presidency; the Ellsburg (psychiatrist's office) break-in, an offer to presiding Judge Byrne of the FBI directorship; charges of political sabotage during the 1962 California gubernational race; a falsified telegram designed to link John Kennedy to South Vietnam President Diem's assassination; the Watergate break-in and cover-up, etc. Nixon's Watergate speech and the reactions it drew (the normally pro-Nixon *Chicago Tribune* editorialized: "The President simply assumed the responsibilities which he could not, in any way, escape") were described, as well as the "Prussians' resignations", Haig's replacement of Haldeman, and Vice-President Agnew as a political security blanket for Nixon to retain the Presidency.

"THE LESSONS OF WATERGATE", an editorial by Revel (p. 155), maintained that this scandal would have disappeared if it had involved just one unfortunate mistake (the break-in), but due to continuing revelations had grown into a full-scale battle between a self-appointed monarchy and a democratic society. The dogged pursuit of justice in the Watergate affair, he posits, is a uniquely American phenomenon made possible by a special combination of American ideas and institutions: the idea that all men, including the President and all other elected or appointed government officials at the highest levels, are subject to the law; the most truly independent (vis à vis the government) and powerful press in the world; a television system not controlled by the government (this was also a back-handed slam at France's state-controlled electronic media system, particularly regarding its news presentations); and an independent judiciary with its Grand Jury system to guard against government or other meddling. Though Watergate had clearly been an important victory and vindication of the *Washington Post* and the American press as a whole, it was, more importantly, a victory for the United States and for democracy:

> And, finally, if [Watergate] has made it necessary to recognize the silliest notion which has ever been concocted in the history of political science, then the crown of martyrdom should be given to the author of the expression, "formal liberties". Indeed, the presence or absence of these very material liberties today constitute the principle for the most fundamental differentiation among the diverse types of civilizations and men which comprise the world in which we live."

Kermit Lansner contributed a "Special Watergate" article, "THE VICTORY OF THE WASHINGTON POST" (pp. 156–59), accompanied by photos of various media heroes and anti-heroes: Woodward and Bernstein; Nixon mouthpiece Ronald Ziegler surrounded by reporters; "Woodstein" with Bradlee;

publisher Katherine Graham and managing editor Howard Simons; Salinger and Revel with Bradlee, Simons and Graham. A Tim cartoon showed Nixon looking guilty and dejected in a dunce's cap concocted out of a folded *Washington Post*, with his oft-caricatured nose evolving into a filing cabinet with the drawer open. For the past 5 years, the article explains, Nixon-via-Agnew has been kicking the press around — particularly the *Post*. If Watergate demonstrates anything, it is how wrong and unwise is political maltreatment of the press and, more importantly, how much a free society needs a free press. The writer describes Bradlee as a "fighting journalist", and details the *Post*'s and Woodstein's role in uncovering the gory specifics of the Watergate tale. He concludes: "The strongest government in the world is bowing before the fourth power: the press. A free press."

For the final article of the May 7 edition, *L'Express* bought exclusive French rights to the Lou Harris poll conducted the day after Nixon's Watergate speech. Central findings: 77% are opposed to Nixon's resignation, even though the majority (54% vs. 37%) think he has lost public confidence to the extent that it will be difficult for him to govern in the future; 78% would like to see a Special Prosecutor independent of Nixon's control; and 64% still consider him a man of "deep integrity".

Three Watergate articles made the subsequent issue. Salinger's "WATERGATE: THE LONGEST CRISIS" (pp. 140—42) was complemented by a full-page Tim cartoon featuring a repentant Nixon in the Statue of Liberty's right hand, one finger of which is pointing to the tablet (Principles of Liberty) in its left. Salinger's introduction: "The televised Senate Watergate hearings begin Thursday. The list of witnesses resembles the White House telephone book."

Henri de Turenne contributed the second article, "FIRST AND FOREMOST, MONEY", explaining that at the bottom of all this wiretapping, burglary and other "jamesbonderies" lies a question of money — a lot of money. "Some examples? The only difficulty is in choosing [from among them]." The milk fund, MacDonald's Hamburger, oil companies and other "political favor" contributions have spurred calls for stricter campaign financing laws.

"THE MEN OF THE HOUSE" (p. 143) by Bertrand de Jouvenel lent Watergate some historical and sociological perspective. There is a great difference, he explains, between executive officials (i.e. cabinet members) trying to make the American government function smoothly, and White House staff members whose sole responsibility and loyalty is to the President. The latter category has been increasing in both numbers and influence since the Franklin Roosevelt era, reaching a pathological culmination with Richard Nixon's enclosed, isolated, autocratic Presidency. What the Watergate controversy truly signifies is America's attempt to revert from presidential politics based on personal power to that founded on public support.

Finally, a scathingly satirical editorial supplemented this edition's news articles. WATERGATE À LA FRANCAISE by Paul Guimard (p. 117) transplanted the Watergate break-in and subsequent events from Washington to Paris — i.e., with a Portuguese (rather than black) nightwatchman surprising the burglars, illegal campaign money laundered in Lichtenstein (rather than Mexico), and the Élysée Palace (rather than White House) denying all wrongdoing. When the Élysée's press spokesman virulently attacks journalists who "look for their news in wastebaskets", some remind him that, in a strikingly analogous situation, the White House spokesman had publicly apologized to the press. His response: "Each nation has its own nature. It does not conform to the French nature that the State look for its models [of behavior] in foreign countries." The scandal continues to build, and:

> Beginning of July: New evidence overwhelms a former minister and several very high officials at the Élysée. Indictments are awaited.

> Mid-July: Three indictments are handed down against Jean-François Revel, editorialist for *L'Express*, Piere Viansson-Ponté, editorial advisor of *Le Monde*, and Wolinski, political cartoonist for Charlie Hebdo, for contempt of the Head of State.

> End of July: Public opinion organizations publish the results of a poll on the preoccupations of the French people:

45%, the victory of Cyrille Guimard in the Tour de France
22%, the engagement of Princess Anne
11%, social conflict
22%, no response.

August 1; Departures for vacation reach a record high.

August 15: Orlando D., (Portuguese) immigrant worker, is escorted to the Portuguese border, his working contract not having been renewed.

The third Watergate cover within 2 months appeared on May 21: a full-page portrait of Nixon, the bottom half in color, the top in black-and-white, titled "THE NIXON TRIAL" and with the biblical quote from Song of Solomon 6:5: "A severe judgment will be exercised on those who command." Again three articles appeared. "WATERGATE: THE FIRE" (pp. 130, 131) by Jean-Jacques Faust, included a Tim cartoon portraying a forlorn Nixon on the witness stand while Leonid Brezhnev, in (French) lawyer's garb, gesticulatingly defends him. The introduction: "Watergate is no longer just an American scandal. It's a fire which threatens to engulf the entire world. In the first rank, Mr. Brezhnev." This article asserted that, since détente had been initiated and to a great extent personalized by Nixon and Brezhnev, and since the latter wanted Nixon in office for continued détente backing in the Soviet Union, perhaps Brezhnev would rush to Nixon's aid as a "fireman" to help snuff out the Watergate blaze.

The cover story by Henri de Turenne and Pierre Salinger (pp. 132—34) was introduced: "Vice is closing in around President Nixon. And now there's a strong chance that no one will show him mercy. Because his crime is a political crime." "Anything can happen now", they begin, because the televised Senate Watergate hearings have blown the issue wide apart. Beginning with first witness Robert Odle from CREEP, the testimony has revealed much more than expected and highly damaged Nixon's position. America is deeply shaken by the implications of it all, but "Everyone is retreating, for the moment, behind the sacred principle according to which any person is presumed innocent until proven guilty. 'Including the President'." This battle between the President and Congress, the writers warn, is to be taken dead seriously, "because, unlike the French Parliament, the American Congress has considerable powers and means of investigation".

The final article, "THE BLIND AND THE PARALYZED" (p. 135), by Pierre Uri, treated the financial consequences of Watergate in terms of European and world economies. "This deterioration of power in America combined with the weakness of the dollar is perhaps the beginning of a crisis which could shake the foundation of prosperity and security in Europe."

"WATERGATE LIVE" by Turenne and Salinger stressed the impact of the televised hearings and recounted testimony to date (5/28 — 114—19). Breaking up this article, a centerfold illustration headlined "RICHARD NIXON'S DOUBLE NET-WORK" included photos and one-paragraph job descriptions of Nixon's former White House staff and CREEP members. Superimposed over each photo was a one-word description of their current situations: "Resigned", "Dismissed", "Convicted", or "Working".

In the same issue, American historian Arthur Schlesinger contributed a full-page editorial. "SO MUCH THE BETTER FOR THE PRESIDENCY" (p. 121) asserted that, when all is said and done, Watergate will undoubtedly have proven itself a good and needed experience in restoring a true balance of powers to the American government.

"WATERGATE: THE NEW TACTICS" by Turenne (6/4 — 124—25) revealed that Nixon had resumed the offensive: whereas he had previously denied all knowledge of Watergate-related events, he now admits to having been informed 6 days after the break-in but suppressed the information for national security reasons. Congress and the press are outraged. Concerning Nixon's offensive defense, *New York Times* columnist James Reston snipes: "This reminds me of the story of the man who killed his parents and then asked for leniency from the jury — because he is an orphan."

"UNITED STATES: THE NET CLOSES" (6/11 — 118—19) included a three-part Tim drawing of Nixon standing at a witness stand reciting "The truth . . .", growing smaller as he swears "The whole truth . . .", and smaller still so that when he says "Nothing but the truth . . ." the stanchions of the witness stand have become prison bars from which he is peering out. The article recounts Dean's testimony claiming that Nixon was promptly and fully informed about Watergate. The White House initially denied this, then reluctantly admitted it. Agnew has been implicated in the ITT affair, Republicans are becoming increasingly worried about Watergate's effect on their party's future survival, and many want Nixon to resign more than the Democrats do.

This same edition carried *L'Express*'s first editorial call — by an American — for Nixon's resignation. Copyrighted by the *New York Times* and *L'Express*, "WATERGATE: AN HONOR-ABLE ESCAPE" By Clark Clifford (p. 120) offered a solution to the Watergate morass. Since the nightmare of Agnew-as-President would probably ensure Nixon's retention of the Presidency — but a weak and sick one no longer able to govern effectively — Nixon should ask Agnew to resign, select a new Vice-President from among three candidates proposed by Congress, after which Nixon himself could step down, putting national interests above his personal interests and thereby living happily ever after in the hearts and minds of the American people.

"RICHARD NIXON IN QUARANTINE" (7/23/73 — 71), an editorial by Jean-François Revel, maintained that the American President had continued a long-standing pattern of abuse of executive power common to all modern democracies. Nixon is now in the hospital (a tactical move for sympathy?) isolating himself from others — including Party conservatives like Goldwater — who are urging him to be more moderate and cooperative in regard to the Watergate investigation. John Mitchell, notes Revel, labelled Nixon's re-election "a sacred duty":

> French citizen, Mr. Mitchell had pursued his career without hindrance by believing in the right to identify the power of one party with State policy, and thus the duty to violate fundamental and penal laws in the interest of this party. American citizen, he found himself reprimanded by Mr. Ervin that no article of the American

Constitution imposes any obligation of the president to run for reelection, and [it] discerns poorly what the "sacred duty" in question could consist of.

Revel explains that the 1950s McCarthy "witch hunts" are not at all comparable to the Senate Watergate Investigation (a common contention in many French news media): the former involved only hysterical opinions and unfounded accusations, while the latter rests on solid evidential ground. His conclusion: "Whatever the Party's unravelling and the extent of its breakdown might be, at worst it is lost. At best, it has lost."

"FROM SCANDAL TO SCANDAL" (8/13 — 60) first broke the news of the Agnew affair to *L'Express* readers. Six weeks later Salinger explained in "ONE VICE-PRESIDENT FOR SALE" that Agnew had been conspicuously ignored and deserted by the White House in order to defer attention from Watergate, to show that Nixon wants justice pursued when there's a true scandal, and to be able to select a new Veep. Connally is the most likely choice, or maybe Rockefeller. In any case, Agnew is undergoing prosecution in Baltimore and his political future looks bleak.

The following week (10/1 — 124–25) "THE NIXON— AGNEW DUEL" provided an hour-by-hour playback of Nixon— Agnew maneuverings leading to Agnew's plea-bargained immunity in exchange for resignation, including Nixon's authorization for Attorney General Elliot Richardson to hand over anti-Agnew evidence to the Baltimore Grand Jury.

"THE PRESIDENT CAUGHT IN A TRAP" (10/29 — 119– 21) detailed the Saturday Night Massacre and its damaging political repercussions to Nixon's presidential future. Art Buchwald lightened up the news with "THE KING'S PROSE-CUTOR" (p. 121). Embellishing the massacre with a royal context, Buchwald quotes the king as saying — after having lopped off his prosecutor's head — that one "can always find a new prosecutor, but where will the people find a new king?"

A rather unique journalistic phenomenon appeared in the November 5 *L'Express*: an open letter from an American, published exclusively in a French newsmagazine, to Richard Nixon, suggesting that he solve the Watergate mess by asking the Supreme Court to organize a new election. The motivation for such circuitous communication remains open to speculation, but its most probable inspiration can be ascertained by a process of elimination: it is doubtful that the letter was seriously intended for Nixon's eyes, as he was not known to regularly read most American media let alone *L'Express*; nor to mobilize relevant public opinion, since the reading public in this case was French. Perhaps significantly, *Time* magazine had published its first editorial (labelled as such) in 50 years, demanding Nixon's resignation following the Saturday Night Massacre. Salinger might have felt upstaged by *Time* and become eager to hop on the journalistic bandwagon via *L'Express*. In any case, both the nature of its communication and the letter's proposed solution are unique. The full-page (p. 90) (translated) text follows.

Open Letter to President Nixon
A SOLUTION FOR THE UNITED STATES

[Introduction] For the first time in 50 years, *Time*, the most influential American weekly newsmagazine, last week published an editorial. To demand the resignation of President Richard Nixon. One more voice increasing the clamor which is rising up, in Republican ranks as well as among Democrats.

Entangled among his contradictions, his denials, his evasions in the Watergate affair, the President nevertheless repeated three times during the past week that he would not resign. No material proof against him exists — yet — which would leave him no recourse. But the United States has lost confidence. What should be done? Pierre Salinger, who was one of President John Kennedy's advisors, suggests a solution. In the form of an open letter.

Mr. President,

The United States is suffering a crisis of authority. You are the center of it. I have devoted most of my 25-year career to leading a political struggle against you, and perhaps you will not attribute great importance to my views. But, just as I will never doubt your devotion to the nation, I am sure that you will not question the patriotic loyalty which today inspires me to write this letter.

Calls for your resignation are increasing on all sides. According to the polls, you have lost two-thirds of your support in one year. And it is not only your adversaries who are demanding your departure. But also, undoubtedly to your sorrow, men and women who had always offered you their friendship and support.

I do not believe that you would ever retreat under fire. These 25 years have convinced me that, the harder the struggle, the harder you fight, with all your forces. I thus do not ask for your resignation. I simply suggest a solution, which will perhaps be more honorable, to the problem which is preoccupying our country.

I thus propose that you, Richard M. Nixon, President of the United States, ask the Supreme Court to hold new elections on the first Tuesday of April 1974.

In this petition you could emphasize that some men working for your cause conducted themselves in such a way that the American electoral system suffered gravely. Which is true. You could also emphasize that the accusations hurled on all sides, once these misdeeds were brought to light, have scarred the country with uncertainty and bitterness. Which is true. And you could assert that in your opinion the best solution would be to give the American people a new opportunity to be heard, by their vote.

Neither party would gain an advantage (over the other) by this. The Democrats today are no better prepared than the Republicans to face a presidential election.

The possibility of provisional presidential elections was not foreseen by the Constitution. But the Supreme Court could, without difficulty, invoke precedent supporting your request. In the past, Justice has annulled elections for fiscal fraud, and ordered new ones.

It is for you to decide — if the Supreme Court grants your request — whether or not you want to present yourself as a candidate again.

If you decide not to enter the race, you will have given the American people an honorable means of resolving the present dispute. You will not have been driven out of the Presidency. Rather, you will have left willingly, voluntarily, as an American who, during a time of profound crisis, holds the country's interest above his own.

And if you choose to run again, you will be able to honorably call on the American people to confirm the support which — as all of your statements maintain — you believe you still deserve.

If, under some pretext, the Supreme Court refuses your request, you will have nevertheless shown your sincerity. And you will have gained from that.

It is not from a frivolous state of mind that I allow myself to submit this suggestion to you. But rather because I sincerely believe that, if you so intend, America will be able to advance a step towards unity and enlightenment from one of the darkest periods in its history.

In the same issue, Salinger contributed the inevitable psychological profile of Nixon. "THE TWO NIXONS" (pp. 133—35) included photos of Nixon addressing a press conference,

Archibald Cox promenading in the countryside, and four adjacent shots of Nixon moods: laugh, smile, worry, anger. "Which is the real Nixon?" the introduction begins, "The great peace strategist? Or the man who drags out Watergate and betrays his friends? America seems to have decided. . . ." Again lapsing into rhetorical questions, the article asks: Is "Richard the Magnificent" and "Richard the Peaceful" the same person as "Richard the Evil"? In terms of foreign policy, "Richard Nixon is decidedly a great President", but he is in increasing trouble domestically, most recently because of two missing tapes and testimony by John Dean, Stephen Bull and Henry Petersen contradicting the White House version of events. Salinger ends his character study by saying that: "the man of international peace is also the man of civil war. Because the people no longer have confidence in him."

This article also cited the comment of Gerald Fox (*sic*), Nixon's vice-presidential nominee, that the impeachment process must continue. Gerald "Fox" was the first of several incorrectly spelled names (some others: Emil Krogh, John Roades, Harry Goldwater, Professor Bruce Maylish) which appeared in *L'Express*. Often, foreign names are adapted to French phonetics (e.g. Brezhnev — the English spelling of a Russian name — becomes Brejnev in French), but none of the above qualify for that legitimate alteration — particularly since they were correctly spelled in other issues. In addition, typographical errors appeared quite frequently within regular copy, and it seems that *L'Express* might cut financial corners with the absence of a proofreading staff. Such shoddy spelling became especially ironic when, in an article describing Nixon's Egypt trip, the magazine condescendingly chortled about Arab misspelling of Nixon's name on welcome posters.

Almost a month passed before "NIXON: THE DOUBLE CRISIS" (12/3 — 129—30) noted that the energy crisis had been heaped upon Nixon's Watergate blues. Gerald Ford (spelled correctly) is all but confirmed for the Vice-Presidency, and many Republicans are leaning toward impeachment due to unending revelations, the latest involving an 18-minute tape gap of suspect origins. Salinger concludes by quoting a Republican leader: "The American people could tolerate corruption, maybe . . . . But corruption and economic disaster, never."

"A CANDIDATE AT THE WHITE HOUSE" (12/10 — 135) included photos of Gerald Ford being sworn in and hiking a football. Framing a political portrait in American football, Salinger began: "To really understand Mr. Gerald Rudolph Ford, it is necessary to be acquainted with *le football américain.* Ford is conservative, honest, solid, a team player, lacking imagination. "In short", the piece ends, "if he were President tomorrow, Mr. Ford would undoubtedly pass the ball to his ministers, like he did when he was center on the University of Michigan football team."

"WATERGATE: THE ARMY TOO . . ." led off the new year (1/21/74 — 70—72) describing still more damaging Watergate-related revelations, some of which even risked tainting Henry Kissinger for the first time. The mysterious 18-minute tape gap continues to gnaw away at Nixon's credibility and public support, and the article ends with a biting quote from the normally pro-Nixon *Washington Star:*

> On criminal grounds, the intentional suppression of an element of proof is, in itself, a crime. It is for Special Prosecutor Jaworski and the grand jury to decide if this crime has truly been committed. There are good reasons, until then, to believe that it has been. Perhaps there is another explanation. Perhaps tomorrow the sun will rise in the West.

On January 28 (pp. 70—71), *L'Express* scooped other European publications with the first interview of new Vice-President Gerald Ford. The chat, which Salinger said left him with the opposite impression from typical Washington gossip deriding Ford's intellectual capacities, covered Détente, European Defense, Energy Crisis, Watergate (in reference to the latter), Latin America, and Impeachment. Regarding the last, Ford said: "The House of Representatives should vote on impeachment of the President as soon as possible. After all that has been said about Watergate, we need a response. Yes or no."

Foreign Minister Jobert's antics at the Washington Energy

Conference won him the February 18 cover: "MR. JOBERT'S
CARDS" pictured the spunky little man sitting frowningly on
a tricolored France which had broken off from the rest of con-
tinental Europe. But *L'Express* took a much less congratulatory
and more analytical view. In the cover story, Marc Ullman
noted the major fallacy in Pompidou's tactics (via Jobert)
for avoiding American "leadership":

> Several ministers at the heart of the government are asking them-
> selves — but silently! — if the best way to assure American preemi-
> nence does not consist, precisely, in serving [it] a divided Europe
> on a platter (p. 32).

In "France at 12 Against 1", Pierre Salinger began:

> Mr. Michel Jobert said no even before the Washington Energy
> Conference began. He repeated no in all tones [of voice] during
> the two and a half days the meeting lasted. And no again in leaving
> the snow-covered American capital. And he was proud of it (p. 37).

On his arrival in Washington, Jobert announced: "I am here
out of courtesy and on the condition that no one steps on my
feet." By that time, most other foreign ministers had already
been in the American capital for a day or two, had their ears
bent by Henry Kissinger, and reached a general consensus.
France refused:

> Obviously there remained a third solution: compromise. But, as
> the French spokesman said: "The only possible compromise would
> be if the twelve others adopted the French view" (p. 38).

"WATERGATE: NIXON FACE TO FACE WITH CON-
GRESS" (3/11 — 96, 97) featured a Suares cartoon of a cracked
and toppling Nixon bust barely supported by makeshift and
creaky wooden scaffolding. There is now no escaping impeachment, the first step toward Nixon's dismissal, Salinger explains.
A recent Democratic electoral victory in Republican strong-
hold Cincinnati has panicked Republicans; the Watergate
Grand Jury has cited Nixon as an unindicted co-conspirator;
after testifying under oath that Nixon said hush money and
presidential clemency for convicted burglars would be wrong,
Haldeman was indicted by Jaworski and the Grand Jury for
perjury. So far, in what Nixon called "a banal affair" following

the Watergate break-in, a Vice-President, thirteen White House counselors, two Cabinet members, eleven members of CREEP, and eight major American corporations have been indicted or sentenced for various misdeeds.

"NIXON BETRAYED BY HIS OWN" (3/25 — 103, 104) included a large photo of Conservative Senator James Buckley and another of Nixon playing with a yoyo on television. The latter was part of Nixon's latest public relations scheme, in combination with singing "God Bless America" at Nashville's Grand Ole Opry, for mobilizing favorable public opinion. Meanwhile, Wilbur Mills declares on television that "Mr. Nixon will no longer be President by the end of the summer" due to explosive revelations forthcoming about his tax returns. Buckley calls for his resignation, and Watergate has now begun showing important effects on Nixon's international power and prestige. In *L'Express*'s only conspiracy *à la* Gosset comment, Salinger concludes:

> In relation to the indictment of Warren Hastings, British governor of India during the last century, Lord Macaulay wrote a phrase which can be applied word for word to Mr. Nixon: "He was assaulted by the most formidable combination of enemies that was ever dedicated to the ruin of one single man."

Salinger contributed two "dance numbers" to the April 15 issue. "NIXON: THE WALTZ OF THE TAXES" (p. 91) began: "Richard Nixon's moves for avoiding taxes; by Dickens" and enumerated his various tax evasion schemes before finishing with the President's dubious claim that "I am not a crook". On the facing page, "NIXON: THE PARIS BALLET" lambasted him for a gross lack of tact in turning French President Pompidou's funeral into an international political forum and fueled French paranoia concerning American hegemony. One excerpt:

> Mr. Nixon took advantage [of the temporary absence of a French government] to attack two of the cornerstones supporting French foreign policy for the past 15 years: Europe's role in relation to the U.S., and Europe's freedom to organize itself and act on world events without necessarily consulting Washington in advance.

"THE CALENDAR OF IMPEACHMENT" (4/29 — 112)

noted that, while fifty-one charges against Nixon had been dropped, five had been retained: fiscal fraud; the milk fund; ITT contribution; Watergate cover-up; and the Ellsburg break-in. All of Washington is now gearing up for the impeachment process.

"THE GODFATHER OF THE WHITE HOUSE" (5/6 — 126, 127) with a photo of Nixon consulting with John Ehrlichman, announced that the published tape transcripts would go on sale publicly that week and be a guaranteed best-seller. They prove politically devastating for Nixon, showing that: he not only knew about the hush money scheme for Howard Hunt, but even encouraged it; he rejected the presidential clemency idea solely because it was politically risky (rather than for moral reasons); he advised his associates to claim loss of memory under questioning; he was very aware of the cover-up. Nixon's only real gain from the transcripts was in creating the first strictly partisan rift in the House Judiciary Committee: the Democrats wanted the actual tapes while the Republicans felt the transcripts should suffice, and the vote to obtain the tapes fell precisely along party lines. This article included portions of the transcripts and, after leading off with one, Salinger wrote that, no, this wasn't a dialogue from the film *The Godfather*, but an actual White House conversation. Quite obviously, he was playing on a pervasive French image of American culture: *les gangsters*.

For 3 straight weeks beginning May 13, *L'Express* recounted the profound and widespread effects of the tape transcripts. "GERALD FORD LEAVES NIXON" (5/13/74 — 127, 128) warned that even staunch supporters were so shocked that they were deserting his cause. "NIXON—CONGRESS: FIGHT TO THE FINISH" (5/20/74 — 122) replayed the *Washington Star*'s exclusive interview containing Nixon's promise that he would go all the way. Republicans, with elections looming in November, now want him out of office more than Democrats. "WASHINGTON PARALYZED" (5/27/74 — 111) with a photo of Nixon and wife cutlined "find the dough, for Chrissake! . . ." noted the important discrepancies between the

White House-released transcripts and the actual tapes — a difference causing even Nixon stalwart Charles Wiggins to groan "It's a bad day for the President. . . ." To make matters worse, Judge Sirica has ordered the White House to concede sixty-four more tapes sought by Special Prosecutor Jaworski. The White House claims it will appeal the decision all the way to the Supreme Court if necessary, but still these and other events have virtually paralyzed the government.

Three weeks later, "NIXON: ESCAPE TO EGYPT" (6/17 — 90—93) replayed Kissinger's emotional Salzburg speech threatening resignation and Nixon's much ballyhooed welcome in Egypt as the latest anti-Watergate tactics. "NIXON: OPERATION KREMLIN" (6/24 — 93—95) followed up on the theme of foreign policy as a deterrent to domestic problems. The American President's foreign policy achievements during his Middle East tour have been so impressive as to invoke praise even from the *Washington Post* and *New York Times.* Nixon is obviously gambling on détente and other foreign initiatives to turn the Watergate tide. His Middle East ventures verify that the power of the United States in the world has not appreciably suffered from Watergate; but whether foreign policy will save Nixon from prosecution remains another matter.

Art Buchwald appeared in the same issue with a column exhibiting nothing short of genius in its depiction of the difficulties inherent in explaining Watergate to a French audience — and in presenting the most efficacious way to do so. In a *Humour* fixture including a photo of Buchwald smirking over his omnipresent cigar, the half-page (p. 95) (translated) text follows.

THE GREAT RECONCILIATION

Good news from France: the French no longer hate Americans. Rather, they are showing sympathy for President Nixon and don't understand why people are making him undergo such misery in Washington.

My old friend François asked me: "What is happening to your poor President?"

— Oh, it's nothing serious, François; Congress just wants to put him on trial.

— The President? But what on earth did he do to deserve that?
François asked me.

— It's hard to explain. The men who were running his electoral
campaign wanted to know the opposition's strategy, so they tried
to bug the Democratic headquarters.

— So what's wrong with that?

— Well, you see, it was also discovered that these men working
for him used a lot of money to illegally sabotage the opposition's
campaign.

— That's only natural, because they wanted to win the election.

— But that's not all. When these men were arrested, everything
was done to suppress the issue so that no one at the White House
would be compromised. The former Attorney General, the head of
the FBI, and several other high officials were involved in the plan.
They had the evidence destroyed. Some of the President's closest
collaborators lied in court and before the Senate Watergate Committee.

— I know, I know. All that has been in the French newspapers,
but you still haven't answered my question: What is the problem?

— You don't understand, François. There's been scandal after
scandal. The Vice-President was forced to resign because of extortion. Nixon forgot to pay his taxes. He cheated the public treasury
out of 465,000 dollars.

— *Vive* Nixon! François shouted.

— Finally, it was discovered that Nixon secretly recorded the
conversations of everyone who came into his office.

— But any French politician has done just as much. You still
haven't explained why you are so implacable towards him.

— François, I didn't want to tell you this, but the tapes revealed
that the President of the United States puts ketchup on his cottage
cheese.

François's eyes popped out of his head.

— So that's it! Why didn't you say so before? Now I understand
why you want to put him on trial.

"NIXON: PORTRAIT OF A MAN WITH NERVES OF
STEEL" occupied the July 1 cover. Below stood a Hemingway
quote: "Man is not made for defeat." Salinger's psychological
portrait (pp. 80—85) emphasized Nixon's solitary nature and
retraced his truly unique political career. Now in Moscow, he
is obviously trying to link his political future to détente, but the
outlook bodes ill. One bad omen: the Russian summit planners
had selected Yalta as the site of some talks; this was changed
at the last minute to nearby Oreanda.

Nonetheless, in the next *L'Express* issue the summit piece
was datelined "From our special correspondents in Moscow

and Yalta." "MOSCOW: THE MILITARIES WIN" (pp. 76—78) by Salinger and Michel Gordey explained that, despite efforts by Kissinger to the contrary, the American and Soviet defense ministers — Schlesinger and Gretchko — had really "won" the summit since the arms race would continue at least temporarily. Watergate had somewhat tied Nixon's hands in that he couldn't afford to jeopardize his remaining conservative support by making military concessions to the Soviets. Though Brezhnev indulged Nixon in several pompous signings of insignificant documents, Soviet officials do not expect the American President to last for his full term. Accordingly, Brezhnev conspicuously kept his distance — for instance, not reciprocating to Nixon's references to their "personal" relationship which implied its indispensability to continuation of détente. Now that Nixon's diplomatic globe-trotting has come to an end, he must face the domestic heat of Watergate again.

"WATERGATE: RICHARD M. NIXON DOSSIER 73—1766" (7/15 — 55—56) with photos of Nixon, Barry Goldwater, and a copy of the "United States Versus Richard Nixon" petition was introduced: "The Supreme Court is going to decide — this week? And in the history of the United States, it has never lost against a President." Nixon's lawyer James St. Clair and Special Prosecutor Leon Jaworski have argued their cases regarding executive privilege and other matters before the Supreme Court, which is expected to decide soon whether or not the President must yield sixty-four more tape recordings. Several other recent revelations and events in Washington have severely damaged Nixon.

"NIXON BEFORE HIS JUDGES" (7/22 — 52—54) appeared with photos of Chief Justice Warren Burger, and Nixon (cutline: "It's for the psychiatrists to judge"), and a Tim cartoon showing Nixon walking away with a stack of tapes in one hand while looking behind him with binoculars in the other. Salinger wrote:

> By unanimous vote, the guardians of the Constitution reminded [Nixon] last Wednesday that no American citizen is above the law. Not even the President of the United States, the most powerful man on Earth. Beautiful lesson in democracy. Especially if you bear in mind that three of these judges were named by Mr. Nixon himself.

The court had voted against Nixon, requiring him to hand over the disputed sixty-four tapes "without delay". The various cogs in the Watergate investigatory wheel are meshing and driving the whole process forward at an accelerating rate: House Judiciary Committee counsel John Doar, until now impeccably neutral, publicly favors impeachment; Maryland conservative Republican Larry Hogan calls for Nixon's ouster; the House Judiciary Committee will accuse Nixon of obstruction of justice and abuse of power violating the Constitution; the Senate clears its agenda for the Watergate trial. Meanwhile, Nixon is isolating himself more and more from both domestic and international events, surrounding himself with his trusty bevy of yes-men, and releasing a 2-month-old conversation with Rabbi Baruch Korff claiming that Nixon was the victim of a political plot led by the press and other political enemies.

Two weeks later, "NIXON: THE HUNT IS ON" (pp. 39—43) began: "For one year the hour of truth has been approaching. . . . It's here: Nixon is now surrounded on all sides." This article included a Tim cartoon depicting Nixon's head as the body of an ostrich (his nose, of course, extending to form the bird's neck and head) running for its life, as well as a reproduction of the famous "WANTED" poster containing mugshots of twenty central Watergate figures. The cutline noted that everyone but Mitchell, Stans and Nixon had been convicted since this poster made its first *L'Express* appearance on June 25, 1973. Compromising events, Nixon's reaction (or lack thereof) to them, and the resulting angry about-face of many previous pillars of support have combined to back Nixon into a no-exit corner.

"NIXON DRIVEN OUT BY AMERICA" occupied the August 12 cover, with a portrait of Nixon under broken glass. In this issue, the entire "World" section was devoted to the Watergate culmination, with six articles covering eighteen pages.

Salinger's cover story (pp. 21, 22) dealt mostly with the transition of power from Nixon to Ford. The lead:

> It's over. Following a bitter struggle lasting two years, during which he had never wanted to yield an inch of ground, the President

elected by 220 million Americans threw in the towel. He no longer had any choice.

Assuring French readers that Nixon's resignation had by no means traumatized the United States, Salinger said:

> It took America two years to drive out this foreign body which attempted to upset the sacrosanct equilibrium of its political system. It succeeded all the same, and the vast majority of Americans today feel proud of this achievement.
>
> The best proof that it concerns only a return of normalcy: the transfer of powers between Richard Nixon and Gerald Ford was accomplished without drama or shock.

Driving the message home again, Salinger concludes his description of the power transition with:

> One president leaves, another comes. Nothing more. With a certain automobile [play-on-words] humor, the new President declared: "I'm only a Ford, not a Lincoln". Everything considered, after the events of the past 11 years, isn't that what America needs?

In "THE COLLAPSE" (pp. 24—27) Henri de Turenne described the crucial roles played by Kissinger and Haig in urging and/ or covering for the President's resignation. "Alone, always alone", the article began, Nixon had recently succumbed to all the pressures and "he cut the last ties linking him with the world of realities". When he fled "Alone" to the presidential yacht *Sequoia*,

> General Haig called a meeting of about 100 White House collaborators and told them, in a pathetic tone: "You must continue your work as usual. The country's business cannot wait." They all understood: practically speaking, America already had no more President. Only a phantom which from that time on haunted the White House.

Again emphasizing that America will survive this crisis, Turenne concludes:

> Thursday, the 37th President resigned. For the first time in the history of the United States. Friday, at the precise moment when a helicopter lifted off from the White House lawn, carrying ordinary citizen Richard Milhous Nixon towards his destiny, the 38th President of the United States took the oath. Under a portrait of Abraham Lincoln, Mr. Gerald Ford, in his turn, swore assumption of the function of President. "Loyally".

"THE TAPE WHICH CONDEMNED NIXON" (pp. 28, 29)

ran a translated version of the bomb and included the introduction:

"I don't want to be implicated in that. . . . Call in the CIA. . . . And play a careful game. . ." Impossible, from that time on, to deny it. Two years of solemn denials collapsed.

L'Express indulged in a little self-advertising with a centerfold spread (pp. 30—31) blaring: "A FABULOUS DETECTIVE STORY: In *L'Express* Starting August 26." With a photo of Watergate-breaking journalists Woodward and Bernstein watching Nixon's televised resignation speech, it announced that the magazine would run the serialized story of their day-to-day Watergate uncovering. Their book, *All the President's Men*, would also appear in a French version published by Robert Laffont.

"THE MEN WHO FELLED NIXON" (pp. 32, 37, 38) was introduced: "Jean-Jacques Faust paints an astonishing gallery of portraits: the average Americans who won the battle for democracy." Faust detailed the roles of primary investigatory figures under the headings of Journalists, Parliamentarians, and Magistrates.

Finally, the magazine granted Pierre Salinger a full page (p. 23) to sigh about the task of trying to explain Watergate to a French audience — and to one last effort to do so. From where Salinger received his feedback remains uncertain, but it was apparently the same essential response any American gets from any French person about the Watergate affair. His text:

THE AMERICAN CEMENT

Since the beginning of Watergate, I have tried to explain to my European friends what this affair has meant to Americans. Without much success. Apparently, they don't understand what it concerns. We're not talking about the same thing.

To understand the fall of Richard Nixon, it is necessary to understand the United States. A relatively young country, composed of men and women who came from all parts of the world to create a new country founded on a certain idea of freedom. They created a contract among themselves whose purpose was to guarantee human rights. This contract is the Constitution. Also, throughout their history, which nevertheless has lasted for 200 years, they have considered as unpardonable only one crime: the violation of this contract, because it represents the cement which unifies them.

That is exactly the crime of which Richard Nixon is held guilty. He systematically misled the American people. He used the Government of the United States to pursue and destroy his "enemies". He showed his contempt for the Congress and the Courts.

The President of the United States is a powerful man, perhaps the most powerful man on Earth. The American people admire and respect him. They are willing to accept many things on his part. For example, they tolerate the fact that their President lives like a king. But not that he acts like one. The Watergate affair demonstrated in a spectacular way that, for Americans, the President of the United States cannot be a man above the law. He must obey it like any other citizen.

Even more important: the American version of democracy is a political system based on the balance of powers. The Judiciary must be independent. Congress must be strong. The press must be truly free, as guaranteed by the First Amendment to the Constitution.

The only person responsible for the fall of Richard Nixon is truly Richard Nixon himself. He committed a series of actions which inevitably led him to his ruin. Without the democratic institutions of America, he could have avoided his destiny. Thank God, they functioned normally.

Finally, some people played their roles in this affair: a courageous Senator, an incorruptible judge, two persevering journalists. But it wasn't so much that individuals or supposed "enemies" of the President succeeded in overthrowing the most powerful man on Earth. Above them and above the institutions they represent, it was the American people who had the last word.

Winston Churchill once said that: "Democracy is the worst system, with the exception of all the others." The Watergate affair confirms this judgment.

The American system is not perfect. Far from it. The United States has some urgent problems to resolve, some glaring injustices to rectify, some abuses of power to correct. But we can hope that the Watergate affair will finally be a fresh start.

The end of Richard Nixon will perhaps mark the end of 11 years of nightmare which began with the assassination of John Kennedy. During these 11 years, the country has been torn by crises: the war in Vietnam, racial conflicts, the deaths of Martin Luther King and Robert Kennedy.

Vietnam showed Americans the limits of their power. Watergate showed the future leaders of this country the limits of power of the White House. Most certainly, the American Constitution is based on the principle of a strong President. But he must respect the law of public opinion. In any case, with the extraordinary developments of mass communications, the times of secret Cabinet politics is finished.

On May 7, 1973, *L'Express*, devoting its cover to the editor of the *Washington Post,* the daily newspaper which was the first to "break" the Watergate affair, tried in doing so to present its readers the magnitude of what it called "the drama of the White House".

Many French people then believed this [affair] to be a politically banal news item. A little corruption, a few wiretaps, a handful of skilled laborers. . . . Fifteen months have passed. *Goodbye* [in English], Mr. Nixon.

"A NEW AMERICA" (8/19) headed *L'Express*'s final Watergate-related cover. Stars surrounded the cover title above a drawing of Ford draped in an American flag; at the bottom, a Jules Laforgue quote: "Ah! How life is daily. . . ."

Salinger's cover story (pp. 21, 22) ebulliently described the immediate post-Watergate atmosphere.

It's "spring in Washington". In one week, everything has changed and an incredible euphoria has inundated the country.

America has turned a page. Relieved and delighted, it contemplates the image of its new President, stepping outside at 6.30 in the morning onto the steps of his suburban home, in blue pajamas, to pick up his *Washington Post.*

Reassured, [Americans] watch him on television swimming in his small private pool after a hard day of work at the White House.

Just imagine! Mrs. Ford refused to have a new dress made for the swearing-in ceremony! She contented herself with an old sky-blue outfit. Her two sons, who timidly presented themselves at the White House door the same day, were stopped by the guards. Their chauffeur had to intervene: "These are the President's kids." There you have a modest family of good middle Americans at the White House. Finally.

Ford chose mostly staunch conservatives for his staff:

But from the old school. No young California wolves, coming from the advertising world, like Mr. Nixon's collaborators. Rather, good provincials from Michigan — like himself — or from neighboring states, from "the country": a former member of his Grand Rapids football team, an old classmate. After the gaudy, conquering and cynical California, this is the Middle West in depth, traditional, nostalgic for isolationism, which is moving into the White House. Middle America. Four of [these men] are former journalists. A striking acquittal of the press, which emerged victorious from the Watergate battle.

Still, about the easiest thing in the world at that time was to look good compared to Nixon. Though Americans are comforted by and ecstatic with the new President's refreshing plainfolks openness and candor, Ford remains largely an unknown entity and there exist some nagging political doubts already beginning to circulate. Salinger concludes with a William Shannon editorial quote from the *New York Times*: "Today the United States has a President who speaks like Eisenhower, thinks like Truman and has economic theories like Herbert Hoover's. A disconcerting mixture."

The other three articles in that issue speculated on the future of U.S.–Soviet détente, now that Nixon had exited the national and international arenas. Michel Gordey's article, "MR. BREZHNEV'S SECRET MESSAGE" (p. 23), was introduced: "The same day that Mr. Ford arrived in power, *Isvestia* published a poem by Yevtushenko entitled 'Détente'. . . ." Despite Nixon's futile attempts at personalizing détente to counterbalance Watergate, U.S.–Soviet relations are expected to continue along the same directions toward easing of tensions. "EAST AND WEST AFTER NIXON" (pp. 24–26) reprinted excerpts from a debate among international relations specialists organized by the *New York Times* following the Moscow summit. Finally, "THE DYNAMICS OF DÉTENTE" (p. 26) by Samuel Pisar, an advocate of East–West commerce and author of *The Arms of Peace*, took the adversary view of those criticizing transfer of Western technology to the Soviet Union because it supposedly reinforces the worst aspects of Soviet society and weakens pressure for internal reform:

> My experience and my convictions are diametrically opposed to this objection: it is precisely the East's current quest for more efficient industry, agriculture, and management, and for an improvement of the standard of living (difficult to attain without Western equipment, know-how and credit) which inevitably leads to a humanization of its internal system and appeasement of its international politics. . . . However fragile it might be, I believe that the dynamics of détente are irreversible, with or without Nixon, with or without Brezhnev. But the question of knowing if Europe will participate in the development of the East–West coexistence, if she will play a true role in the construction of peace, and who will lead her in this historic role, is of primary importance.

Summary and analysis

During the roughly 70 weeks that Watergate existed as a hot

international news item, *L'Express* thoroughly covered the crisis in forty-nine of its issues, devoting more than 100 pages for over sixty articles. The amount of weekly coverage naturally varied with events, but the typical *L'Express* reportage was thorough, explanatory, and usually embellished with several photographs of prominent figures or events. In addition, six Watergate covers appeared.

Besides its own correspondents, *L'Express* uses the wire services of Agence France-Presse and the Associated Press, and has special accords with the *New York Times, Washington Post*, and *Los Angeles Times*. During Watergate, the magazine relied heavily on American writers and media. Not only did Pierre Salinger contribute the bulk of news articles, but room was given to other Americans as well: Art Buchwald contributed several humorous parodies of the Watergate mess; politico Clark Clifford suggested a round-about resignation scheme copyrighted by both *L'Express* and the *New York Times*; historian Arthur Schlesinger editorialized on Watergate's consequences on the U.S. Presidency. American newspaper, magazine and television stories were often quoted, and the first cover ever awarded to a journalist went to Ben Bradlee.

Though Salinger got the call for most news reporting, the majority of Watergate editorials were written by Frenchmen. For the most part, these remained more explanatory than judgmental, indulging in a little historical, sociological or political theory in order to make Watergate more understandable and palatable for fellow French people. The various writers pointed out similarities and differences between the French and American societies and governments, dabbled in political character studies, analyzed the long-standing trend in all modern democracies toward consolidation of executive power which sometimes reaches a pathological state, and generally treated Watergate as a beneficially analyzable and instructive series of events — rather than wishing it would either disappear or explode. When these editorialists did take sides, their comments normally praised the American system's crisis functioning and often betrayed a certain envy toward the American press's power and independence. In this regard, Henri de Turenne once commented in a news article that White House press conferences are "more like a boxing match than the exchanges of capped [fencing] foils" typical of those at L'Élysée Palace.

The "major" criticisms of *L'Express*'s Watergate coverage amount only to nitpicking. Several names — and everyday French words — were misspelled, their writers (including Salinger) occasionally lapsed into rhetorical questions or rather puerile language (Richard the Magnificent, Richard the Evil), and some questionably necessary snide cocktail-circuit jokes (e.g. Salinger's mention of the Lyndon Johnson quote deriding Ford's intelligence: "Ford isn't capable of doing two things at once. In fact I think he has trouble walking and chewing gum at the same time") cheapened otherwise serious copy.

Although some French journalists contributed news reports, Salinger was clearly *L'Express*'s big gun on week-to-week Watergate coverage. Such heavy reliance by a French news-magazine on an American's reporting might be considered a journalistic cop-out, but might equally reflect some sound — if not totally correct — reasoning. Salinger is a well-known and highly experienced politician—journalist who could provide years of inside knowledge highly useful in explaining a very complex series of events and systemic functioning — versus someone with only a textbook awareness of American politics. The important interpreting involved not language, but different institutions and a different mentality. *L'Express* probably reasoned, quite logically, that a qualified American with French connections and understanding could more accurately interpret an American domestic crisis to a French audience than could a French person lacking experiential knowledge.

For an American reader already familiar with Watergate, this holds true. Salinger's coverage is difficult to criticize from that point of view, but in some very important ways he may have left his French audience wondering — like Art Buchwald's poor François — what all the fuss was about in Washington. In essence, Salinger reported on — and excellently — the American system's functioning during the Watergate period: the respective roles played by the press, Congress, the Courts, Nixon, his staff, and the American public. He explained congressional involvement — Senate Watergate hearings, House Judiciary Committee findings, impeachment procedures, influential opinion within Congress, etc. — most thoroughly week by week; the Judiciary system — lower courts, the Supreme Court, the Special Prosecutor, legal implications and procedures, etc. — received extensive coverage also. Salinger conspicuously underplayed the press's role — though it was covered elsewhere by French journalists — perhaps mindful of general French cynicism regarding the "unscrupulous opportunists" in that profession.

Where he most probably misled and possibly angered French readers was in his oft-repeated use of the term "Watergate" and a relatively scanty explanation of all the diverse scandals implied by this term. "Watergate", of course, began with the unsuccessful burglary in the apartment complex so named, but also served as a semantic umbrella for a cornucopia of subsequent — or at least subsequently revealed — Nixon-related misdeeds. In the second *L'Express* issue with Watergate coverage, Salinger provided a detailed rundown of the scandalous events which had been uncovered by that time (April 2, 1973). However, a reader is not likely to recall this plethora of crimes unless he receives repeated mention in following weeks. Salinger, while going heavy on systemic functioning and often mentioning that certain of Nixon's closest aides or collaborators had been accused of crimes, indicted, or found guilty, went light on explaining subsequent scandals — and specifying that they were all part of what is called "Watergate" for the sake of simplicity and lack of a better term. Thus for a French person — used to government and other scandals, and to ignoring them — Watergate could easily have been much ado about nothing or, worse, a political conspiracy which had blown "a banal news item" into a political assassination.

Certainly, Salinger was limited to a certain amount of space and could not hope to cover every sinister aspect of Watergate in detail. And, Monday-morning quarterbacking is much simpler than Sunday-afternoon decision-making, so retrospective criticism ignores many of the pressures he faced as a journalist. The point is that *L'Express* gambled on the idea of placing an American perceptual filter rather than a French one between American events and French audience, believing this would provide a more accurate — but still understandable — picture. Judging by Salinger's full-page sigh, they might not have lost, but they certainly didn't win either. Ironically, the absurdly slanted and inaccurate reportage of the Gossets might have made more sense to French people because the perceptual filter was one they share to a much greater extent.

Le Monde

Le Monde ("The World") accurately reflects this unique newspaper's sphere of both content and distribution. Probably the world's most internationally oriented daily, *Le Monde* took over the material assets and location of *Le Temps* — outlawed for wartime collaboration — and ran its first edition on December 18, 1944. Since then, distribution has climbed annually, with the exception of one year, from 120,000 to over 400,000 by 1974.[59] Roughly half of these copies circulate in the provinces, making *Le Monde* the least *"parisien"* of all Paris-based dailies, and nearly 20% are exported to other countries. In addition, the paper runs a special monthly edition (*Le Monde Diplomatique*) and a weekly issue containing its best articles and translated into English.[60] Fully 90% of its weekly edition is exported.[61]

The archetype of an "elite" newspaper, *Le Monde* never prints photographs and its austere presentation reflects a seriousness of tone and purpose. Its format, a hybrid of tabloid and broadsheet, readily distinguishes *Le Monde* from other papers on the newsstand. The paper typically runs thirty to forty pages except on Saturday when circulation drops sharply, and on Sunday no paper appears. Advertising of various sorts occupies about one-third of the surface; of space devoted to news and information, more than one-third carries international politics, followed by economics and domestic politics.[62]

Le Monde's working journalists exercise more editorial and financial control over their publication than any other French newspaper staff — and perhaps more than any other in the world. In 1951, the paper's two major stockholders demanded the resignation of director Beuve-Méry. Outraged journalists formed a union (*société de rédacteurs*), appealed through the paper to its readers, recruited public figures and political groups for support, and refused to accept Beuve-Méry's resignation. Their very successful campaign resulted in the journalists' union gaining nearly 30% of *Le Monde*'s holdings and virtual veto power over internal policies; since 1968, the journalists have controlled 40% of the paper's capital. This example spurred roughly thirty other journalists' unions into existence, but none have come close to gaining as much control or professional leverage.[63]

The by-lined diversity of opinion and style within *Le Monde*'s pages backs its claim that journalists are accorded considerable independence in their reportage, as well as responsibility for it. *Le Monde* is clearly the paper of record in France, carrying exhaustive — and, at times, exhausting — accounts and commentary on major issues and events. Its back-page index of major articles ("One Day in the World") is a researcher's dream, but the convoluted literary writing style often makes for tortuous reading, particularly for an anglophone.

Le Monde is probably the most internationally oriented of all watchdogs. Its typical news budget includes articles under the headings: "Europe", "The Americas", "The Middle East", "Asia", "Oceana", "Africa", "Diplomacy", "Politics", "Economics", and several other categories covering French society. The overthrow of Salvador Allende in Chile and Juan Perón's return to Argentine political life often eclipsed Watergate in the "Americas" section.

As an afternoon paper, *Le Monde* faces less deadline pressure so is able to take a more analytical approach — more in-depth than the succinct newsmagazine summaries and less headline-oriented than morning dailies. Indeed, its headlines are anything but terse or sensational: "UNITED STATES: THE COUNSEL FOR THE JUDICIARY COMMITTEE OF THE HOUSE OF REPRESENTATIVES DEMANDS THE IMPEACHMENT OF PRESIDENT NIXON" headed a three-paragraph wire report on John Doar's stance (7/22/74 — 6). *Le Monde*'s obvious concern with accuracy and balance is exhibited by related practices: its wire-service stories often came from two or three agencies — such as AFP, AP and Reuters — possibly to cross-check accounts. Footnotes at the end of the story often explain procedural technicalities, historical precedent, and so forth. During Watergate, the paper often cited American media reports, and ran lengthy sections quoting presidential speeches, tape transcripts, etc. Frequently the original American terms — e.g. Rules Committee, indictment — were parenthetically included next to the French translation. Reporters repeatedly made it clear that the term "Watergate" did not apply exclusively to the break-in, and often referred to the overall crisis as scandals "annexed to Watergate". *Le Monde* also devoted much space to international press commentary on Watergate and other major issues, and opened its pages to a wide range of opinions on various topics.

Foreign news editor Michel Tatu contributed a handful of Watergate articles during peak crisis periods. Chief Washington correspondent Henri Pierre's reporting was often supplemented by that from special correspondents Jacques Amalric, André Clément and Alain-Marie Carron. All these reporters exhibited a variously subtle skepticism regarding Richard Nixon's innocence and carried some individual attitudes into their coverage. Amalric's accounts were normally balanced, except for a clear distaste for John Dean; André Clément often used the unrolling of Watergate to get in some digs at the American system. Robert Escarpit, who writes a two- or three-paragraph fixture on the front page ("From Day to Day") also contributed some slurs and some glaring misinterpretations of Watergate and the American system.

Le Monde's view of American foreign policy and the European Community differs less in substance from other French publications than in presenting it with more sophistication and a broader range of opinion. As one isolated example, a handful of articles appearing around the time of the Washington Energy Conference deserve note.

"THE IMAGE OF FRANCE" by Alfred Grossier followed France's surprise announcement of the floating franc — not long after then-Finance Minister Giscard had informally assured German counterpart Helmut Schmidt that this would not happen. Excerpts:

> We can always counterattack. The deutschmark floated too. The strikes in England. The absurd Belgian conflicts. And Mr. Nixon. But on the condition of first listening to what is being said about us in other countries and to take into account the constant deterioration of the image of France. Also on the condition that we attach importance to this deterioration, to not just see in it the proof that the others are bad, that they wanted it to happen, that one more time France is misunderstood.

> We claim to want to create Europe and yet we would be insensitive to the growing distrust that our policies inspire? "France deserts the European Community each time that she doesn't find it to her advantage": there's a rather positive description from the day after our monetary decision.

> But the least that one can say is that we don't appear to be a model of democracy. When . . . we compare the wiretapping [in France] to that of Watergate, it's not in our favour.

> But [foreign tensions] are also due to the simple fact that the image of France is tarnished by the reproachful view attached to it. A reproach that we would do well to attribute to our policies before bitterly taking an inventory of the reproaches that can be addressed to others.

In contrast to this self-criticism, Philippe de Saint-Robert geared up *Le Monde*'s readership for the WEC with "NO TO THE NEO-ATLANTIC OPERATION" (2/12/74 — 2). One paragraph:

> French people, another effort! The big operation of Atlantic recovery of which we are the victims will become divisive as soon as we ridicule it, as soon as we refuse to enter into the American game. This American game is currently to assure itself control of the energy resources of Europe, to replace a worn-out military tutelage with an economic tutelage at the sources in using the means of the international oil companies which, in reality being multinational, are completely and uniquely Anglo-Saxon. Any self-respecting European country has the means to shatter this expropriation

because, for the first time, we aren't without possible alliances with other nations [the Arab countries], those which, precisely, produce these goods which are vital to us.

In the next day's edition, *Le Monde* used its daily (unsigned) editorial column to look at Jobert's stance and France's relations with the U.S. and other European countries. Typically, this editorial cited various positions, and their pros and cons, before deciding that the French viewpoint is the best. Some excerpts from "ALONE . . ." (2/13/74 — 1):

> Must Europe be Atlantic or European? Doesn't it have the right to exist unless it integrates itself into a West directed by the United States, or is it an end in itself? That is the question. . . .
>
> Undoubtedly, in the same solitude in which General de Gaulle took delight, Mr. Jobert, who was authorized by President Pompidou at his departure from Paris, to "re-pack his little suitcase" and break away, [and] if he deemed it necessary, to repeat: "And if there's only one left, I'll be that one." To be alone when one is convinced of the justness of his cause, why not, indeed? What good is it to "create Europe" — an objective proclaimed and little contested in all French politics — if it's necessary to mean by that the consequences of a dependence in deeds and rights? . . .
>
> [French opposition] is not justified, however, unless it is not systematic, unless the refusals of Mr. Jobert are not a goal but a weapon.

With a beautiful touch of irony, the article concludes:

> That Europe be European, that she strains with all her forces towards independence, so be it. But she doesn't have any chance of succeeding unless the governments, starting with that of Paris, accept a strict community discipline.

A few weeks earlier, a similar editorial chided other European countries for succumbing to Washington's influence. "WHY WASHINGTON?" (1/24/74 — 1) gave both the American and French arguments about energy crisis tactics, and pointed out that Foreign Minister Jobert had proposed a European—Arab oil conference before the Washington meeting was even suggested. Jobert's plan never hatched, though, because: ". . . it's the [other] European countries [rather than the Arabs], traditionally oriented towards Washington, and who fear creating competition against the Kissinger project, whom it is difficult to convince."

Le Monde's normal coverage of American internal affairs is an unpredictable melting pot of events and people, ranging from Martha Mitchell's latest harangues (7/4/72) to ex-Black Panther Bobby Seale's bid for the Oakland mayorship (7/20/73) to a retrospective on what's happened to the American black movement since Martin Luther King's assassination (2/10—11/74) to a six-page spread on the State of Illinois (6/29/74). The latter is part of the paper's admirable attempt to get the world acquainted with itself, an effort particularly evident in the monthly *Le Monde Diplomatique*.

Coverage of the Watergate affair was thorough in *Le Monde*'s particular way. Again cross-breeding the daily deadline with newsmagazine reflectiveness, the paper usually ran short wire stories of several events before one of its correspondents contributed a longer and more interpretative analysis of these events. From June 22, 1972 when the break-in first drew mention, and especially from March 1973 when it beat most other European publications to latching onto Watergate, *Le Monde* left few stones unturned. Its reporters examined the scandal aspects of Watergate as offshoots of the American political system, and its prosecution as the flip-side of the coin. They followed its consequences in terms of domestic politics and foreign policy, regularly gauged public opinion, detailed America's crisis functioning, tapped the congressional mood, outlined judicial functioning, and footnoted institutional procedures and idiosyncracies. For the most part their interpretative reporting provided an essential context for the "facts" of a story. Still, they occasionally overstepped the fine line separating interpretative — or in-depth — reporting from personal opinion, and exhibited some distinct attitudes about people, events or procedures.

Henri Pierre was particularly skeptical about Nixon's actions and reactions, never hesitating to point out contradictions between word and deed — or word and word. In his piece covering Nixon's 1974 State of the Union message, Pierre wrote:

"One year of Watergate is enough!" declared Mr. Nixon, as if it concerned a trivial affair which shouldn't prevent the President from accomplishing his great peace mission abroad and, at home, resolving the energy crisis, reducing inflation and maintaining prosperity. Previously, Mr. Nixon had emphasized that he intended to cooperate with the investigators in furnishing to the Special Prosecutor all the necessary items to "condemn the guilty and clear the innocent. . . ." But, of course, this cooperation will be limited to those things which wouldn't weaken the presidential functioning. . . .

After citing Nixon's promise to ensure safeguards against government snooping on private citizens through wiretapping, etc.:

Mr. Nixon speaks admirably on the matter. Never, previously, had the practice of clandestine eavesdropping been as highly developed and encouraged as during his administration (2/1/74 — 4).

On Nixon's view of executive privilege:

It's to protect the presidential institution — which he confuses with his person — and to defend the confidential character ... [that Nixon refuses to release documents] (3/31/74 — 3).

After Nixon declared that any errors on his tax returns were committed without his knowledge or approval, Pierre commented:

That's a little like what the President hasn't ceased to claim in regard to Watergate and related scandals. Apparently, he has no better luck in the choice of his fiscal advisors than in choosing his closest collaborators, currently indicted, on trial or already in prison (5/4/74 — 12).

When Nixon balked before handing documents over to various investigatory bodies:

But, once again, instead of actively and voluntarily contributing to the investigation, the President waited until the last minute, and almost under threat, before giving an ambiguous response. . . . He's fleeing one more time behind procedural guerilla warfare, which contradicts his declared intention to permit the investigators to rapidly finish their work (11/4/74 — 8).

Other reporters deepened this skepticism, particularly Jacques Amalric. Predicting the resignations of Haldeman, Ehrlichman and Dean a good month in advance, he wrote:

The indignant denials of the White House convince no one any longer, even in Congressional Republican ranks, for the President has already been caught flagrantly lying about this affair. Another method of defense — for example, a severe purge of the President's entourage — risks soon becoming inevitable. Senate investigators affirm, in fact, that James McCord is only at the beginning of his revelations and that other names, again from the White House, are going to follow (3/28/73 — 5).

When Nixon finally dropped the nomination of Patrick Gray for FBI chief:

Rather sacrifice a friend — after all too talkative and much too naive — than to allow Mr. Dean to explain his strange behavior. . . . Thus ends the short "national" career of Mr. Gray, victim of his compliance regarding the White House, then of his incapability to hide the truth (4/7/73 — 6).

After Nixon pulled his first come-clean act in purging the White House staff:

The problem for Mr. Nixon is that it took 10 months to revise his position. In fact, he affirmed that it was because of a "personal" inquiry that he had discovered the grave suspicions weighing down on his collaborators. But how can one forget that since the summer not one day has passed without a newspaper or television station bringing some information to light on the ramifications of the scandal? How can one forget that all the names cited today had already been cited for several months? How can one believe that Mr. Nixon doesn't read the press, particularly the *Washington Post*, which has been the most tenacious in the search for the truth? (4/26/73 — 3).

Following the purge, in an article headed "THE WHITE HOUSE EXERCISED DIRECT AND REPEATED PRESSURES", Amalric led off:

Three steps forward, two back. . . . Mr. Nixon hasn't modified his method of defense in the Watergate affair, and the day has not yet come when the White House will cooperate entirely in the search for the whole truth (5/10/73 — 4).

John Dean's testimony and the White House's embarrassed response convinced Amalric that: "the Watergate fiasco wasn't an accident, it was the logical culmination of a quasi-totalitarian conception of power." (5/16/73 — 5.) Whether Nixon's actions are the result of "total incompetence in the choice of his collaborators, or prolonged duplicity" matters little because neither explanation is "royal or glorious" (5/23/73 — 5). Nixon's repeated "national security" rationalizations don't hold water since that is "a universal notion which isn't any better defined on this side of the Atlantic than in France" (5/27/73 — 4). Nixon is obviously more "a man of law ready to use all the science's resources, than a President desirous of winning back the confidence of his constituents" (5/24/73 — 4).

Amalric also reserved some special barbs for "officious White House spokesman" Ronald Ziegler (5/6/73 — 5) and the fuzzy ethics of John Dean's desertion of the White House. In an article with the subtitle "The Blackmail of Immunity," he wrote:

> ... since he began collaborating with the judiciary and the Senate Watergate Committee ... Mr. Dean has carefully organized leaks, revealing by bits and pieces most of his accusations against Mr. Nixon (5/27/73 — 3).

Prior to that, Amalric had described Dean as the "Judas" of the Watergate affair, and someone "far from being a likeable person" (5/14/73 — 7).

André Clément added more skepticism — some directed at Nixon, but more toward the American system in general. But at first, some astonishment:

> One remains confounded in the face of these unlawful, sordid or puerile activities incessantly employed by the "committee" for the reelection of a politician while all the forecasts at that time indicated he had already won (6/7/73 — 3).

Clément said that Watergate had created the "impression among the public that the institution of the Presidency had been 'profaned' " (1/8/74 — 3). Responding to the State of the Union speech and alluding to the Besançon watch factory uproar in France, he wrote: " 'Lip, c'est fini' 'One year of Watergate is enough': The major capitals have the secret of definitive formulas" (2/5/74 — 6). After Wilbur Mills stuck to his contention that Nixon's tax matters would be more damaging than Watergate, despite White House rebuttals, Clément reminded his readers:

> You will remember that the under-secretary of the Treasury, Mr.

Edward Morgan, who approved the most contestable fiscal deductions of Mr. Nixon, recently handed in his resignation and is not
making a mystery of his bad conscience (3/14/74 — 6).

More often, Clément's criticism fell onto the American system
and its Watergate functioning. Following Agnew's resignation,
he wrote in "A CONSTITUTIONAL LABYRINTH":

> The crisis opened by the Watergate affair wouldn't provoke such
> interest in the United States — where it has been the star for several
> months, and isn't finished yet — if it wasn't a living commentary
> on a political system that is complex and rigid at the same time.
> Rigid because, contrary to parliamentary democracies, it excludes
> the "recourse at the ballot box". The election dates are fixed to
> barely one day by the Constitution and it would be sacrilege —
> simply unthinkable — to move them ahead. Complex because this
> Constitution, to which people refer as to the Holy Writ, neither
> said nor forecast everything: the Supreme Court is there, precisely
> to decipher gradually the dialectic revelation of its message (10/12/
> 73 — 1).

Clearly disturbed by what he considered to be American insensi-
tivity to fallen politicians like Spiro Agnew, Clément said that
whether or not Nixon is eventually deposed:

> ... is, for the honest American, almost a clinical alternative. Mr.
> Nixon never made hearts throb. And besides, what does it mean
> *the morning after* [in English], the day after a sentence without
> appeal? Mr. Agnew, who for four years was the most capable star
> for electrifying Republican listeners, fell into the trap of unworthi-
> ness (by scandal). Without a shiver, without a noticeable stir among
> millions who formerly applauded him, he simply disappeared from
> news columns (10/12/73 — 1).

The Senate Watergate Committee, he said, was divided "in
agony" over whether to continue public hearings, but in any
case has already fulfilled its role in providing "major documents
of self-criticism of which the American society is capable".
Nixon was in trouble because he "refuses to play the 'straight
game' by the written and unwritten rules of American democracy". An eventual vote on impeachment is and will remain
unpredictable, he said, because "the American [political]
parties, being what they are, in other words of nebulous interests
and tendencies", prevent the kind of strict party-line votes
characteristic of France. "The procedure of impeachment in

itself is neither glorious nor ignominious", but it is unfair since "the rights of the defense are practically ignored in that it's the House which investigates and indicts" (1/18/74 — 3). When the Ervin Committee's public hearings were cancelled in order not to prejudice jurors in the Mitchell—Stans trial, Clément put tongue in cheek in describing the " 'virginity of spirit' which members of an American jury are supposed to maintain in order to render a verdict in all impartiality" (1/29/74 — 3). Once Watergate was over, he back-pedalled a little to explain that the different institutions, ideals and procedures which had manifested themselves during the crisis constituted "the core of that which attaches Americans to *their* democracy, and not to ours" (8/10—11/74 — 1).

Other writers also took potshots at the American system. Near the end of the crisis, Henri Pierre wrote:

> Finally, the Ervin Committee, often criticized and whose role was quickly eclipsed by the various developments in the affair, attacked the roots of the evil in establishing something which many Americans wish to ignore, to know that Watergate isn't so much an exceptional accident as it is a normal manifestation of these politics whose uncontrolled financial pressures play an inordinate role (7/17/74 — 5).

Jacques Amalric, noting that James McCord's testimony took place behind closed doors, sniped that "the Senate hardly knows how to keep a secret, and the essence of his declarations is now public knowledge" (3/28/73 — 5). Jean-Alain Royer wrote in *The Eagle*:

> Having washed its dirty linen in public, the American democracy, stronger and healthier than ever, will be able to continue giving lessons in morals to the entire world. Does anyone imagine that *The Eagle*, one day, would lower its head? (5/12/73 — 1).

Robert Escarpit often used the "From Day to Day" box to take jabs at America. One example, just before Nixon's resignation:

> President Nixon confessed and people say he's going to make his act of contrition. But puritan civilizations grant absolution less easily than Catholic civilizations.
> One thinks of the novel by Nathaniel Hawthorne, *The Scarlet Letter*, whose theme is hidden sin and in which a pastor wears a black veil over his face during his entire life, until the moment

when the letter engraved into his flesh reveals him as a sinner.
A long time ago President Nixon's veil of respectability was
torn by all the winds of the political storm. But America feared
discovering that the red mark was inscribed in its own flesh and
that a scapegoat wasn't sufficient to erase it (8/8/74 — 1).

Le Monde's front-page editorials variously criticized and compli-
mented the American system. Following Agnew's resignation:

> It is true that if this affair illustrates hardly enviable political morals,
> it also bears witness to Americans' good citizenship ever since
> justice began doing its job (10/12/73 — 1).

In reaction to the Saturday Night Massacre:

> . . . attitude of defiance, which the American presidential system
> encourages by its rigidity. In no parliamentary democracy would
> Mr. Nixon still be the first person of the State. The American
> Constitution gives him a *de facto* impunity more exorbitant than
> all the "executive privilege" invoked by him. Mr. Nixon's cause
> being morally understood, it's now up to Americans to open the
> trial [impeachment] of this obsolete Constitution (10/23/72 — 1).

After Nixon's resignation, André Fontaine contributed
"Sacrilege" (8/10/74 — 1, 2). Some excerpts:

> We no longer knew it, we no longer wanted to believe it. But there's
> still at least one nation on this earth where the law, decidedly, is
> stronger than men, where, just named by the President, some judges
> were capable of making some decisions against him, where a party
> can prefer the manifestation of justice over maintaining one of
> their own in power. . . .

> Also the idea that the President of the United States must give
> up his place to the liberties he took with the truth doesn't leave
> [Americans] astonished. As for the Watergate scandal, we have
> heard much that the wiretapping at *Le Canard* is only a weak replica,
> [but] the fact is that France has had some others.

> Our old Catholic countries, by dint of frequenting them, have
> become very indulgent toward sins. But the Americans, despite the
> excesses of competition and counterculture . . . haven't yet loosened
> the cocoon of moralism, into which the puritans put their political
> life. . . .

> At the bottom, if [Nixon] was a traitor to the American dream
> he was also, to a certain extent, the victim. In a system which
> exalts to such a great extent the individual and the struggle for
> life, which professes that every citizen can . . . ascend to the highest
> responsibilities, how many, each day, burning in the flame, of whom
> no one ever speaks, because, less tough or more scrupulous than
> Richard Nixon, they become discouraged earlier. . . .

Le Monde's journalists often noted the differences in cultural outlooks and ideas as making Watergate difficult to understand for Europeans and particularly the French.

> Of course a foreigner, especially a Frenchman, can become astonished at how far this [affair] has come, following what was only, at the start, a sordid wiretapping incident (5/10/73 — 4).

The inevitable question "IS A 'WATERGATE' POSSIBLE IN FRANCE?", by Pierre Viansson-Ponté (6/5/73 — 1, 3) again drew a negative response. There are several reasons: America is a much more open society where "individual liberties are better guaranteed than in France, with all the consequences that brings in one sense or the other for each person". Public life in the U.S. is much more exposed, and exchanges between officials, the press and other agencies much more candid and rude. The press is less respectful and therefore more respected, and it is much less encumbered than the French press with libel laws and their strict enforcement. Still, it's not inconceivable that these cultural and institutional obstacles could be overcome. But, he concluded, there is one final factor which cannot be overlooked:

> Everything leads us to believe that in its own manner, within the practical, legal and moral limits to which it is assigned, a French newspaper could have found the means to uncover a Parisian Watergate. But it must be immediately added that, whether skeptical or resigned, in any case too used to the way power uses and abuses illegal procedures, arbitrary measures, exceptional jurisdictions, secrets and propaganda, the French are quicker to speak ironically about the misdeeds and turpitudes of those who govern them than to be truly indignant.

After Nixon released the final tapes proving that he really knew about everything all the time, André Clément wrote that most Europeans were baffled not only by the enormity of his misdeeds, but even more so by the prosecution of Watergate and the "kind of parliamentary decapitation to which he is now exposed". Then he chided *The Times* of London for taking so long to realize that impeachment, " — a word nevertheless of purely British origin — was not a barbarous recourse". Not only do people on the Continent lack the semantic and historical guidelines of Britishers, but "on this side of the English Channel, it's in good form to profess a certain skepticism regarding all institutional sanctions of political power" (8/7/74 — 1, 2).

When Nixon finally resigned, *Le Monde* reported that American journalists in Paris were seeking French man-on-the-street views, while French reporters were scurrying to American hangouts. Said Nan Robertson of the *New York Times*:

> For two years, people have often asked the paper to interview French people about Watergate. In general, the most frequent reaction is: after all, all governments are more or less corrupt, everyone knows that, it's always been like that . . . . In short, one sometimes gets the impression that the French judge us as being a little naive to get upset about it. And that is extraordinary. . . ."

The article, titled "WHERE ARE THE CYNICS?", concluded that "the gaulois cynicism incessantly feeds and comforts the 'corruption' which it pretends to put up with" (8/10/74 — 9). Finally, in a classic case of missing the point of what Watergate was all about, Robert Escarpit said in "DEMOCRACY AND THE PALACE REVOLUTION":

> The great leap in American democratic conscience which led Mr. Nixon to his resignation at the same time placed in the Presidency of the United States, for two years and probably more, a man who was not elected to the office and for whom the Vice-President will also be co-opted.
> That isn't to say that Mr. Ford won't be a good President. The fact that he isn't a political monster but a simple professional rather falls in his favor.
> There is still no less irony in the fact that the American people, even if they were well-informed, weren't called on to vote and that one of the biggest decisions [of the country's history] in the final analysis had the dimensions of a palace revolution and a settling of accounts at the heart of the political class (8/11—12/74 — 1).

Summary

Escarpit wasn't alone in missing the point, though he was often the farthest from it. All of *Le Monde*'s journalists at one time or another stated or hinted that the way America was handling the scandal left a lot to be desired, and perhaps it should become a little more like Europe. André Clément said that while "politics is a sport" in America, European governments consist of "technicians, in general honest" (5/5/73 — 4). An obsolete Constitution was blamed for injecting rigidity into the American political system and giving exorbitant powers to a President who would never have survived the scandal that long in a parliamentary democracy. Not only were *Le Monde*'s journalists convinced that the scandalous aspects of Watergate were inextricably rooted in the American political system, but they were also impatient with and often critical of its prosecution. In this sense, they missed or misread many points.

First of all, it remains highly debatable — given *Le Monde*'s own reportage of domestic politics — that top officials in the French government (where patronage likewise plays a substantial role in recruiting a new administration) are any more "generally honest technicians" than their American counterparts. Secondly, it may be reasonably argued that it's precisely the American Constitution's flexibility which has accounted for its survival and guaranteed political stability during social evolution. The fact that it is constantly being interpreted hardly lends support to its alleged obsolescence. And the Constitution does not grant the President exorbitant powers: Nixon simply took them, with the help of several predecessors who consolidated power in the Executive Branch over the years. Whether or not a President would have survived for as long in France once a comparable scandal surfaced remains a moot question since — as *Le Monde* and the other French media pointed out — it's highly unlikely that it would surface in the first place, for reasons ranging from press restrictions to power balances and public cynicism. Most importantly, the fact that Americans didn't go to the polls to elect a new President after Nixon's resignation is simply irrelevant. Other mechanisms were functioning with public approval and confidence: the Twenty-Fifth Amendment, enacted after John Kennedy's assassination, constitutionally sanctioned Ford's Vice-Presidency; when Nixon stepped down, Ford took over. That both the new President and Vice-President, for the first time in history, had not been elected caused little concern. The transition of power was undramatic and smooth — probably more so than either Harold Wilson's replacement of Edward Heath as Prime Minister of Great Britain or the more recent political turnover in Australia — and even *Le Monde*'s correspondents expressed surprise at this. And, contrary to Escarpit's imagery, Watergate was hardly a "palace revolution". Few, if any, political issues in the United States have ever aroused the widespread public interest or the amount of integrated functioning of the American political system that Watergate did. If anyone could have survived a palace revolution, Richard Nixon could have. And he did not survive.

A few other attitudes deserve brief mention. First, some largely unsubstantiated assumptions about the pervasiveness of corruption in American politics. Nixon and his entourage of "politicians and shady figures getting together to exchange styles of corruption" (4/24/73 — 3) reflected the "normal and almost inevitable venality of the political milieu" (5/2/73 — 2). André Clément wrote:

> Isn't American politics thus, at the bottom of things, only "banditry", each new President bringing with him a court of astrologers, experts, favorites, agents with no political responsibility and who bring in their wake an army of clients, debtors and beggars?
> It's always more or less that (5/5/73 — 4).

These and similar comments presented Watergate as simply the latest manifestation of longstanding and widespread political corruption in the United States. Sometimes this image was backed up with specific historical examples, but more often it was left hanging as a "fact".

A related image created by *Le Monde* might be called the "cowboy": a picture of Americans and American life as being fierce, unruly, cut-throat, violent and crude. The Nixon—Agnew battle leading to the latter's resignation provided "an unprecedented scene for a European" (10/3/73 — 5). Political maneuvering between people or institutions was often described as "guerilla warfare", impeachment was repeatedly referred to as "decapitation", either of Nixon or of the entire United States

(11/23/73 — 1), and James Buckley was quoted as saying that if the House impeached Nixon, it would "deliver him to the electronic lions of the Senate [which would] become the Coliseum of the twentieth century" (3/31/74 — 3). Some spectators lining the Supreme Court steps seemed to want to transform the Jaworski—St. Clair tapes debate into a boxing match (7/10/74). Watergate was a "manhunt" (8/9/74 — 1). One of the reasons its prosecution was possible, said Pierre Viansson-Ponté, was the openness of public life in the United States:

> ... the tone and climate of public life are much more harsh in America than in France. On television, before the press, the [White House] directors and the President himself gladly express themselves with a brutality, a harshness, a crudity sometimes on the attack or in retort, which [in France] would make one gasp. They are very far from our padded, allusive debates, from our disputes with capped foils, from our conventional attitudes, like elsewhere the customs of courtesy and formality practiced in the British Parliament (6/5/73 — 3).

This lack of courtesy bothered Alain-Marie Carron, who said about Nixon's tax returns that "one cannot help but be somewhat upset in seeing the petty calculations of the President of the United States exposed to the whole world or, at the very least, in front of tens of millions of television watchers ..." (8/1/74 — 2).

Le Monde never indulged in a conspiracy theory, but occasionally threw hints in that direction. André Clément described Nixon's support in helping Conservative Senator James Buckley defeat *"enfant terrible"* Goodell for Bobby Kennedy's old seat. Leading a campaign against Nixon in March 1974, he became "James Buckley or Brutus ..." (3/22/74 — 7). Henri Pierre said "It's necessary to go back to Roosevelt to find a President who aroused such hatred" and "partisan passion" (3/31/74 — 1). Alain-Marie Carron maintained that the Democratic majority of the commission investigating Nixon's tax returns had intentionally scheduled its hearings for prime time on television (8/1/74 — 2).

Similarly, the paper steered clear of sweeping character

studies while noting a Nixon trait here or there. A front-page editorial responding to the State of the Union discourse began:

> No American President, in the situation in which Mr. Nixon finds himself, could have done it better than he. While his main collaborators of yesterday are being indicted or appearing before their judges, while some of their subordinates are in prison, while he himself is under threat of being deposed and in violation of the public treasury of his own country, Mr. Nixon had no other resource than to put the multiple worries "in parentheses" and to move on to the agenda for the year 1974 (2/1/74 — 1).

The final paragraph in a description of Nixon's Black List said that: "It was undoubtedly by treating evil with evil that certain members of Mr. Nixon's team intended to save the country from the attempt at general demoralization launched by decadent liberals" (6/29/73 — 4). Much of the comment on Nixon leaned toward the idea that he got what was coming to him because of his own behavior:

> It wasn't so long ago that, to the frequent applause of his listeners, Mr. Spiro Agnew subjected to public derision the "effete snobs" of the press and other liberal circles. In Chicago, his successor to the Vice-Presidency didn't mince his words about the "arrogant adolescents" of the "Committee for the Reelection of the President". But everyone understood: Mr. Nixon has had the [public] servants he deserves (4/2/74 — 1).

Le Monde's reporters clearly disliked Nixon, but also exhibited a variation of respect based on his uncanny ability to wriggle out of tight situations or turn the tide in his favor. Alain-Marie Carron may well have been projecting his own feelings onto "the people" when he wrote:

> The people gathered [at the Capitol] are breathtaken by a rebounding intrigue, worried and seduced at the same time by the idea that, in some still unknown way, the "villain" will succeed, by some miraculous trick, in eluding his destiny or simply delay infinitely the hour of the last judgment (8/2/74 — 4).

Finally, *Le Monde*'s attitude toward the American press fell between those of *L'Est Républicain* and *L'Express*. Regarding its crucial role in uncovering Watergate, the American press was complemented and sometimes defended by *Le Monde*'s reporters. Jacques Amalric reminded readers that without the press, "the Watergate operation would have been definitively buried" (5/3/73 — 1), and maintained that although justice would be a long time in coming for the Watergate affair, "an injustice was rectified" when the *Washington Post* received the Pulitzer Prize for its work (5/9/73 — 3). Michel Tatu defended the press's aggressiveness at White House press conferences by saying:

> Those who judge this behavior as "irresponsible" simply haven't understood that such a press has to be responsible before nothing other than that which it believes to be the truth of the matter (5/16/73 — 4).

In answering the question of whether or not Watergate could occur in France, Pierre Viansson-Ponté compared the American press to its French counterpart:

> Inclined by temperament and incited by professional competition to incessantly search in order to be in the know, American journalists are less respectful than their European colleagues and, because of this, they're more respected (6/5/73 — 3).

Henri Pierre was a little less enthusiastic, due mainly to a number of journalists who, feeling "the spirit of Judas or Robin Hood", jumped on the Watergate bandwagon after Woodward and Bernstein had started it rolling. Still, he said, the sour relationship between the press and White House fell every bit as much on the latter due to its secrecy and non-cooperation. As a final word, Pierre criticized a Supreme Court ruling which denied equal-space access for rebuttals of political candidates, as well as America's financially-based media system. The Court's decision, he said:

> . . . gives priority to the defense of a free press, even if insufficient or abusive, over the public's right to be informed most completely and most objectively, and to make itself heard among media controlled by financial fiefdoms (7/4/74 — 4).

REFERENCES

1. Morgan, Betty T., *Histoire du Journal des Scavans*, Paris, Presses Universitaires de France, 1929.
2. Albert, P., and Terrou, F., *Histoire de la Presse*, Paris, Presses Universitaires de France, 1974, pp. 37, 80.

3. Frémy, Dominique, and Frémy, Michèle, *Quid? 1975*, Paris, Éditions Laffont, 1975, pp. 1049, 1131.
4. Albert, Pierre, *La Presse*, Paris, Presses Universitaires de France, 1973, p. 80.
5. Albert and Terrou, p. 12.
6. Albert and Terrou, pp. 15, 20.
7. Albert and Terrou, p. 25.
8. Albert and Terrou, pp. 28—30.
9. Albert and Terrou, pp. 66—69.
10. Albert, p. 80.
11. Albert and Terrou, pp. 77—79.
12. Albert and Terrou, pp. 106—22.
13. Albert and Terrou, pp. 78—86.
14. Frémy and Frémy, pp. 1057—58.
15. Albert, p. 86.
16. Albert, p. 61.
17. Albert, pp. 92—93.
18. Frémy and Frémy, p. 1055.
19. UNESCO in Fischer and Merrill, p. 276.
20. Albert and Terrou, pp. 121—22.
21. Albert, p. 76.
22. *Cinéma 75*, numéro 196, pp. 63—64.
23. Hardt, Hanno, "The Plight of the Daily Press in Western Europe," in Fischer and Merrill, p. 289.
24. Albert, pp. 17—18, 90—94.
25. Albert and Terrou, pp. 83—113.
26. Hardt in Fischer and Merrill, p. 289.
27. Albert, pp. 78, 81.
28. Frémy and Frémy, p. 1057.
29. Albert, pp. 82—83.
30. Albert, pp. 44—46.
31. Albert, pp. 19, 67.
32. Albert, pp. 94—96.
33. Frémy and Frémy, pp. 1061—64.
34. Albert, pp. 88, 96.
35. Albert and Terrou, p. 122.
36. Albert, p. 48.
37. Albert, pp. 48—55, 81.
38. Albert and Terrou, p. 114.
39. Albert, p. 54.
40. Frémy and Frémy, p. 1057.
41. Frémy and Frémy, p. 1200.
42. Albert, p. 66.
43. Albert, p. 36.
44. Frémy and Frémy, p. 1055.
45. Albert, p. 35.
46. Frémy and Frémy, p. 1055.
47. Albert, p. 36.
48. Frémy and Frémy, p. 1054.

49. Albert, p. 42.
50. Frémy and Frémy, pp. 753, 1124—30.
51. Albert, p. 76.
52. Albert, p. 93.
53. Frémy and Frémy, p. 1072.
54. Frémy and Frémy, p. 1027.
55. Albert, p. 94.
56. Frémy and Frémy, pp. 1221, 1227.
57. Timothy Crouse, "The Great Pro-American Novel," *Esquire*, December 1975, p. 27.
58. Boris, Claude, *Les Tigres de Papier: Crise de la presse et (auto) critique du journalisme*, Paris, Éditions du Seuil, 1975, pp. 164—67.
59. Boris, p. 142.
60. Albert, p. 90.
61. Frémy and Frémy, p. 1071.
62. Boris, pp. 144, 145.
63. Boris, pp. 143, 144.

4. The Legitimization Function of the Press: Perspectives on Watergate

> The formation of a party — if this party is not properly represented by a well-known newspaper — remains to a significant degree just words.
>
> V. I. Lenin

The question of the "effects" of the mass media is one that has haunted journalists, politicians and social scientists alike for decades. Just exactly what does a newspaper do to a person who reads it? Does it, or any other medium, have the power to change attitudes, opinions, or behavior? Is this supposed power more important than what it can do to a powerful politician who is about to make an important decision concerning his career, his party or his nation?

The role that the mass media play in a modern democratic society is an elusive one, but its importance cannot be denied. In these next two chapters, we will be taking a look at what that role is and how we can better understand it.

There used to be little doubt about what sort of effect the mass media in a literate society could have. It was seen to be all-encompassing and all-powerful. It was a bandwagon of public opinion which, once rolling, could rarely be stopped. Press baron Lord Northcliffe summed it up, saying: "The whole country will think with us when we say the word."[1]

The frightful experiences of Nazi Germany in the thirties sealed this picture into our heads. Hitler's minister of information, Dr. Goebbels, had gained control of the nation's mass media and had so distorted the messages they sent out that a nation of decent, industrious and intelligent people was turned into a pit of racial hatred with a fanatical desire to make war. It was all so obvious for most of us that it needed no further verification. The verification was to be found in the 55 million people thought to have lost their lives as a result of World War II.

The coming of television only increased the general public's wariness toward the "effects" of mass media. Here was a new persuader, brought easily and cheaply into our homes, able to sway the unassuming public with even greater efficiency. Again, we did not need much verification for our attitudes. It came early with Richard Nixon's "Checkers" speech. With just half an hour of talking straight into the camera, Nixon had saved his political career and turned himself into an asset for, rather than an anchor to, the Eisenhower presidential ticket. Richard Nixon had spoken directly to us, and we had immediately responded, doing exactly as he had bid us.

About this same time, social scientists were approaching the question of mass media "effects" from their own perspective. They were surveying, interviewing, and speculating on just what it was that led people to make political decisions. Many concentrated on the mass media, asking in any number of ways if what a person read in a newspaper or saw on a television screen made any difference in the kinds of political actions he or she took.

They found that, in general, it didn't.

Joseph Klapper summed up 20 years of mass communications research in 1960 and listed two of the conclusions that could be drawn from this research:

1. Mass communication ordinarily does not serve as a necessary and sufficient cause of audience effects, but rather functions among and through a nexus of mediating factors and influences.
2. These mediating factors are such that they typically render mass communication a contributory agent, but not the sole cause, in a process of reinforcing the existing conditions . . . .[2]

Klapper had formulated what two later researchers called the "law of minimal consequences",[3] and those familiar with social science literature were reduced to arguing that the mass media could not change our attitudes but could only reinforce the ones we already held.

That litany did not catch on with the general public, however. Nor did the message ever really get through to politicians. The belief that the mass media could change us, that it did have some effect, never really died.

Actually, neither view of the mass media — that they act as an all-powerful persuader or that they only reinforce — makes much sense when applied generally. All of us, from our own experience, know of cases where the press has definitely changed attitudes and others where it has singularly failed to do so. Social scientists had possibly made the mistake of putting too much emphasis on, or misreading, Harold Lasswell's communications formula: who says, what, through what channel, to whom, with what effect. Though useful in many ways, the formula is, in the words of Colin Seymour-Ure, "narrow and static" and has forced us to focus on audience analysis in mass communication research. Consequently, we have ignored studying the press in the context of its political or social environment.[4]

AGENDA-SETTING

Researchers have recently vaulted themselves past the studies of the forties and the fifties and are again taking up the subject of effects. Accepting the basic results of these studies that only in rare instances is there a direct, measurable response to information or opinion in the mass media, they have found a different, more reasonable kind of "effect": agenda-setting. The elements of the mass media "help at least choose the subject we have views *about*, regardless of the question whether they decide *what* views we have".[5]

That periodic chronicler of presidential campaigns, Theodore White, recognized the agenda-setting role of the press in his book about the 1972 election:

No great act of the American Congress, no foreign adventure, no act of diplomacy, no great social reform can succeed in the United States unless the press prepares the public mind.[6]

And what has been said on a journalistic level, communications researchers have taken up on a research level. In surveys taken in the Charlotte, N.C. area, remarkable correlations were found between what subjects newspapers and television presented and those uppermost in the minds of individuals interviewed.

> . . . People do learn from mass communication. Not only do they learn factual information about public affairs and what is happening in the world. They also learn how much importance to attach to an issue or topic from the emphasis placed on it by the mass media. Considerable evidence has accumulated that editors and broadcasters play an important part in shaping our social reality as they go about their day-to-day task of choosing and displaying news. In their reports both prior to and during political campaigns the news media to a considerable degree determine the important issues. In other words, the media set the "agenda" for the campaign.
>
> This impact of the mass media — the ability to effect cognitive change among individuals — has been labeled the *agenda-setting function of mass communication.* Here may lie the most important effect of mass communication, its ability to structure our world for us. In short, the mass media may not be successful in telling us what to think, but they are stunningly successful in telling us what to think *about.* [7]

In outlining some of the relationships between the press and the formulation of U.S. foreign policy, Bernard Cohen also talks about the agenda-setting functions of the press. The State Department, he says, may place certain priorities on issues with which they have to deal, but once those issues go into the public forum, the priorities may have to change.

> . . . under certain circumstances the order of priority that the press attaches to policy items may be superimposed upon the significance originally and ordinarily attached to them in the State Department and elsewhere and eventually even come to supercede those original estimations.[8]

With Congress the press is even more powerful in this regard. Because of the lack of expertise in foreign policy on Capitol Hill and the minimal contacts between State Department officials and Congressmen, legislators depend heavily on the press not only for information but also for priorities.

> It would seem that their [Congressmen's] own dependence on the
> press is so complete that they absorb most of the ordering of impor-
> tance that takes place in a newspaper as an original form of reality,
> . . . the order that is in the press becomes *their* order. . . . [9]

As important a function as agenda-setting is, we are left with
the feeling that there is something more about the "effects"
of the press that we should know. The mass media almost
certainly order our world and define its limits to a great extent,
but in doing that, what are some of the spin-off effects?

Taking up this question, Colin Seymour-Ure has examined
the role of the press in the context of British parliamentary
government. The British political system relies more heavily on
the cohesiveness of party groups than does the American system,
and Seymour-Ure studies some of the roles that the British
national press plays and the effects they can have within this
context of cohesiveness. He concludes, not surprisingly, that
mass media are so embedded in the political system, and the
system so dependent on them, that political activity could not
take place without them; and that the "effects of a communication process may vary according to the level of political relationships considered".[10] The author also presents several case
studies demonstrating the perceived powers of the press and
the role of lateral communications among politicians.

WHO DO YOU TRUST?

That ungrammatical question was the name for a daytime
game show popular on American television several years ago.
Lightly put, it provided amusement for participants and audience
alike.

The question takes on crucial importance in the political
realm, however. In fact, the answers to it form the basis for
survival of a political system and the institutions within it.
Political systems continue, in great part, because people trust
them; they have credibility; they have *legitimacy*.

Legitimacy of political systems has often been linked with
development. Beginning political systems must gain credibility

with those they are trying to govern. As Karl Deutsch has written, they must gather the "symbols of legitimacy".[11] But gaining legitimacy is not a one-time thing. Like communication itself, it is an on-going process with which governments and institutions are — and should be — consistently concerned.

One of the symbols of legitimacy of a political system is the mass media. The traditional view of the mass media in a democratic society is summed up by Fredrick W. Frey:

> The media function as an integral part of the governing mechanism, checking and controlling the main branches of formal government and parties by giving publicity to their operations, supplementing official communications and providing essential information to diverse actors — especially to those outside the government but also to those within it.[12]

The information-giving role of the press is certainly a vital one, as is the agenda-setting role, but it is not the only one. There is a more subtle role which we may call *legitimization*. Legitimization combines information-giving, lateral communications among political actors (including journalists themselves), and agenda-setting. In short, by the simple process of presenting or reproducing ideas, the press "legitimizes" them for discussion within the political arena. A statement produced in a newspaper, for example, may take on much greater importance because those reading it will perceive that others, too, are reading it, that others are thinking about it, and that a politically astute editor has thought enough of it to allow it to get into print.

Cohen gives a good example of this in his analysis of the press and foreign policy. In the 1950s certain members of Congress were becoming increasingly distrustful of the presidential proclivity to make executive agreements with other nations. Since these agreements were not treaties, they did not need Senate approval. To stop this, a constitutional amendment, known as the Bicker Amendment, was introduced. One Senate staff member told Cohen that no one took much notice of the Bicker Amendment until a newspaper began writing stories on it, "thereby establishing an importance for it". The staff member is quoted as saying: "The important thing is . . . . the fact that coverage is there to keep . . . an issue alive among the people."[13]

It is unlikely that the Bicker Amendment stirred the hearts of many Americans. The "people" to which the staff member was really referring were those interested in the subject. Because the press had given its attention to the amendment, and because of the perceived powers of the press to mirror what others are thinking about, the issue — for all its lack of merit — had become a topic of heated debate. Not only had it made the agenda, but it had also been legitimized for discussion.

Legitimization can be a cumulative thing, too. The Bicker Amendment took on an importance all its own because it had been given the attention of certain reporters and editors. Soon Congressmen and Senators were talking about it, and then other editors and reporters began writing about it. Alternatives were suggested; counter and watering-down amendments were proposed. This activity stemmed not necessarily from the proposal itself but from the attention it had been given, the legitimacy it had received.

To do their work, journalists must make certain assumptions about the people and stories they cover. These assumptions are rarely questioned; they are simply accepted, and in the hectic world of daily journalism, they are reinforced by the constant interaction of reporters with one another.

Sometimes these assumptions are implausible or even inaccurate. Once they are accepted by journalists and appear in print, however, they take on a legitimacy which may make them unassailable. The danger then is that journalists, editorial writers and readers may build interpretations and conclusions on what may be the shifting sands of ignorance rather than the more solid ground of logical thinking.

In covering Watergate, British and French journalists developed a set of assumptions about the story and the people within it, which on closer inspection were inaccurate or at best questionable. (These assumptions were often shared with, or originated by, their American colleagues.) While much of the massive coverage given to Watergate by the British and French press was fair and accurate, these assumptions prevented journalists and editorial writers from correctly interpreting what was happening in Washington, and legitimized beliefs that were not justified.

WATERGATE AS APOCALYPSE

The possible consequences of the Watergate crisis spread themselves like the tentacles of a giant, fast-growing octopus. Very quickly, they became national and international in scope. Just what effect was it having on the President and on the Presidency? Could Nixon and Kissinger maintain their foreign policy initiatives? Could Nixon and the Cabinet deal effectively with Congress and the bureaucracy? These were questions which no journalist could ignore when covering the Watergate story.

In dealing with these questions, a definite attitude developed among French and British journalists which viewed Watergate as the possible apocalypse. There was the tendency to overstate the possible consequences of the Watergate crisis without any explanation or qualification.

"America", that amorphous mass of people, buildings, hills, trees, attitudes, opinions and accents, was selected by the *Daily Mirror* as the "saddest victim of Watergate" (4/22/73 — 16). Just who or what America was and how it was being victimized and being made the "saddest victim" of Watergate is never explained.

Gauging the mood of "America" with sampling techniques such as "several days of travelling", the Gossets in *L'Est Républicain* wrote that forces, like the press, pursuing the Watergate investigation were doing so "against the current of public opinion" of people who eventually became "weary to the point of nausea" (7/24/74 — 14). The French journalists of *L'Express*, in contrast, continually touted Watergate as a triumph: a "victory of America over itself" (5/7/73 — 77), a conquest for the U.S. and for democracy, a reestablishment of public support rather than personal power as the basis for a strong government. *Le Monde* maintained that "the crisis was too hot to not leave profound wounds in the body of America and the part of the world it dominates" (8/10/74 — 2).

If all America is the victim of Watergate, then something is happening, or is about to happen to it. This, too, is not explained. We are simply left with the feeling that we are to feel sorry for America, whatever that means, for her victimization, however that is taking place. For the most part, French and British journalists just left the subject twisting slowly in the wind.

The "people of America", in various stages and forms, were often pictured as having doubts about their government and political system. The Senate Watergate hearings, *The Times* said, were "sapping confidence in and within the Government" (7/6/73 — 8). The Gossets concluded the same thing when they heard their house painter groaning about "all our leaders" (7/16/73 — 14). Here again, we are left without adequate explanation — only some one-shot impressions, asserted without any solid backing.

Two other examples of the journalistic jargon floating around at the time were Nixon's "inability to govern" and a "paralysis of government". The *Observer* spoke darkly of a 3-year "paralysis of America" which would do the world no good (5/20/73 — 10). The *Daily Telegraph* said that Watergate was "destroying America's international influence" (5/19/73 — 14), but as the chief defender of Richard Nixon among the British press, the paper also worried about his becoming like Charles II, in respect of his "inability to govern" (6/7/73 — 18).

"CAN NIXON STILL GOVERN?" and "AN UNGOVERN-ABLE AMERICA?" headlined two *L'Est* articles examining Watergate's effect in curbing presidential power vis à vis other institutions. The Gossets complained that every time Nixon exercises his "Constitutional" powers, "everyone cries dictatorship" (10/27/73 — 18). *L'Express* once proclaimed "WASHINGTON PARALYZED" in talking about the tape discrepancies (5/27/74 — 110). More often, however, the magazine noted a more limited paralysis — that of Nixon himself. He was reluctant to push détente too far; he was losing conservative support in Congress, etc. *Le Monde* warned that Watergate was "paralyzing the American executive at the moment it needs to catch its second wind" (5/2/73 — 2), "shaking the pillars of power" (5/5/73 — 4), and headlined that "THE WATERGATE SCANDAL PARALYZES THE WHITE HOUSE" (5/12/73 — 1).

All of these examples point to some real definitional problems facing journalists in covering Watergate. Just what is an "inability to govern"? Richard Nixon continued to function in most of the roles of President for most of the Watergate crisis. He continued to propose, sign, and veto legislation. His vetoes, more often than not, were upheld. He kept command of the armed forces, as evidenced by the worldwide alert in October 1973. As head of the diplomatic corps, Henry Kissinger continued to work with his support.

This is not to say that Nixon stood aloof from Watergate. His performance was definitely affected by incidents in the crisis. Despite trips to Europe and the Mideast, where crowds gathered by the million to see and cheer him, his prestige did suffer among world leaders. His increasing dependency on Kissinger was readily apparent. At home, much legislation went unproposed and many appointments were left unfilled. Yet all of this was simply categorized under the heading of "inability to govern" and readers were left with a vague feeling that all was falling apart.

And what is "paralysis of government"? The Congress continued to pass laws and the bureaucracy continued to function all during Watergate. Money was spent at an ever-increasing rate by the U.S. government. Certainly a lot of man- and woman-hours were lost within the bureaucracy by people huddled around television sets watching the Ervin hearings, but does this constitute a "paralysis of government"? The same thing happens whenever there is an exciting World Series baseball game, a cricket test match, or a World Cup soccer game. Probably the most rigorous test of governmental paralysis is the ceasing of a government to collect taxes — and that certainly didn't happen at any time during Watergate.

Was America being destroyed by Watergate? To have read parts of the British and French press, one might have thought so. The *Daily Mirror*, a master of the gloomy overstatement, constantly talked about the American political system being "doomed" (4/30/73 — 2). But even a paper with the even-handed coverage that the *Evening Standard* gave sometimes fell into that trap. Their Washington correspondent said that the "fabric of government threatened to be irretrievably damaged" by Watergate (5/2/73 — 6).

The Gossets warned early on that the "institution of the Presidency itself is in danger", that the "destruction of Richard Nixon risks being the destruction of the System itself" (5/15/73 — 14), and later lament that "never has such a tragedy been produced from such a banal news item" (7/27/74 — 14). *Le Monde*'s foreign news editor Michel Tatu diagnosed "THE UNITED STATES DISEASED WITH SCANDAL" in a two-part article (4/16, 17/73).

Numerous reasons emerged for journalists generally being unable to define the problems and possible consequences of Watergate. The Watergate story took place on a number of simultaneous fronts, and it was obviously impossible for one journalist to be at the Federal courthouse with Judge Sirica, on Capitol Hill with Senator Ervin, and at the White House press room with Ron Zeigler at the same time. There were also several missing pieces to the story, which we now know but which we did not always know. The unpredictability of the President always had the ability to keep journalists off balance. Finally, in Washington during the 2 years of Watergate, there was always a sense of impending crisis, of the coming cata-clysm, which would envelope the nation and the world. This was reflected in — and often fed by — the reports that journalists themselves wrote for their own publications.

THE PICTURE OF AMERICA

Foreign correspondents face a universal problem. What can a foreigner (or a native, for that matter) say about the people of a nation? Specifically, what can a French or British journalist, who spends most of his or her time in Washington or New York, say about the people of America that would have any validity? And, more importantly, how does that journalist know he's right?

This major dilemma for foreign journalists covering Watergate was accentuated by the kind of story Watergate was. As has been mentioned before in other parts of this book, Watergate constituted an extremely complex domestic political situation, which to be even partially understood had to be fully explained. A vital part of the story was the reaction of the American people to the actions of its leaders in Washington. The journalist covering Watergate, then, had to do a lot of speculating on what "the people" — whoever they are and wherever they are — were thinking.

Many British and French journalists did so willingly and totally without shame. They set themselves up as people who were fully in touch with Early, Middle, Late and Late-late Americans, and who knew almost at the instant something would happen just how Americans would or should feel about it.

Early in the Watergate story, British journalists proclaimed the American people apathetic. *Daily Telegraph* reporters and commentators predicted that the American people would soon grow jaded over Watergate and that "the factor of boredom" would save Nixon (6/30/73 — 14). Even after the Saturday Night Massacre, the Agnew resignation, the Ervin hearings, and the revelation of the tape gaps, the *Daily Telegraph* announced confidently — along with Nixon in his State of the Union message — that the American people were ready to "bring the investigations to an end" (2/1/74 — 16). Reluctantly, the editors and reporters had to admit the very next day that Watergate simply "refuses to be buried" (2/2/74 — 6).

The Gossets repeatedly noted the "formidable innocence" and "fundamental placidity" (10/27/73 — 18) of Americans who were "thinking only about their vacations" (7/16/73 — 14) and tuning in on football games instead of the President's

televised speech following the Saturday Night Massacre (10/27/
73 — 18). *Le Monde* often cited "the lassitude of the general
public" (3/31/74 — 3) whose boredom with Watergate bordered
on "reactions of fatigue, even nausea" (7/4/74 — 4).

Even as early as the day Richard Nixon was re-elected President, the *Daily Mirror* correspondent wrote off most Americans
saying they "simply cannot be shocked anymore" (11/7/72 —
12). And after 2 years of the crisis, the *Guardian* correspondent
led off his story about possible television coverage of the House
Judiciary Committee's impeachment hearings with this sentence:

> To the undoubted relief of both the American public and the
> members of the Judiciary Committee, it is beginning to look as
> though there will be no television coverage of the next phase of the
> impeachment inquiry (6/1/74 — 2).

From this, the only thing we know for sure is that this particular
correspondent was relieved. *Le Monde* claimed the Ervin
Committee was divided in "agony" over whether to continue
public hearings (1/18/74 — 3).

The easy assumptions about America's apathy flew in the
face of some of the direct evidence that journalists could have
used, especially in the later stages of the crisis. Public opinion
polls, which were published regularly in the British and French
press — including *L'Est* — showed a steady decline in the
President's personal popularity, an increase in the number of
people who wanted him to resign or be impeached, and a
general satisfaction with the work of the Senate investigations
committee and the work of the Special Prosecutor. Besides
these trends in public opinion throughout Watergate, there
were specific incidents all during the crisis to which public
reaction was fairly evident, such as the Agnew investigation,
the Saturday Night Massacre, the President's tape transcripts,
and the House Judiciary Committee hearings.

None of this is evidence for American apathy about Watergate. It instead points to a keen and continuing interest that
Americans took in Watergate. There were few public demonstrations or street marches concerning the events of Watergate;
unlike the war in Vietnam, major portions of the public never

felt the need to react in that way. This absence, however, constitutes no evidence for apathy.

New World Monarchy

Explaining the relationship between the American people and the Presidency was another part of the Watergate story. Unfortunately, this relationship turned out to be as elusive as public opinion about Watergate. Journalists were forced to ask themselves the often unanswerable questions: how do Americans feel about their President, both the office and the man who holds it? and do they distinguish between the two?

What European journalists said about this relationship probably says more about them than it does about the American people. For the basis of their attitudes toward the American Presidency, we may logically go back to John F. Kennedy. To a great many Europeans, Kennedy was everything a President should be. He was an articulate moral advocate, a man who appreciated "the best" of things in the European sense. He had tremendous personal charm, a beautiful wife and children, and his family was one of wealth and tradition. In short, he was royalty.

It is no surprise then that Europeans are likely to equate a President with a king (or queen), and it does not take much of a logical leap to expect European journalists to superimpose their own attitudes onto the American people. Throughout Watergate, Richard Nixon was referred to as the king of America. References to Nixon as king were especially proliferate during the 1972 Republican convention when nearly all the papers in Britian said that "King Richard" was about to be "crowned". And in his lead paragraph on the day of Nixon's re-election, the *Daily Mirror* correspondent wrote: "Today after a lapse of 196 years, the Monarchy will be restored to America and Richard Milhous Nixon will be king..." (11/7/72 — 12).

In *L'Est* the Gossets trumpeted the "New Crowning" (1/19/73 — 13) of Richard Nixon, a "Modern Monarch", while at the same time scoffing at Americans for their "great innocence" in supposedly regarding the Presidency as a New World Monarchy (5/15/73 — 14). They then wrote that those people "sticking their noses" into the presidential coffer and other matters exhibit the "bad taste" of ungrateful subjects lacking "elementary decency" (4/14/74 — 16; 7/16/73 — 14). Even *L'Express* could not steer completely clear of the royalty labels ("Richard the Magnificent", "Richard the Evil"), although the editors there were more conscientious about it than those of other publications (11/5/73 — 133, 134).

Once Americans had been officially endowed with this attitude about their Head of State, British and French journalists wrote about the divine right to govern that Americans had given to their President, and speculated that this would allow Nixon to remain in office. They tended to assume that because crowds often gather to see and cheer the President, they are also cheering and supporting the man who holds the office. When Nixon went to campaign for a Republican candidate in Michigan in 1974, he was accompanied by a correspondent of *The Times*. The entourage was met by large cheering crowds, and the correspondent was so disgusted with what he saw that he wrote: "A skeptical Englishman finds the idolatry Americans accord their Presidents both dangerous and silly" (4/18/74 — 1). A skeptical journalist might have looked closer and found something besides idolatry. Even near the end, *Le Monde* thought that "the image which American citizens create" about the Presidency might save Nixon (5/19/74 — 4).

One would be hard pressed to deny that there is a class structure in America. But it would also be difficult to equate this economically based structure with the traditional, family class structure of many European countries. For these reasons Americans may tend to be more egalitarian and feel that the man who is President is "just as good as we are". In writing about this for *L'Express*, Salinger put it another way, saying Americans are willing to accept the fact that the President lives like a king, "but not that he acts like one" (8/12/74 — 23).

Other correspondents might have done well by brushing up on their de Tocqueville:

In order to form a clear and precise idea of the position of the President of the United States it may be well to compare it with that of one of the constitutional kings of France. . . . In the exercise of the executive power the President of the United States is constantly subject to a jealous supervision. He may prepare, but he cannot conclude, a treaty; he may nominate, but he cannot appoint, a public officer. The king of France is absolute within the sphere of executive power.

The President of the United States is responsible for his actions; but the person of the King is declared inviolable by French law.[14]

Gangsters

One of the most persistent pictures of America that Europeans carry in their heads is that of crime-ridden America: Is it safe to walk the streets at night? they will ask American travellers. Do you carry guns? Have you ever been mugged or robbed?

What was happening with Watergate fits rather neatly — or at least seemed to — with this image. Here were five men caught in an obviously illegal act, trying to place listening devices in the offices of a political opponent. They were being paid by an organization to re-elect the President of the United States. What more proof does one need?

In the first story printed about the Watergate break-in, the correspondent for the *Guardian* wrote:

Bugging for political purposes is an ancient and well tried practice in this country and traditionally reaches a high point of artistry at political conventions. . . . The bugging practitioners, however, are rarely caught in the act (6/20/72 — 1).

That assumption caught on and was used throughout the British press to explain why Watergate was happening. The *Daily Mirror* concluded that "corruption and lying in high places has always been a tragically familiar feature of the American scene" (4/22/73 — 16).

L'Express fed this same stereotype in the French press and carried it further with the gangster (pronounced gong-STARE) image. Nixon was called the "GODFATHER OF THE WHITE HOUSE" (5/6/74 — 126). And for the Gossets, the United States comprised one enormous Mafia. "Corruption is standard practice, notorious, a quasi-traditional institution — if not a respectable one" (10/12/73 — 16). The Watergate crisis represents nothing "new or original in American politics" (7/27/ 74 — 14) and is "certainly not without precedent" (10/27/ 73 — 18). Internal political maneuvering among "Family" members upset these correspondents much more than mere corruption. Conspirators constantly lurked in the shadows, assassination plots proliferated, coups were always imminent. *Le Monde* cited the "normal and almost inevitable venality of the political milieu" (5/2/73 — 2) which makes American politics merely another form of *"bandatisme"* (5/5/73 — 4).

One might fairly assume that the American political system is not totally clean, but the generalizations about how corrupt *everything always* is should have had some backing. For instance, a quote from someone who had worked in many political campaigns saying (even anonymously) that the regular practice was to bug opponents and play "dirty tricks" on them would have lent more support to these statements. But no such support was ever printed; bugging goes on all the time in political campaigns and that's something "everybody knows".

But is it? The contrary assumption might have as easily been made. Political campaigns are notoriously understaffed and underfinanced. The Committee to Re-elect the President was unusual, if not unique, in that it found the money to carry out these espionage activities. Such a line of reasoning, however, does not fit in with the image of crime in America.

Again, we are not saying that the stereotype of crime in America is totally wrong. The problem is an acute one and is often insufficiently dealt with. The question here is: does the image of "crime in America" have anything to do with Watergate? For many reasons, violence and crime in America occur on an individual level; the violent acts of the individual are often sanctioned and sometimes rewarded by American institutions (witness the film *Walking Tall* as an example). Crime and violence occur as the result of the passionate arousal of emotions in many cases.

Watergate, on the other hand, was the systematic undermining of the political structures in America by a group of men who were anything but passionate. This organized disregard for the law and for the rules of the political game has little to do with what we normally think of as the crime problem in America.

Crime and violence remain a primary problem in America and are an integral part of the image of America held by the rest of the world. That image is reinforced in many ways — especially by the media in other countries. For instance, each year on British television there are more and more American detective shows, drawing larger and larger audiences. Women freak themselves out over Telly Savalas's language and bald head when he plays *Kojak*, and men stay glued to the pedestrian antics of Angie Dickinson in *Policewoman.* Is it any wonder, then, that the girl on the bus in Belfast told her American visitor that she would never live in New York City "because it's too violent"?

Imported American television shows and particularly films similarly contribute to the gangster image of America in France. *Columbo* draws nearly as many viewers as TV1's evening news[15] and old Edward G. Robinson or Humphrey Bogart flicks often fill the film-of-the-week slot. *The Godfather* (parts I and II) and *The French Connection* (parts I and II) typify a host of films depicting crime as America's national pastime.

IMPEACHMENT: FEARING THE UNKNOWN

Clause 4 of Section 2, and Clauses 6 and 7 of Section 3 of Article I of the United States Constitution, set forth fairly clearly the way a President may be removed from office. The House of Representatives has "the sole power of impeachment", that is, bringing charges against the President. The Senate has "the sole power to try all impeachments". The only penalty which can be imposed is the person's removal from office, but that person is still subject to judicial proceedings. While impeachment (the word often used to describe the entire process of removing a President and so used here) is the big gun that Congress has and is certainly not as American as apple pie, it is a constitutional process and one of the potential "duties" of any Congress.

To have read the British and French press during Watergate, one might have come to a very different conclusion.

Impeachment seemed to be one of the most misunderstood and consistently miscalled parts of the Watergate story. The press helped legitimize a feeling that impeachment was not an option viably open to the opponents of Nixon, that it would be a destructive, divisive, rending process from which the American political system could not recover. Politicians and journalists on both sides of the Atlantic wrung their editorial hands and made the direst predictions about what impeachment would do to us all.

The *Daily Telegraph* referred to it as "this great danger" (8/9/74 — 16), while *The Times* thought of it as a "public agony" (7/13/74 — 14) and a "most damaging process" (9/17/73 — 14). The *Daily Mirror*, which probably wouldn't have minded it all that much, called it a "long and harrowing ordeal" (8/9/74 — 3). *The Times* once quoted Senator Barry Goldwater, not noted as an authority on impeachment, as saying it would be "two or three months of televised horror" (5/21/74 — 6), and the *Observer* said after the Saturday Night Massacre that Americans were now having to "think the unthinkable" (11/4/73 — 7).

The Gossets in *L'Est* also presented impeachment as a vicious self-righteous tool of political blackmail, being used by Nixon's opponents. Nixon "surrendered" in agreeing to turn over the first tapes following the Saturday Night Massacre, they wrote, "because the wolfpack of his political enemies unleashed the big word 'Impeachment' " (10/27/73 — 18). The House of Representatives, "playing Pontius Pilate", was expected to impeach Nixon (a latter-day Christ, one might fairly presume) and thereby wash their hands of the matter by passing final responsibility for his fate on to the Senate (5/10/74 — 16). While academically describing impeachment as "the sole mechanism foreseen by the Constitution" for deposing a President and in itself neither "glorious nor ignominious" (1/18/74 — 3),

Le Monde warned that it would "shake the whole American system" (5/16/73 — 1) and "practically decapitate the United States" (11/23/73 — 1) by irreparably damaging the Presidency (5/19/73 — 4).

The fear of impeachment as something almost extraconstitutional can trace itself back to America's only other presidential impeachment, that of Andrew Johnson in 1868. Then the Congress accused Johnson of not satisfactorily carrying out the laws it had passed. After a vicious, acrimonious debate, the Senate failed to convict the President by only one vote. The charges against him were obviously "political". That he had really done little or nothing illegal had not stopped firebrands in Congress from rolling out the constitutional cannon and firing it at him. When they just barely missed, the country lurched ahead bitterly and irretrievably divided.

Journalists, politicians and historians have looked back on that time and silently vowed to themselves "never again". To compare that situation to what was happening during Watergate, and to predict the downfall of the nation if the impeachment process is carried out, is falacious, however. The nation was already divided at the time the Johnson impeachment was initiated. Less than 3 years before, it had been engaged in a civil war that had left thousands dead and a whole region's economy in ruins. Figuratively and literally, many of the nation's wounds were still open and bleeding. It was not impeachment, then, that divided the nation. The impeachment of Andrew Johnson was a *result* of the nation's divisions, not the cause of it.

Contrast that with what was happening during Watergate. An increasing number of people were believing that Richard Nixon should be removed from office. As early as March, 1974 *The Times* was forced to comment on the public "acceptance of impeachment" (3/8/74 — 7). Even as the House Judiciary Committee was beginning to debate the charges, there were those who were predicting division. Yet, when the impeachment hearings were concluded, the Judiciary Committee was lauded for the calm reasonableness of both sides. There was no evidence to conclude that the country was being torn apart. Indeed, the *Observer* commented that the American people had actually discovered that "toppling a President is not so terrible after all" (8/4/74 — 7). Perhaps instead, it was the press and the politicians who had found that it wasn't so terrible.

Even *L'Est Républicain*, after the Gossets had so unflinchingly warned of the cataclysm (and then vanished from *L'Est*'s pages before it occurred), had to reverse its position by admitting that Americans were not at all traumatized by the process and, well, yes, maybe Watergate was a good thing after all. "The public", said *Le Monde*, perhaps looking in a mirror, "is reacting with mixed feelings of anxiety and liberation [to] . . . the end of the manhunt. . ." (8/9/74 — 1).

Impeachment is a prime example of how an attitude can be legitimized and reinforced by the press. For nearly 2 years there was nothing good said about the process of impeachment. In fact, it seemed to have become the "in" thing to talk about how terrible it all would be. (You could show real concern for the fate of America and appear very statesmanlike if you said that.) No doubt, supporters of Nixon used such talk and fed it to protect him. But even those very much opposed to the President and disgusted with what his administration had become were urging resignation (or almost anything) rather than impeachment. That impeachment was constitutional, that it was useable, and that it was not necessarily divisive were ideas which were never rushed into print.

Impeachment, in short, was not what the press told us it would be.

REFLECTING ON WATERGATE

It Couldn't Happen Here

The press of Western democracies prides itself on being the watchdog of society, protecting the people from the consequences of repressive or incompetent government. Certainly, the role that the American press played in Watergate heightened this image for journalists, politicians and the public alike. The American press was lauded as never before for having broken the story, pursued the evil and eradicated the disease. In many senses the British and parts of the French press were cheering their colleagues in America.

The reason they were cheering is that members of the British and French press were seeing themselves in the same role. They, too, are watchdogs on their own governments. And even if the British press stands watch on the wrong door — that of Parliament rather than Whitehall (the bureaucracy) — as Colin Seymour-Ure puts it, the press is still watching.[16] The French press also serves as a public watchdog on the government, but for many reasons and to the chagrin of most journalists, its bark is far worse than its bite.

Yet, curiously, instead of the British press's sensitivity being sharpened by the events of Watergate, it was dulled. Many elements of the British press concluded that Watergate was purely an American phenomenon and that it could not happen in their own country. The *Evening Standard* printed a striking editorial to that effect (5/2/73 — 21), and the *Daily Telegraph* saw Britain as Watergate-proof since "party political activities are rigorously separated from Government activities" (5/2/73 — 18). The *Daily Telegraph* even implied that it wouldn't hurt the Americans to reshape their political system so that it more closely resembled the British one.

A certain amount of jingoism may inevitably result when a foreigner looks at the troubles of another country. "At least", he may say to himself, "that sort of thing wouldn't be happening in my country." Where this attitude becomes dangerous is when a journalist, one of society's watchdogs, so assimilates this attitude that he fails to draw what parallels there may be available for his own nation.

Certain aspects of Watergate, of course, could not occur in the British system. At the first hint of a scandal, the government would have resigned, and if there had been criminal investigations, all comment in the press would have ceased. Even if the Prime Minister had tried to keep his government in power, he would have had to appear before the House of Commons to answer questions about his activities. These safeguards may have prevented certain aspects of an American Watergate; they would not have prevented a similarly corrupting situation. For a government to resign could just as well have the effect of sweeping a scandal under the rug, and a man who becomes the prime minister has, by definition, become a master at evasion of pointed questions in Parliament.

There is nothing about the British political system which naturally breeds honest politicians. In fact, one could argue that the low pay and the increasing workload of politicians makes them more vulnerable to corruption than their comparatively well-heeled American colleagues. The concept of "conflict of interest" is not as strongly held in Great Britain as it is in America. The fact that the British governmental system is so closed to public view and that there is little of the adversary relationship between the press and the government offers little guarantee against a British Watergate.

And if there was corruption in government in Britain, would the watchdog be watching? Yes, he would, but there is little chance that he would be barking. The laws governing the press in these situations (reviewed in a previous chapter) are relatively restrictive, and the unwritten laws of the establishment to which Fleet Street journalists belong would close the door on almost any disclosure.

None of this is predicting that Britain is about to have her own Watergate. (She could, in fact, be having it, but we're not saying that either.) It is to say that when the British press says it could not happen in their country, they are missing the main lesson of Watergate and legitimizing a very dangerous assumption for their readers. The crisis represented not a failure for a political system but a failure of the men within that system. The American political system is based on men of goodwill acting in good faith with one another. Watergate was the result of a systematic disregard of this principle. The British system, too, is based on politicians' respect for the rules of the game and the rights of the "loyal opposition". No political system, no matter how cleverly devised, can sustain itself unless these principles are maintained.

French journalists also repeatedly claimed that "it couldn't happen here", but they meant something entirely different. Political corruption and power-brokering occur frequently within the French government, but abuse of power normally goes unchecked by the press and other forces. Perhaps the French public's worldly-wise "shrugging of the shoulders", as the Gossets put it, is an effect of the former and a cause of the latter. In any case, the *scandale* part of Watergate could easily happen in France, but not its prosecution.

Indeed, several French political scandals surfaced and then faded away during the Watergate period. The Dega affair involved the imprisonment, without trial, of a Parisian tax investigator who held potentially embarrassing information about the tax returns of some top Pompidou government officials, including current Prime Minister Jacques Chirac. Shady electoral contributions purchased political favors, and a lower-level abuse of executive power escalated into the Aranda affair. State-controlled television, allotting right-wing Gaullists and the left-wing coalition of Communists and Socialists 90 minutes each, while giving the centrist Reform Movement only 7 minutes of air time, "fixed" the 1973 parliamentary elections by solidifying France's political "bipolarization". Agents from the *Direction de la surveillance du territoire*, a French equivalent of the FBI, were caught red-handed in a bungled wire-tapping attempt on the satirical weekly newspaper *Le Canard Enchaîné* ("The Chained Duck"). Sued by *Le Canard* and cornered by a tenacious judge, the DST eventually snuffed out the affair with a national security blanket.

A cover-up of possible fiscal fraud by government officials. Questionably legal electoral contributions. Abuse of executive power. Election fixing. Government wire-tapping for national security reasons. Sound familiar?

The difference between these events and Watergate is that the diverse collections of alleged or proven misdeeds lumped under the latter all revolved around one small group of men:

Nixon and his White House "palace guards". Still, even if Georges Pompidou had been similarly tied to all of France's scandals, it remains highly likely that "it couldn't happen here".

French journalists of varying persuasions offered essentially the same reasons for this. In *L'Est Républicain,* Georges Mamy ("AND IF IT HAD HAPPENED IN FRANCE . . .", 5/7/73 — 1) pointed to the American press's greater independence, political neutrality of the judiciary assured by the grand jury system, and the close liaison between the two as making the Watergate prosecution a uniquely American phenomenon. The *Canard* affair would simply fade away, predicted Philippe Marcovici, because the French press lacks the power to really pursue the matter (12/10/73 — 16). A true balance of power and a strong Congress, said *L'Express*'s Jean-François Revel, would ensure that Watergate wasn't swept under the presidential carpet; the lack of those elements in France promoted the opposite effect (4/23/73 — 57). Congress's investigatory confrontation with the President is serious business, warned Salinger and Turenne, "because, unlike the French parliament, the American Congress has considerable powers and means of investigation" (5/21/73 — 133). *Le Monde* cited fewer individual liberties, more press restrictions, a more closed system of public life, and particularly a general cynicism regarding political corruption as major obstacles to a French Watergate (6/5/73 — 1, 3).

The Watergate crisis sparked the extraordinary functioning of a complex and unique political system, an intricate interplay of opposing and/or combined forces. True, the French Parliament may, in ordinary times, lack the power necessary for a presidential confrontation, and the judiciary may be tainted by political pressure, but neither fact excludes the possibility that they could rise to the occasion of a domestic crisis like Watergate. What greatly precludes that from happening, however, is the French press.

To a great extent, Watergate was brought out by two reporters who refused to let go of a story; who worked for a powerful newspaper in the capital city; and who had the strong backing of their editors. Their continued reporting convinced official Washington that something was amiss, and the investigatory wheels began turning. It is highly unlikely that the press could, or would, play the same role in France.

An adversary press system predates the American revolution and has always been part of the American political system. The French press, in contrast, has often suffered as a victim of the country's turbulent history. Though occasionally vociferous, French publications have served variously as Kings' proclamation sheets, Emperors' house organs, Republics' information networks and wartime propaganda pulp. The French press generally followed the changes in government rather than initiating them, and the lack of political stability has prevented any one press system from putting down roots. The contemporary French press dates back only to the end of World War II, and although the Fifth Republic's Constitution guarantees "freedom of the press", the government has curbed its power by retaining many official and unofficial sanctions.

The press's political diversity also hinders its development into a major force. The population in France covers a much broader political spectrum — ranging from reactionary monarchists to left-of-Communist radicals — than that of the United States or Britain, and each major subgroup adheres to one or more ideologically correct publications. Although the political party press has largely vanished since World War II, its vestiges remain, and the gap between "leftist" and "rightist" publications in France dwarfs that in America and Great Britain. The political diversity often spurs divisiveness, even among non-strange bedfellows: the Communist—Socialist power battle in Portugal created a major rift between French Communists and Socialists — whose previous coalition came within 1 percentage point of defeating Giscard for the Presidency — and their respective party organs, *L'Humanité* and *L'Unité*. The French press, in short, simply cannot get together on any issue.

The French connotation of "political opposition" fuels this divisiveness within the press, population, and government. As Eugene Ionesco puts it:

What is there to say of the political opposition, like that in France for example, which does not want the government to restore any economic equilibrium and does its best to prevent this, otherwise it would lose its purpose? The politicians' fight has to continue at our expense.

The press operates under this definition as well, often erupting in bitter inter-publication bickering and, inevitably, an unending stream of government criticism by the out-party press. For the opposition press, the Administration provides daily scandals simply by instituting policies. Very possibly, the word *scandale* has suffered overkill and lost its power to arouse French readers.

Finally, it is not inconceivable that, even if the French press did have enough power vis à vis the government and could overcome its internal squabbling, French journalists themselves would shy away from the implications of initiating the fall of a Head of State. During its 200-year history, the United States has survived a devastating civil war, participation in two world wars and other international conflicts, a severe economic depression and countless other domestic crises with the same form of government intact. For centuries, France has seesawed back and forth among monarchies, empires, republics, revolutionary governments, military occupations and variations on these themes. Political stability has never been a French characteristic. As late as the post-World War II era, France struggled to get on its political feet: between 1947 and 1958, a span of only 11 years, the country had twenty-two prime ministers. One of them lasted a mere 13 days.[17] Only the autocratic rule of Charles de Gaulle ushered in a period of relative stability, which so far has lasted almost 20 years.

The American press, whatever its vices and virtues, has traditionally been one of the stabilizing forces in a very stable political system. It has taken on an adversary role, as evidenced by Watergate, which is both natural and necessary. Never was there any danger of the system collapsing. But while political stability is often taken for granted in America, for the French it is a new, precious and fragile thing. The country's future would be much less predictable if Watergate had happened here.

Perhaps this is why, as Henri de Turenne said, instead of the "boxing match" atmosphere at the White House press conferences, verbal exchanges between the press and government spokesmen at the Élysée Palace rather resemble a gentlemanly fencing match with "capped foils" (8/27/73 — 61).

CONCLUSION

In this chapter we have outlined some of the consequences or "effects" of the press in a given societal structure. As we have seen, there is little evidence that the press has a direct stimulus—response effect on its audience. Rather, information that comes from the media must go through a number of filters before it reaches its destination.

This does not preclude a set of "effects" that the press can have, however. In many cases, the press may *set the agenda*, structuring our world for us and introducing the subjects we are likely to think about. Related to this function is that of *legitimization*, which refers to the power of the press to make items worthy of discussion in a public forum. The "perceived power" of the press is important to this concept in that a reader who sees something in a newspaper will attach an importance to it because he or she feels that other people, too, are reading and thinking about the same thing.

The press also serves other functions, such as *crystalizing* and *stereotyping*. By crystalizing, or integrating, information, the press can draw attention to a particular subject by reporting on just part of it. In this instance, stories about Watergate often lead to stories about other American problems, such as crime, economic problems, the Vietnam aftermath, etc.

Since the press must choose from a vast array of information it often uses stereotypes — or creates its own — as a form of journalistic shorthand. These stereotypes are likely to fit into the journalist's individual preconceptions of events, such as the "King Richard" image with which Nixon was anointed.

Related to this is what we may call the *journalistic-fallacy* function of the press. This function is inherent within the nature of the job journalists must do. In covering stories which have wide ranging consequences, journalists are often reduced to making grand assumptions ("apathetic Americans") or creating jargon ("government paralysis") which do not suffer close scrutiny.

All of these concepts are especially important in understanding the dynamics of international communications. On a domestic level, the power of the press to set the agenda or perform any of these other functions may be diluted by numerous intervening variables, such as information that comes from other sources than the press. On an international level, however, the power of the press to do all of these things is heightened.

The extent to which a press system can perform any of these functions is dependent on the role the press plays in a particular society. In comparing or studying different press systems, this factor is often forgotten or ignored. Instead, evaluations of press systems have often hinged on how much "freedom" a press system has. Westerners talk about "freedom of the press" with regard to freedom from government control. Soviets talk about freedom from economic control. Both evaluations tend to get caught up in ideological jargon and miss an extremely important question: what role is the press expected to play in a society? Instead of asking, freedom *from* what, we should be asking, freedom *for* what. We will try to examine some of these issues in the final chapter.

REFERENCES

1. Colin Seymour-Ure, *The Press, Politics and the Public*, London, Methuen, 1968, pp. 276—77.
2. Joseph Klapper, *The Effects of Mass Communication*, Glencoe Free Press, 1960, p. 7.
3. Maxwell E. McCombs and Donald L. Shaw, "A Progress Report on Agenda Setting Research." Paper presented to the Theory and Methodology Division, Association for Education in Journalism, San Diego, California, August 19, 1974, p. 3.
4. Colin Seymour-Ure, *The Political Impact of Mass Media*, London, Constable, 1974, p. 42.
5. Seymour-Ure, 1968, p. 301.
6. Theodore White, *The Making of the President 1972*, New York, Atheneum, 1973, p. 245.

7. McCombs and Shaw, p. 19.
8. Bernard Cohen, *The Press and Foreign Policy*, Princeton, Princeton University Press, 1970, pp. 226—27.
9. Cohen, p. 230.
10. Seymour-Ure, 1974, p. 63.
11. Karl Deutsch, *The Nerves of Government*, New York, Free Press, 1966, p. 209.
12. Fredrick W. Frey, "Communication and Development", in Pool, I. *et al.* (eds.), *Handbook of Communications*, Chicago, Rand McNally, 1973, p. 383.
13. Cohen, p. 229.
14. Alexis de Tocqueville, *Democracy in America*, Vol. 1, pp. 127, 129.
15. Frémy, Dominique, and Frémy, Michèle, *Quid? 1975*, Paris, Éditions Laffont, 1975, p. 1130.
16. Seymour-Ure, 1968, p. 311.
17. Frémy and Frémy, p. 448.

5. Freedom of the Press: A Search for Boundaries

An enemy of Socialism cannot write in our newspapers — but we
don't deny it, and we don't go around proclaiming a hypothetical
freedom of the press where it doesn't actually exist. . . . Furthermore,
I admit that our press is deficient in this respect. . . . Not that I
would tell you we delude ourselves that under present circumstances
journalism can have any other function more important than that
of contributing to the political and revolutionary goals of our country.
We have . . . an objective to fulfill, and that objective essentially
controls the activity of the journalists.

Fidel Castro to Lee Lockwood, quoted from
Castro's Cuba, Cuba's Fidel

As the Vietnam war broke the mold of Cold War assumption
and opened many closed issues to new debate, so did the
Watergate scandal's impact upon American society and polity.
One of its most profound consequences was the debate it
generated about the freedom of the press in Western democracies.
The Watergate coverage by both the American and the West
European communications media raised in bold type the
biggest communication issue of them all: What is the role of
the press in our post-industrial society?

The Watergate revelations, combined with both America's
and Europe's economic and social problems, produced a considerable amount of lamenting about the state of Western democratic systems. But this was in part balanced by widespread
admiration for the way the press and certain political institutions handled the scandals. Western press interpretations of
Watergate were, of course, filtered through the national experi-

ences of the beholders. And in the case of the European press —
especially the British and the French which shared certain
philosophical and historical values with their North American
counterpart — the greater significance of its Watergate coverage
was the light it threw on comparative meanings and concepts of
press freedom across the national boundaries.

The impact of Watergate upon the freedom of the press
is examined from two major perspectives in this chapter. The
first perspective assesses the degree to which certain characteristics of the Anglo-American-French press have been illuminated
as a direct consequence of Watergate reporting. The second
perspective examines the consequences of Watergate on the
institutional and behavioral processes of the press systems and
attempts to present a framework for comparative analysis of
press freedom and control.

THE PRESS AND POLITICAL CULTURE

The Anglo-American press and to a great degree the French
press share several characteristics that are directly related
to their role in providing information about, and their tendency
to affect the conduct of, national and foreign affairs:

(1) They perceive that their primary enterprise is that of
reporting the most important news and events of the world.
They see their task as being the source of "all the news that
is fit to print", in the case of the *New York Times*, or "the
newspaper of record", as it is thought of *The Times* (London),
or as the carrier of "real information, fast and complete", as
Le Monde once declared. Because of this self-image, and because
of the advance of technology and the multiplicity of world
news, they have been overwhelmed by the very torrent of
events and facts and thus overloaded by opinions and variety
of items.

(2) They believe in some kind of "neutrality" syndrome,
"fair treatment", or simply journalistic "objectivity" in the
separation of news and editorials.

(3) They are extremely vocal about their rights and preroga-

tives in what may be called the cult of disclosure.

(4) They see themselves as the "Fourth Estate" or the "Fourth Branch of Government".

The myth widely accepted by the public is that the most important news of the world, if not the entire stream of events, is in the columns of their daily newspapers or may be found on their television screens. But in fact, close observation supports the hypothesis that the selection and dissemination of what constitutes "the most important news of the day" is a function of the nation's national culture and political norms. The uneven coverage of the 1956 Suez War by the British press and the Algerian liberation movement by the French press, the silence of the American press at the Bay of Pigs invasion, and the suppression of news of East European uprisings by the Soviets, are all well documented.

In the Watergate affairs the press as a whole accepted much of the credit for exposing the scandal. But as we know, press credit is due primarily to the Washington press and a handful of other papers and journalists whose systematic reporting and persistence in pursuing facts and inquiries led to the disclosure of a series of corruption and irregularities at the highest level of American government.

It is argued here that the press and the journalists working for them do exhibit cultural biases and often do internalize national interest. In this case the crisis for the government is a crisis for the journalist also. What we mean by this is that there is a possibility that reporters who are at work in their home country are naturally more involved in the politics of the land of their birth. Indeed, the press in the United States, Britain and France is often referred to as the "Fourth Branch of Government" or the "Fourth Estate", a phrase which lends testimony to the seriousness of purpose which is generally regarded as an important characteristic of the press systems of the countries examined in this book.

This crisis involvement separates a nation's own press and the foreign journalists stationed there. A foreign journalist is unlikely to become as emotionally involved in covering events in which he has no natural involvement due to nationalist sympathy as a reporter who is evaluating his own political system. The results of this difference, already demonstrated in the case of Watergate, may be seen further in the following case.

THE MYTH OF NEUTRALITY

During the week of the My Lai disclosures that the American press was playing down the story in favor of several salient others, the front pages of the British newspapers were filled with cries of moral outrage over the incident. While the angle taken by American newspaper coverage was that of the "inquiry" or "probe" into the "alleged massacre" of Vietnamese civilians, the British press churned out banner headlines about the American "atrocities".

A comparison of editions of a sampling of American and British newspapers from the same day following shortly after the initial disclosure of the My Lai incident is illustrative of the difference.

On November 22, 1969, a few days after the My Lai story broke, the main My Lai story in the American newspapers reported a Pentagon news conference at which the Army's chief legal counsel outlined the conduct of the military investigation of the incident and its legal intricacies. The story — variously headlined "24 INVESTIGATED IN VIETNAM CASE" *(New York Times)*, "VIETNAM PROBE WIDENS" *(Washington Post)*, "ARMY WIDENING ITS PROBE INTO ALLEGED U.S. MASSACRE" *(Baltimore Sun)*, "MASSACRE PROBE BROADENED" *(Philadelphia Inquirer)* — was given little column space on the front page, if it appeared there at all. The main stories of the day concerned the Senate rejection of Clement Haynsworth as Nixon's nominee to the Supreme Court, and another American space triumph — the start of the Apollo 12 astronauts' return to earth after another successful venture on the moon.

Interestingly enough, the next most common My Lai-related

story in the American papers that day concerned the furor the story had created in the British press. Each of the above-mentioned papers carried a story about the British reaction, variously headed "ATROCITY CHARGE STIRRING BRITISH" *(New York Times)*, "SHOCK EXPRESSED OVER VIET SLAYING" *(Washington Post)*, and "FOREIGN PRESS GIVES BIG PLAY" *(Baltimore Sun)*. The *only* My Lai story the *Chicago Tribune* carried on November 22 was a report from London: "U.S. MASSACRE REPORTS STIR BRITISH PRESS."

The British press has indeed responded vigorously to the allegations of a massacre at My Lai. In striking contrast to American press treatment, the My Lai story quickly displaced the Apollo 12 mission headlines in the British newspapers, and in their place appeared banners reading "MASSACRE THAT CHILLED THE WORLD" *(Daily Mirror)*, and "WAR CRIME — IF THIS CAN HAPPEN AMERICA HAS LOST" *(Daily Sketch)*. Editorial — and political — reaction was swift and severe. For example, the conservative *Daily Telegraph* editorialized: "Even if they [the allegations] are substantiated to the extent of only 1%, they would leave forever a blot on American military honour." The *Daily Sketch* noted: "The killer instinct, that dark side of the American character, has been unleashed by the brutality of the Vietnam war to such a point that the very purpose of fighting that war is now lost." And the tabloid *Daily Mirror*, the country's biggest-selling newspaper, wrote: "If the ghoulish allegations are true, how have they been hushed up for 20 months? American Army Law will have to take its course. And clearly there will have to be a ruthless inquiry into just how ugly the ugly war has now become."

Nor did the reaction in the British press quickly abate. On the same day, November 22, that American newspapers were running the above noted stories, *The Times* of London, for example, was devoting half of its front page, including a four-column picture of an American G.I. looking at photographs of the massacre in an American newspaper, and half of its editorial space to the "American tragedy". The lead story described an angry disagreement among Labour Party members over the proper channel of protest of the atrocities, a political reaction whose immediacy and intensity was, again, well in advance of that in the U.S.

This disparity between the American reaction, in the press and in general, and the British reaction to the story of the My Lai massacre was itself the subject of some commentary. In the November 22 issue of *The Times* noted above, its Washington correspondent wrote: "There has been little editorial comment, and fewer headlines than could have been expected. As far as the men involved are concerned, the case is still *sub judice*, but in the past this has rarely prevented the American press from expressing its views. One must assume a collective embarrassment, if not disbelief."

Anthony Lewis, writing from London in the *New York Times*, reported: "A number of commentators remarked that the concern about the charges seemed more intense here than in the United States, and were puzzled at the relative coolness with which the charges were being reported and discussed in America."

Lewis went on to quote the assessment of the BBC's Washington correspondent, Charles Wheeler, of the "relatively calm reaction" in the United States: "Seen from here, it seems that the conscience of America rests in the House of Commons and Fleet Street."

THE UNEVEN FLOW OF NEWS

Cultural filters are not the only element affecting the "veracity" of cross-national news reporting. The very structure of the international news-gathering effort is an important element.

Recently, the asymmetry in the modern global system has emerged as a primary focus of discussion and controversy. A significant amount of journalistic content and research effort has been devoted to the analysis of the implications and consequences of the unequal distribution of the world's resources. This inequality in distribution applies not only to natural or financial resources, but also to the flow of information between and among nations. Just as the internalization of production and finance as embodied in the multinational corporation has not resulted in optimal economic rationing, so the expansion and integration of the global communications system has not brought about an optimal allocation of information resources.

That the flow of news and information between nations is governed by certain basic realities of technology and wealth cannot be denied. What is important from our point of view are the patterns of concentration and of omission that seem to have a bearing on the volume and direction of news from the United States to the rest of the world. Thus a recent study examining the source of the differential treatment of events by the press concluded the following:

> Although the number of correspondents stationed in the United States has increased from a modest 300 in 1956 to an all-time high of almost 900 in 1974, this upsurge of foreign journalists and media communicators has not led to a better diversification of international media representation in Washington and New York.
>
> For example, the foreign press corps in Washington includes no correspondents from black Africa. Israel is represented by 23 correspondents in New York and Washington, while the Arab countries of the Middle East have only 13 full-time and part-time journalists, including the Egyptian press with only three representatives. Nationalist China has more registered correspondents (23) in the United States than either India (10) or Pakistan (1). (Of course, there is yet no correspondent in the United States from the People's Republic of China). And while there is a total of 43 correspondents from the Canadian media in both Washington and New York, there are only eight journalists from Mexico. With the exceptions of Argentina and Brazil, few Latin American countries maintain any press representative whatsoever in the United States.
>
> By contrast, we can note several structural features of the geographical diversity of correspondents from Western Europe and Japan.
>
> First, there is a large concentration of British, German, and Japanese correspondents in Washington and New York. In fact, Western Europe accounts for more than 50 per cent of all the foreign correspondents covering the United States. Second, there are relatively few correspondents from Latin America, the Middle East, or Asia. Third, there is the total absence of correspondents from several countries and regions, including Communist China, for reasons of government policy at both ends, or economic and financial considerations.[1]

Table 3
Foreign Correspondents Stationed in U.S. (1974)

Region	Number of countries	%	Number of media organizations	%	Number of correspondents	%
Western Europe	18	25	285	52	465	54
Asia	11	15	78	14	132	15
Latin America	21	29	66	12	77	9
Middle East	9	12	44	8	53	6
Eastern Europe and U.S.S.R.	7	10	33	6	46	5
Canada	1	1	21	4	42	5
Australia and New Zealand	2	3	10	2	33	4
World-wide	—	—	7	1	9	1
Africa	4	5	6	1	8	1
Total	73	100	550	100	865	100

(Percentages are rounded off to nearest whole numbers)
Source: Hamid Mowlana, "Who Covers America?", *Journal of Communication*, Vol. 25:3 (1975), p. 87.

The implications of this imbalance were clearly demonstrated in the case of the Watergate coverage. The rest of the world received what news it did about Watergate from largely American or Western European sources, whose interpretations of the events varied along the lines we have noted but which also shared certain cultural views of the relationship between government and the press. This may explain in part the little attention paid to Watergate events in the major Communist press systems: they were virtually silent on this issue. The stance of "non-involvement" taken by the Soviet Union as a result of détente and other foreign policy considerations blocked the interpretation of Watergate in that part of the world.

THE "DISCLOSURE CONCEPT"

The Times of London in 1851, in response to Lord Derby's complaint about the responsibility of the press, published a classic editorial:

The first duty of the press is to obtain the earliest and most correct intelligence of the events of the time and instantly, by disclosure of them, to make them the common property of the nation. The press lives by disclosure. [It continued:] The statesman's duty is precisely the reverse. He cautiously guards from the public eye the information by which his actions and opinions are regulated.[2]

In a different context, recently, the U.S. Central Intelligence Agency's director, Mr. William Colby, wrote a letter to Washington columnist Jack Anderson saying that: "The successful conduct of both intelligence and journalism depends upon the ability to protect sources." Anderson's response was that such "a cozy relationship between the CIA structure and the press apparatus" will make the reporters "become lap dogs

Table 4
Countries with the Largest Number of Foreign Correspondents in the U.S.

Country	Number of correspondents representing Radio/TV and Photo-film		Press/News Agency		Total	
		%		%		%
Great Britain	11	7	91	16	102	14
Federal Republic of Germany	30	20	68	12	98	13
Japan	30	20	52	9	82	11
France	13	9	59	10	72	10
Italy	8	5	48	8	56	8
Canada	16	10	27	5	43	6
Australia	7	5	26	5	33	4
Switzerland	3	2	23	4	26	4
Soviet Union	2	1	24	4	26	4
Spain	5	3	21	4	26	4
Taiwan	3	2	20	3	23	3
Israel	3	2	20	3	23	3
Sweden	6	4	17	3	23	3
Netherlands	6	4	11	2	17	2
Turkey	2	1	14	2	16	2
Argentina	3	2	11	2	14	2
Brazil	1	1	10	2	11	2
Denmark	2	1	9	2	11	2
Norway	1	1	10	2	11	2
India	—	—	10	2	10	1
Total	152	100	571	100	723	100

Source: Hamid Mowlana, "Who Covers America?", *Journal of Communication*, Vol. 25: 3 (1975), p. 88.

rather than watchdogs", and called it "an attack on American liberties".[3]

The fact remains that contemporary public diplomacy, new international relations, public opinion, and domestic considerations will not permit a public official in the United States, Britain, or France to take so luxurious a view, and assert a right to tell only what he pleases. In fact, as the amount of information in these societies increases, the tendency is toward a more investigative reporting and a trend to disclose secrecy. The contemporary history of domestic and international affairs of the three countries is full of such disclosures, and there is no need to illustrate them here. What is important from our point of view is the demand put on the political systems through these processes, and the ability and adaptation of each political system to accommodate and respond to these demands. It is here that the media or political crises in each political system can be a testing ground of the durability and vulnerability of Western democratic systems.

As was shown in the previous chapters, in the early part of the Watergate affair the British and the French, although much interested in the scandal, tended to dismiss it as different only in degree from what they knew about the American politics. Furthermore, the disclosure of Watergate was interpreted by the British and the French in the framework of their political and legal systems. For example, under the British laws of libel and very strict rules for preventing the prejudicing of cases which are *sub judice*, it would have been quite impossible for the British press to report the stories which were being published daily in the *Washington Post*. As Peter Jenkins of the *Guardian* put it: "What I think *The Times* of London failed to understand, and what many Britishers at that time failed to grasp, was that the ability of the courts to do justice was gravely at issue as the results of an obstruction of justice being conducted by the President of the United States."[4] But the same cultural and political norms once intensified in the heat of the Watergate controversy triggered the British consciousness. Jenkins explains this succinctly:

What finally excited the British to the realization of what was going on here — the nature of the crisis — was the sacking of the prosecutor by the accused. This brought dramatically home what was at issue, and in my view had been at issue throughout. The Europeans — the Germans, in particular — have deep, abiding memories of the consequences of executive overthrow of an independent prosecutor; it had the air of a coup d'état, and I for one reported it as such.[5]

COMPARATIVE STUDIES OF MASS MEDIA SYSTEMS

In the comparative study of press systems, the tendency in the United States has been to categorize the communication systems of various societies into Western, Communist, and non-Communist developing models, or to see them in the tradition—transition—modernity continuum. For over a generation, the prescriptive and normative framework of mass communication systems formulated by a group of American scholars has been the backbone and common denominator of analysis of national communication models by students of the press and mass communication.

Their four categories of communication systems include: (1) authoritarianism from the birth of modern communication in 1450 to development of authoritarian society; (2) libertarianism, born through struggles in the sixteenth and seventeenth centuries; (3) the Soviet Communist system developed by Marx and Lenin; and (4) the social responsibility model newly developed in the current century as a response to criticisms on the performance of libertarian press, all of which have their roots in political and ideological philosophies.[6]

In Western Europe, similar theories have been expressed in a neat descending order of control of communication channels: authoritarian, paternal, commercial, and democratic.[7]

When compared with the American models, two interesting features of the European concepts seem to stand out. They are the concept of paternalism, as a halfway house between the authoritarian control and the laissez faire approach, and the emphasis on the weaknesses of the commercial system, which are discussed far less comprehensively by the Americans, with their presentation of the system emphasizing self-control and responsibility. These features obviously reflect the West European socialist approach to socio-economic organization, which is different from the mainstream of American ideology that stresses self-control and autonomy rather than public control in any discussion of abuses of freedom by mass media.[8]

As has been observed, there is a tendency to generalize the problems and situations of both developed and developing (or Communist) nations at the cost of a careful consideration of their diversity. When all the varied difficulties and pitfalls in development efforts are lumped together, regardless of the obvious variety in the cultural, social, economic, and political backgrounds, the resultant weight of the problems appears no doubt appalling and unbearable. There are many countries, for example in Western Europe, where authoritarian, paternal, commercial, and democratic modes are *all* to some extent active. It may be easy to see the differences between libertarian and authoritarian systems, but a model like the social responsibility theory is unclear at best. Practically any media system in the world could justify its behavior as socially responsible to its people and polity.

The problem has moved into sharper focus in recent years as the students of mass communication have sought to operationalize and compare press freedom and national development, and as political scientists have used such a measure as an index and adjunct of political development and integration. In some instances, the comparative study of communication systems has been linked with democracy — raising further difficulties, since even the attempts to operationalize democracy have resulted in separate sets of indicators which are not highly correlated.

For example, in cross-national studies of press freedom, researchers have not used a standard set of criteria for each country, nor have they considered factors other than those of obvious governmental interference. Comparative mass media systems research has been concerned mostly with variables dealing with the relationship of the media and government. There are, however, a multitude of other factors which can inhibit press freedom.

In one study, for example, carried out in the United States, there is such excessive reliance on legal and/or governmental factors that with the exception of the United States and several European countries, the rest of the world is at a disadvantage: seventeen of the twenty-three factors used in measuring press freedom are either directly or indirectly related to government regulation.[9] In many countries government is the *only* social entity with sufficient resources to maintain any form of communication network.

There also is a tendency among researchers to separate the press — predominately newspapers — from other media such as magazines and broadcasting.[10] In making this analytical distinction, one necessarily limits the applicability of one's measure of free press, or on a broader scale, freedom of information. If one encounters a situation in which government control over media varies in different areas, one may find a free press alongside a severely restricted broadcast system.

The point is that if one is examining the relationship of a free mass media system to other variables one should define and operationalize free press in such a way as to include all of its dimensions. In many cases the assumption regarding freedom of the press has already been made before the researcher has embarked upon data gathering and analysis.

Every generalization about mass media systems of nations and societies as disparate as those in the Middle East, Latin America, Asia, and Africa is subject to many exceptions and qualifications. Yet, if the danger of over-generalization of the mass communication systems of various countries as being authoritarian, Communist, or libertarian is obvious, the danger of regarding each nation as totally unique and with no common features must also be avoided.

Central to the study of comparative mass media systems is the search for some acceptable definition of mass communication variables. Many of the present definitions have been challenged for being based on Western values and institutional structure, which themselves may be rejected by other societies as meaningless and undesirable. Yet the concern for the development of mass communication theory and the collection of data in a non-ethnocentric fashion, and on an empirical basis, is obvious.

Several years ago, Hamid Mowlana proposed a paradigm in an attempt to present a framework for the non-normative and comparative study of mass communication systems throughout the world. Mowlana's paradigm has been discussed in detail elsewhere.[11] Here we will outline the scheme of this paradigm and show how, in the light of the data and discussion presented in the preceding chapters, the anatomy of press freedom can be mapped out and how the freedom and control of mass communication channels can be measured and compared.

MOWLANA'S PARADIGM

In Mowlana's paradigm, a mass media system is viewed as a complex social system consisting of actions carried out within the context of external social conditions of the community and society in which it operates. The operation of no one part of the mass media system and process can be fully understood without reference to the way in which the whole itself operates. The operation of any particular mass media channel may be viewed according to the following schema:

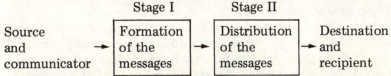

One crucial departure Mowlana's approach makes from the previous modes of press system analysis is in focusing upon the *distribution*, rather than the *formation*, of messages as the critical variable. The traditional Western normative approach to the study of the press, with its preoccupation with the rights of individuals and groups to *formulate* and *produce* their desired messages, has resulted in the considerable neglect of the distribution variable. Yet the growth of communication technology, the expanding national and international market, and the creation of institutional policies and regulations have all made distribution the most important sequence in the process of mass communication. Thus, Mowlana's emphasis is upon not only the rights of individuals and groups to produce their desired messages — the traditional politico-philosophical under-pinning of the press freedom — but also on their rights to distribute and receive the produced messages in their environment.

The second important difference in Mowlana's approach is its focus upon the descriptive variable of *control* in contrast to the traditional approach's concern with *press freedom*, the normative weighting of which has already been discussed.

The paradigm, in its entirety, is an analytical framework embracing eight broad areas pertinent to both stages of the communication process — message formation and message distribution: (1) types of ownership; (2) types of control; (3) sources of operation; (4) disposition of income and capital; (5) complexity of media bureaucracy; (6) perceived purpose of the media; (7) messages or numbers of the media; (8) types of content. For purposes of the present discussion, however, the rest of this chapter will focus upon the first two of these elements: types of ownership and types of control.

Types of ownership

Ownership of formation and distribution agencies of a given mass media system varies from country to country, and the type of ownership may influence the content. Government owned media facilitate researchers' analysis of the respective government policies and positions. It must be stressed that in most cases, even when ownership is completely private, governments have some degree of control over the distribution of the messages (especially through licensing and legal control).

A relatively new phenomenon is the extensive ownership of media in one country by predominantly private interests in another country. The five television stations comprising the Central American Television Network are 51% owned

Table 5
Mowlana's Paradigm for Comparative Mass Media Analysis (Stage I)

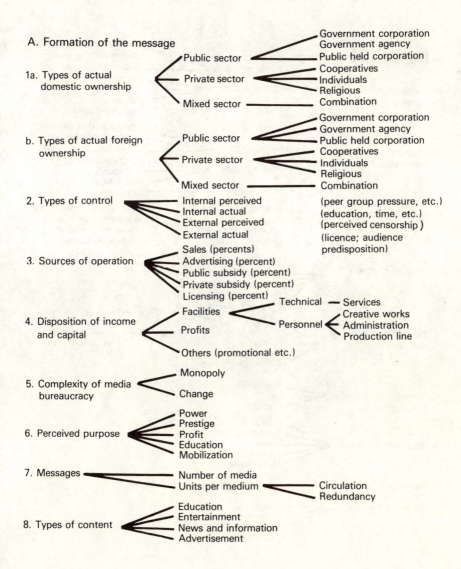

Table 6
Mowlana's Paradigm for Comparative Mass Media Analysis (Stage II)

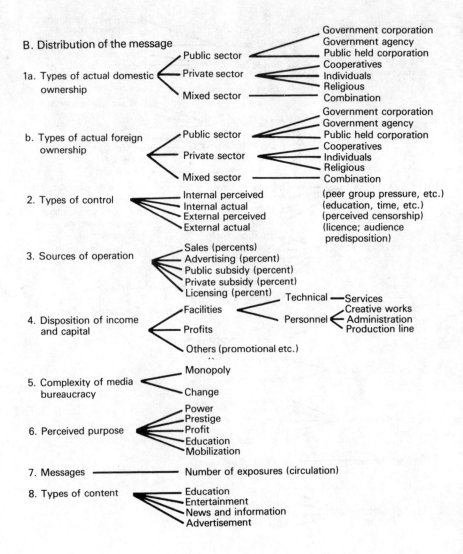

subsidiaries of the American ABC (American Broadcasting Company) network. This same company owns the American Television International Network Organization, which operates in six countries. Both the American television networks CBS (Columbia Broadcasting System) and NBC (National Broadcasting Company) also operate internationally. The British Lord Thomson owns close to 400 media outlets, predominantly newspapers, including some major elite or quality papers from around the world.

In assuming the degree of freedom of a press system one must, therefore, also pay attention to the level of ownership and monopoly in both the production and distribution levels and may examine the economic structure of the press in such sectors as public, private, or mixed.

Types of control

In the formulation and distribution stages of a given mass media system, the control aspect is by far one of the most significant variables in its complexity and measurement. Control over the system can take many forms: it comes from within the structure of a given mass media system, as well as being exerted from the outside. Some controls are actual, others are perceived. (Control here is the process of deleting or limiting the content or distribution of any of the media of communication.)

Although the process of perceived control has become more organized and consciously applied during the past 4 centuries, it has existed as an informal check in all societies. This control of the media system is applied not only by authoritarian, legal, or economic restrictions, but also by individuals' and the organization's mental processes.

These standards, existing in the conscious mind, reject alien and dangerous subjects. For example, a newspaper reporter or a broadcaster, having observed the standard of his employer or organization or culture, limits his observation to what he should do, see, and write, and after a time may be quite unaware of the limitations upon his observation. This informal or perceived control in the interest of the social system or of folk values is pervasive and insidious. In many countries and societies this form of control is usually far more effective than the formal control of a ruler or a hierarchy. Thus, in the paradigm, Mowlana distinguishes four types of control for any mass media system.

(1) *Internal actual control.* These are specific rules and regulations such as education, professional qualification, internal rules, and hierarchy created and institutionalized formally by the mass media system itself, to which members in a media system subject themselves.

(2) *Internal perceived control.* Social control in the newsroom, peer group pressure, perceived gatekeeping functions, and unwritten but understood rules of the internal conditions of the organization are examples of perceived control. These are the so-called "rules of the game" and consist of all those arrangements that regulate the way members of the mass media system must behave within the perceived institutional boundaries of the unit they work.

When, for example, Harrison Salisbury became national news editor of the *New York Times* some of the correspondents correctly perceived what this editor expected. "He wanted more imagination, more mobility and drive from his correspondents, more jet journalism and less waiting for events to occur in their own backyards",[12] we are told. A gatekeeper's study about NBC television's controversial Tet offensive film demonstrates the control exercised by an American television executive producer of the Huntley-Brinkley Report when he carefully cut the "too bloody" film in which Brigadier General Nguyen Ngoc Loan "blew the brains out of a prisoner". By mere accident John Chancellor happened to see the film prior to its airing and, due to the great mutual respect between commentator Chancellor and producer Northshield, Chancellor's reservations were heeded and the film revised.[13] This is an example of peer group pressure, or perceived internal control.

One illustration of perceived editorial influence among the British press during the Watergate reporting was the conflict and the differences of view between Mr. Fred Emery, *The Times*'s Washington correspondent, and his editor's support of Nixon. *The Times*'s editor, who apparently favored for some time Nixon's continuation in office, had published a leader denouncing the American press as contributing to the President's problems. As the Watergate events unfolded, several of Emery's stories were not published, presumably because their content was unfavorable to Nixon, although in the stories which did appear his views were never altered or deleted. What is important from our discussion point of view is this perceived internal screening in the editorial room which every working journalist can face from time to time. Yet there is also another element of perception that can be observed in the elite or prestige papers and also in the case of *The Times*: that correspondents feel that they are elites themselves writing to their peers and as such they jealously guard their own rights to put forth their opinions.

Institutional and professional self-control also has come to the attention of both liberal and conservative advocates of press freedom. It is being attacked increasingly on all fronts — the left, the right and the center. Thus, in a recent book Professor John Merrill of the University of Missouri who takes a very strong view of traditional concept of journalistic autonomy has this to say:

> Most American journalists think they are free. Actually, they are giving up their freedom, adapting to institutionalism and professionalism, and demeaning their individuality and rational self-interest. They are escaping from freedom and self-responsibility into the comfortable sanctuary of social ethics and fuzzy altruism. American journalists, like most journalists in the Western world, while still chanting the tenets of liberalism, are marching into an authoritarian sunset under the banner of "social responsibility."[14]

(3) *External actual control.* Direct censorship, licensing and other external legal, professional, governmental, or external institutionalized factors form this category. Further subcategories can be established here to divide external actual control into such areas as constitutional, legal, economic, and political factors.

(4) *External perceived control.* In every society we have such systems as culture, social structure, and economic and political elites. Each of these can constitute a major set of factors in the process of demands entering a mass media system. Not all demands and influencing factors have their major locus inside the institutional system of mass communication. Important factors in determining the outcome of both the production and distribution stages of a media system stem from constraints and unwritten rules of the environment. Predispositions and wants of readers and audiences, reactions to perceived political preferences and idiosyncracies, and pressures exercised by elites and organizations in the society are examples of this type of control.

During the Cold War of the 1950s, journalists, aware of their publishers' aversion to Communists (internal perceived control), and aware of the readership's suspicion of anything that may be interpreted as reflecting favorably on Communists (external perceived control), were under perceived constraints. Their product was a reaction to perceived political preferences and idiosyncracies. Social controls in newsrooms occur at all levels. This was most dramatically revealed in Clifton Daniel's speech regarding the Bay of Pigs story, recalling that "editors were fuming and disagreeing with one another over how the pre-invasion story should be played" on the front page of the *New York Times* in that particular evening in 1961. The final decision was a result of external perceived control. Publisher Dryfoos, worried about possible consequences, ordered self-censorship on grounds of national security. He misperceived the external factors: President Kennedy conceded that "if the *Times* had printed all it knew about the invasion, he would probably have called it off."[15]

The journalist's perception of his sources as well as his audience illustrates the notion of external perceived control: Who does he perceive his audience to be, and does the reporter—source relationship in any way affect his reporting? The popular and mass press is after the large circulations; the quality or elite press is after readers of discernment and influence. In a recent study of foreign journalists stationed in the United States it was shown that: "interpersonal and group communication among foreign correspondents, as professional colleagues, tend to play an important role in the evaluation and transmission of news. At times, this seems to be more important than the relation each correspondent has with the indigenous environment."

One of the most interesting aspects of the Watergate affair was why the White House press corps failed to get the story. One reason was that the journalists covering the White House had become prisoners of their sources. It is known among the reporters that the most difficult story to write is not usually the kind that angers editor or government officials, but one that dries up the source to the extent that the reporter no longer has that precious commodity called "the scoop". Charles Peters, in describing the constraints under which the White House reporters work, illustrates this point:

> In 1971, *Newsday,* the Long Island newspaper, ran a series of exposés on the financial affairs of Bebe Rebozo, concluding with the editorial comment, "Let's face it, the deals made by Bebe Rebozo and the Smathers gang have tainted the Presidency."
>
> Ron Ziegler would not speak to *Newsday*'s White House correspondent, Martin Schram, for three months afterwards and excluded Schram from the China trip . . . .
>
> Bill Moyers recalls that Lyndon Johnson once forbade him to give any White House exclusives to the *St. Louis Post-Dispatch*'s James Deakin, simply because Johnson thought Deakin's questions at press briefings were too tough.[16]

Peters believes that "one of the most important things the reporters could have done to prevent Watergate was to have alerted the public about their inability to report the Presidency".[17] He cites Mel Elfin, Washington Bureau Chief of *Newsweek*, who was never able to get an interview with H. R. Haldeman. Elfin was not alone; James Reston of the *New York Times* had not been granted an interview with Nixon, Haldeman, or Ehrlichman since 1968, and did not report this fact in his column to his readers. On the other hand, what gave Reston and some other journalists the upper hand on other issues was the fact that they extended the "periphery" of their sources beyond the top officials in Washington. Reston received most of his first-hand information from the gap created between the formulation of a policy and its announcement. Sy Hersh uncovered the My Lai story from the lower echelons of the bureaucracy, as did the two *Washington Post* reporters who investigated the Watergate affair.

The traditional concept of press freedom, its meaning, and its measurement, has its roots in the Industrial Revolution. The new meaning and assessment of a free and democratic press are being nourished in the Information Revolution. Will the press survive the Information Revolution as vigorously as it did the Industrial Revolution? Can an institution which is so heavily dependent on others be truly free?

Despite the so-called communication revolution with its new technologies, we have not become informationally affluent. As the demand for the supply of news and information has soared, the press and other channels of mass communication are already experiencing the phenomenon of "information overload". This is not to say that the society has too much information; it has too little. What is happening is the clumping of news and editorial around old points and institutions no longer able to handle the flow, either because the information is poorly chosen (irrelevant) or because the formation and distribution ends are inadequately organized and controlled.

In our modern industrial society, the learning and the kind of socialization that people receive from the media far outweigh the little education each generation acquires from the formal education system and the family. The need for understanding this important and changing institution is obvious. But in analyzing our mass communication systems, a new focus is required, as we have shown. As Professor George Gerbner of the University of Pennsylvania has observed: "The real question is not whether the organs of mass communication are free, but rather: by whom, how, for what purposes, and with what consequences are the inevitable controls exercised?"[18]

REFERENCES AND NOTES

1. Hamid Mowlana, "Typewriter-Ambassadors: Explaining America to the World", *Intellect*, Vol. 104, September—October, 1975, p. 120. See also, Hamid Mowlana, "Who Covers America?", *Journal of Communication*, Vol. 25, Summer 1975, pp; 86—91.
2. Quoted in Robert Manning, "International News Media", *International Communication and the New Diplomacy*, Hoffman, Arthur S. (ed.), Indiana University Press, Bloomington, Indiana, 1968, p. 148.
3. Jack Anderson, "An Attack on American Liberties", *Washington Post*, October 26, 1975.
4. Peter Jenkins, "Britain Looks at American Politics", Speech given at the American University, Washington, D.C., December 10, 1973.
5. Peter Jenkins, "Britain Looks at American Politics".
6. Fred Siebert, Theodore Peterson and Wilbur Schramm, *Four Theories of the Press*, Urbana, Illinois, University of Illinois Press, 1956.
7. Raymond Williams, *Communications*, New York, Barnes & Noble, 1967.
8. For a detailed discussion see Hamid Mowlana, "Toward a Theory of Communication Systems: A Developmental Approach", *Gazette: International Journal for Mass Communication Studies*, Vol. XVII, No. 1/2, 1971, pp. 17—28.
9. Ralph L. Lowenstein, "Measuring World Press Freedom as a Political Indicator", unpublished Ph.D. dissertation, University of Missouri, Columbia, Missouri, 1967. See also, his chapter "Press Freedom as a Political Indicator", in Heinz-Dietrich Fischer and John C. Merrill, (eds.), *International Communication: Media, Channels, Functions*, New York, Hastings House, 1970, pp. 129—40.
10. For example see Raymond B. Nixon, "Freedom in the World's Press: A Fresh Appraisal With Data", *Journalism Quarterly*, Vol. 42, Winter 1965, pp. 3—14.
11. Hamid Mowlana, "A Paradigm for Source Analysis in Events Data Research: Mass Media and the Problems of Validity", *International Interactions: A Transnational Multidisciplinary Journal*, Vol. 2, July 1975, pp. 33—44. See also, Hamid Mowlana, "A Paradigm for Comparative Mass Media Analysis", in George Gerbner (ed.), *Current Trends in Mass Communication*, 1976.
12. Gay Talese, *The Kingdom and the Power*, New York, The World Publishing Company, 1966, p. 299.
13. George A. Bailey and Lawrence W. Lichty, "Rough Justice on a Saigon Street: A Gatekeeper Study of NBC's Tet Execution Film", *Journalism Quarterly*, Vol. 49, Summer 1972, p. 221.
14. John C. Merrill, *The Imperative of Freedom: A Philosophy of Journalistic Autonomy*, New York, Hastings House, 1974, p. 4.
15. Gay Talese, *The Kingdom and the Power*, p. 5.
16. Quoted in Charles Peters, "Why the White House Press Didn't Get the Watergate Story", *Washington Monthly*, July/August, 1973. This article has been reprinted in David C. Saffell (ed.), *Watergate: Its Effects on the American Political System*, Cambridge, Mass., Winthrop Publishers, Inc., 1974, pp. 26—33.

17. Charles Peters, "Why the White House Press Didn't Get the Watergate Story".
18. George Gerbner, "Communication and Social Environment", *Scientific American*, 1972, pp. 152—62.

Bibliography

ALBERT, Pierre, *La Presse*, Paris, Presses Universitaires de France, 1973.

ALBERT, P. and F. TERROU, *Histoire de la Presse*, Paris, Presses Universitaires de France, 1974.

ALLPORT, G. W. and L. POSTMAN, *The Psychology of Rumor*, New York, Holt, Rinehart & Winston, 1947.

ALMOND, Gabriel and G. B. POWELL, *Comparative Politics*, Boston, Little, Brown, 1966.

AYERST, David, *Guardian*, London, Collins, 1971.

BAGDIKIAN, Ben, *The Information Machine*, New York, Harper & Row, 1970.

BERTRAND, Claude-Jean, *The British Press*, Paris, O.C.D.L., 1969.

BORIS, Claude, *Les Tigres de Papier: Crise de la presse et (auto) critique du journalisme*, Paris, Editions du Seuil, 1975.

BOSTON, R., *The Press We Deserve*, Routledge & Kegan Paul.

BROWN, George, *In My Way*, Harmondsworth (U.K.), Penguin, 1971.

BRYSON, Lyman (ed.), *The Communication of Ideas*, New York, Harper, 1948.

BUCHANAN, W. and H. CANTRIL, *How Nations See Each Other*, Urbana, University of Illinois Press, 1953.

BUTLER, David and Michael PINTO-DUSCHINSKY, *The British General Election of 1970*, London, Macmillan, 1971.

CATER, D., *The Fourth Branch of Government*, New York, Vintage, 1959.

CENTRAL OFFICE OF INFORMATION, *The British Press*, London, C.O.I., May 1966.

CHERRY, C., *On Human Communication (A Review, a Survey and a Criticism)*, The Technology Press of M.I.T. and John Wiley, 1957.

COHEN, Bernard C., *The Press and Foreign Policy*, Princeton, Princeton University Press, 1970.

COMMISSION ON FREEDOM OF THE PRESS, *A Free and Responsible Press*, University of Chicago, 1947.

COOPER, Kent, *The Right to Know*, New York, Farrar, Straus & Cudahy, 1956.

CRANSTON, M., *Freedom: A New Analysis*, London, Longmans Green, 1953.

DANCE, F. E. X. (ed.), *Human Communication Theory*, Holt, Rinehart & Winston, 1967.

247

DEFLEUR, M. L., *Theories of Mass Communication*, New York, David McKay, 1966.

DEUTSCH, Karl W., *The Nerves of Government: Models of Political Communication and Control*, New York, Free Press, 1966.

DEUTSCH, Karl W., *Nationalism and Social Communication: An Inquiry into the Foundations of Nationality*, Cambridge, M.I.T. Press, 1968.

DEXTER, Lewis Anthony and David Manning WHITE (eds.), *People, Society, and Mass Communication*, New York, Free Press of Glencoe, 1964.

DUIJKER, H. C. J. and N. H. FRIJDA, *National Character and National Stereotypes*, Amsterdam, North-Holland Publishing Co., 1960.

DUNCAN, H. D., *Communication and Social Order*, Oxford, Oxford University Press, 1962.

FAGEN, Richard R., *Politics and Communication: An Analytic Study*, Boston, Little, Brown, 1966.

FARRELL, John C. and Asa P. SMITH (eds.), *Image and Reality in World Politics . . .* , New York, Columbia University Press, 1967.

FISCHER, Heinz-Dietrich, and John C. MERRILL (eds.), *International Communication: Media, Channels, Functions*, New York, Hastings House Publishers, 1970.

FLETCHER, Winston, "Britain's National Media Pattern", in Tunstall, Jeremy (ed.), *Media Sociology*, London, Constable, 1970.

FRÉMY, Dominique, and Michèle FRÉMY, *Quid? 1975*, Paris, Éditions Laffont, 1975.

FREY, Frederick, "Communication and Development", in Pool, I.S. et. al. (eds.), *Handbook of Communications*, Chicago, Rand McNally, 1973.

GAMMON, Franklin Reed, *The British Press and Germany, 1936—1939*, Oxford, 1971.

GREENBERG, B. S., and E. B. PARKER (eds.), *The Kennedy Assassination and the American Public: Social Communication in Crisis*, Stanford University Press, 1965.

HALLORAN, J. D., *The Effects of Mass Communication*, Leicester, Leicester University Press, 1965.

HALLORAN, J. D. (ed.), *The Effects of TV*, London, Panther, 1970.

HALLORAN, J. D. et al., *Demonstrations and Communication*, Harmondsworth (U.K.), Penguin, 1970.

HALLOWELL, A. I., "Cultural Factors and the Structuralization of Perception", in Rohrer, J. H. and M. Sherif (eds.), *Social Psychology at the Crossroads*, New York, Harper, 1951.

HARRISON, Stanley, *Poor Men's Guardians*, London, 1974.

HERSKOVITS, Melville J., *Cultural Relativism: Perspectives in Cultural Pluralism*, New York, Random House, 1972.

HIRSCH, Fred and David GORDON, *Newspaper Money*, London, Hutchison, 1975.

HOPKINS, Mark W., *Mass Media in the Soviet Union*, New York, Pegasus, 1970.

INKELES, A., *Public Opinion in Soviet Russia (A Study in Mass Persuasion)*, Cambridge, Harvard University Press, (second edn.) 1950.

INTERNATIONAL PRESS INSTITUTE, *The Press in Authoritarian Countries, IPI Survey,* Zurich, 1959.

JENNINGS, H. S., *Behavior of the Lower Organisms,* New York, Columbia University Press, 1906, Reprinted at Bloomington, Indiana University Press, 1962.

KATZ, Elihu and Paul LAZARSFELD, *Personal Influence,* New York, Free Press, 1955.

KELMAN, Herbert C. (ed.), *International Behavior: A Social-Psychological Approach,* New York, Holt, Rinehart & Winston, 1965.

KEY, V. O., *Public Opinion and American Democracy,* New York, Knopf, 1964.

KING, Cecil, "The Newspaper in Europe", *Journalism Today,* Vol. 1, No. 1, Autumn 1967.

KLAPPER, Joseph, *The Effects of Mass Communication,* Glencoe Free Press, 1960.

KLINEBERG, Otto, *The Human Dimension in International Relations,* New York, Holt, Rinehart & Winston, 1964.

LASKI, Harold J., *The Rise of European Liberalism,* London, Allen & Unwin, 1936.

LASSWELL, H. D., N. LEITES and Associates, *The Language of Politics,* Cambridge, M.I.T. Press, 1949.

LEE, Alfred McClung, *The Daily Newspaper in America: The Evolution of a Social Instrument,* New York, Macmillan, 1937.

LENIN, Vladimir, *What Is to Be Done?,* New York, International Publishers, 1943.

LIEBLING, A. J., *The Press,* New York, Ballantine Books, 1961.

LIPPMAN, Walter, *Public Opinion,* New York, Macmillan, 1927.

McCOMBS, Maxwell E. and Donald L. SHAW, "A Progress Report on Agenda Setting Research". A paper presented to the Theory and Methodology Division, Association for Education in Journalism, San Diego, California, August 19, 1974.

McLUHAN, Marshall, *Understanding Media: The Extension of Man,* New York, McGraw-Hill, 1964.

McQUAIL, Denis (ed.), *Sociology of Mass Communications,* Harmondsworth (U.K.), Penguin, 1972.

MACDOUGAL, Curtis D., *The Press and Its Problems,* Dubuque, Iowa, William C. Brown, 1964.

Mass Media and Violence, Volume IX, A Report to the National Commission on the Causes and Prevention of Violence, prepared by Robert K. Baker and Sandra J. Ball, Washington, U.S. Government Printing Office, 1969.

MATSON, Floyd and Ashley MONTAGU (eds.), *The Human Dialogue: Perspectives on Communication,* New York, The Free Press, 1967.

MERRILL, John, *The Elite Press,* New York, Pitman, 1968.

MERRITT, Richard L. (ed.), *Communication in International Politics,* Urbana, University of Illinois Press, 1972.

MILTON, John, *Areopagitica and Other Prose Works,* New York, E. P. Dutton, 1927.

MORGAN, Betty T., *Histoire du Journal des Scavans,* Paris, Presses Universitaires de France, 1929.

250   *Watergate: A Crisis for the World*

MOWLANA, Hamid, *International Communication: A Selected Bibliography*, Dubuque, Iowa, Kendall/Hunt Publishing Company, 1971.
MOWLANA, Hamid, "A Paradigm for Source Analysis in Events Data Research: Mass Media and the Problems of Validity", in *International Interactions: A Transnational Multidisciplinary Journal*, Vol. 2, No. 1, July 1975, pp. 33—44.
MOWLANA, Hamid, "A Paradigm for Comparative Mass Media Analysis", in George Gerbner (ed.), *Current Trends in Mass Communication*, 1976.
MOWLANA, Hamid, "The Communication Dimension of International Studies in the United States: A Quantitative Assessment", *International Journal of Communication Research*, Vol. 1, No. 1, January 1974, pp. 3—22.
MOWLANA, Hamid, "Trends in Research in International Communication in the United States", *Gazette: International Journal for Mass Communication Studies*, Vol. XIX, No. 2, 1973, pp. 79—90.
MOWLANA, Hamid, "Toward a Theory of Communication Systems: A Developmental Approach", *Gazette: International Journal for Mass Communication Studies*, Vol. XVII, No. 1/2, 1971, pp. 17—28.
MOWLANA, Hamid, "Who Covers America?", *Journal of Communication*, Vol. 25, No. 3, 1975, pp. 86—91.
MOWLANA, Hamid, "Typewriter-Ambassadors: Explaining America to the World", *Intellect*, Vol. 104, 2368, September—October 1975, pp. 119—22.
NIXON, Richard M., *Six Crises*, London, W. H. Allen, 1962.
RESTON, James, *The Artillery of the Press*, New York, Harper, 1966.
ROSENAU, James, *Public Opinion and Foreign Policy: An Operational Formulation*, New York, Random House, 1961.
SALINGER, Pierre, *With Kennedy*, New York, Avon Books, 1967.
SCHILLER, Herbert I., *Mass Communications and American Empire*, New York, Augustus M. Kelley, 1969.
SCHRAMM, Wilbur (ed.), *The Process and Effects of Mass Communication*, Urbana, University of Illinois Press, 1954.
SCHRAMM, W. (ed.), *Mass Communication*, University of Illinois Press, 1960.
SCHRAMM, Wilbur, *One Day in the World's Press*, Stanford University Press, 1960.
SEYMOUR-URE, Colin, *The Press, Politics and the Public*, London, Methuen, 1968.
SEYMOUR-URE, Colin, *The Political Impact of the Mass Media*, London, Constable, 1974.
SHERIF, M., *The Psychology of Social Norms*, New York, Harper, 1936.
SIEBERT, Fred S., Theodore PETERSON and Wilbur SCHRAMM, *Four Theories of the Press*, Urbana, University of Illinois Press, 1956.
SMITH, A. C. H., *Paper Voices*, London, Chatto & Windus, 1975.
SMITH, Anthony (ed.), *The British Press Since the War*, London, David & Charles, 1970.
STAGNER, Ross, *Psychological Aspects of International Conflict*, Belmont, California, Brooks/Cole, 1967.

TAYLOR, A. J. P., *Beaverbrook*, London, Hamish Hamilton, 1972.
TERROU, Fernand and Lucien SOLAL, *Legislation for Press, Film and Radio*, UNESCO, Paris, 1951.
The Times, History of the Times, London, The Times Publ. Co., 1952.
TUNSTALL, Jeremy, *Journalists at Work*, London, Constable, 1971.
TUNSTALL, Jeremy (ed.), *Media Sociology*, London, Constable, 1970 (1).
TUNSTALL, Jeremy, *The Westminster Lobby Correspondents*, London, Routledge, 1970 (2).
WADE, John, *Journalism and Government*, London, Macmillan, 1972.
WADE, John, *The Half-Shut Eye: Television and Politics in Britain and America*.
WEBER, Max, *The Theory of Social and Economic Organization*, Glencoe, Ill., Free Press, 1947.
WEISS, Walter, "The Effects of the Mass Media of Communication", in G. Lindzey and E. Aronson, *Handbook of Social Psychology*, Reading, Mass., Addison-Wesley, 1969.
WHITE, Ralph K., *Nobody Wanted War*, Garden City, N.Y., Anchor Books, 1970.
WHITE, Theodore, *The Making of the President 1972*, New York, Atheneum, 1973.
WIENER, Norbert, *The Human Use of Human Beings; Cybernetics and Society*, Boston, Houghton Mifflin, 1950.
WILLIAMS, Francis, *The Right to Know: The Rise of the World Press*, London, Longmans, 1969.
WILLIAMS, Francis, *Dangerous Estate*, London, Longmans, 1957.
WILLIAMS, Francis, *Press, Parliament and People*, London, Heinemann, 1946.
WILLIAMS, Raymond, *Communications*, London, Chatto & Windus, 1966.
WILLIAMS, Raymond, *The Long Revolution*, London, Chatto & Windus, 1961; Penguin, 1965.
WILLIAMS, Raymond, *Culture and Society*, Harmondsworth (U.K.), Pelican Press, 1961.
WOLF, John B., "Man's Struggle for Freedom Against Authority", in *Social Sciences and Freedom*, Minneapolis, University of Minnesota Press, 1955.
WRENCH, John Evelyn, *Geoffrey Dawson and Our Times*, London, Hutchinson, 1955.

Index